I0560771

Anyone who knows Amber sees grace and joy flowing out of her. Her story shows that God loves to give "a crown of beauty instead of ashes, the oil of joy instead of mourning, and a garment of praise instead of a spirit of despair" (Isaiah 61:3). If you are seeking to let go of the chains of the past and to walk in new freedom, this story will inspire you with hope!

Dr. David Newman—Pastor and Author of *The Shining Light: the man, mission and movement of the YMCA*

Always Amber is a gripping and unfiltered story of heartbreak, rebellion, and radical redemption. Amber's journey is gut-wrenching and inspiring. Her transformation is a stunning testament to the truth that no life is too broken for God to birth a breathtaking comeback.

Jenny Donnelly—Founder, Her Voice Movement

From shattered and shackled to redeemed and restored, Amber shares her heart-wrenching account of one trauma leading to another. This stunning story provides insight into why women choose abortion, what abortion does to women and men, and how healing provides peace. May you enjoy this engaging story as much as I did!

Cheryl Krichbaum, award-winning author of *ReTested* and founder of MybodyMyworship

Always Amber captivated me from beginning to end. With complete vulnerability, Amber addresses the pain of losing a father, the trauma that follows an abortion, and a past filled with unhealthy relationships. Her memoir is truly a powerful story of redemption, illustrating how, even in our brokenness, God lovingly pursues us for forgiveness, healing, and complete renewal!

Tiffany Seifman—Executive Director/Pathway to Hope Pregnancy Care Center, Hamilton, Ohio

ALWAYS AMBER

A story of redemption from the
shackles of shame & trauma

AMBER LERAAS

My body My worship!

© 2025 Amber Leraas. All rights reserved.

Printed in the United States of America

Published by MybodyMyworship, MybodyMyworship.com

All rights reserved. No part of this publication may be reproduced, stored in a retrieval system, or transmitted in any form or by any means—for example, electronic, photocopy, recording—without the prior written permission of the publisher. The only exception is brief quotations in printed reviews.

Cover photo by Bailey Rizk. Author photo by Megan Ivery.

Library of Congress Control Number: 2025910737
Paperback ISBN: 978-1-966744-00-9
Hardcover ISBN: 978-1-966744-01-6
E-book ISBN: 978-1-966744-02-3

To protect the privacy of the many people who are part of my story, some details and most names have been changed. In addition, any internet addresses (websites, blogs, etc.) in this book are offered as resources and are not intended in any way to be or imply an endorsement by MybodyMyworship or Amber Leraas, nor does MybodyMyworship vouch for the content of these sites for the life of this book.

Scripture quotations marked (AMP) are taken from the Amplified® Bible (AMP), Copyright © 2015 by The Lockman Foundation. Used by permission. www.Lockman.org.

Scripture quotations marked (ESV) are from The ESV® Bible (The Holy Bible, English Standard Version®), copyright © 2001 by Crossway, a publishing ministry of Good News Publishers. Used by permission. All rights reserved.

Scripture quotations marked (MSG) are taken from The Message, copyright © 1993, 2002, 2018 by Eugene H. Peterson. Used by permission of NavPress. All rights reserved. Represented by Tyndale House Publishers.

Scripture quotations marked (NASB) are taken from the New American Standard Bible® Copyright© 1960, 1962, 1963, 1968, 1971, 1972, 1973, 1975, 1977, 1995 by The Lockman Foundation. Used by permission.

Scripture quotations marked (NIV) are taken from the Holy Bible, New International Version®, NIV®. Copyright © 1973, 1978, 1984, 2011 by Biblica, Inc.™ Used by permission of Zondervan. All rights reserved worldwide. www.zondervan.com The "NIV" and "New International Version" are trademarks registered in the United States Patent and Trademark Office by Biblica, Inc.™

Scripture quotations marked (NKJV) are taken from the New King James Version®. Copyright © 1982 by Thomas Nelson. Used by permission. All rights reserved.

Scripture quotations marked (TPT) are from The Passion Translation®. Copyright© 2017, 2018, 2020 by Passion & Fire Ministries, Inc. Used by permission. All rights reserved. ThePassionTranslation.com.

BAND-AID is a registered trademark of Kenvue Inc. Chevrolet Cavalier is a registered trademark of General Motors LLC. Clorox is a registered trademark of The Clorox Company. The Floor is Lava is a registered trademark of Goliath IP Stichting. Google is a registered trademark of Google LLC. Jager is a registered trademark of Mast-Jägermeister SE. Hostess and Twinkies are registered trademarks of Hostess Brands, LLC. Kraft Mac & Cheese is a registered trademark of Kraft Foods Group Brands LLC. Mountain Dew is a registered trademark of PepsiCo, Inc. Ms. Pac-Man is a registered trademark of Bandai Namco Entertainment Inc. Ping-Pong is a registered trademark of Indian Industries, Inc. Taco Bell is a registered trademark of Taco Bell IP Holder, LLC. Tuna Helper is a registered trademark of Eagle Family Foods Group LLC. Uber is a registered trademark of Uber Technologies, Inc. U-Haul is a registered trademark of U-Haul International, Inc. Whac-A-Mole is a registered trademark of Mattel, Inc.

for

My Daughter

Audrey Marie

d. August 1994

You will always be in my heart.

&

My Dad

September 18, 1947 – August 16, 1991

I will always be your little girl.

TABLE OF CONTENTS

LOSING LOVE

LOSING MY WAY

LOSING MYSELF

INVITED

FINDING HEALING

FINDING FREEDOM

FINDING PURPOSE

REDEEMED

THE END

APPENDICES

LOSING LOVE

Remember also your Creator in the days of your youth, before the evil days come and the years approach when you will say, "I have no pleasure in them."
(Ecclesiastes 12:1 NASB)

1
FATERLESS AMBER

I gazed sleepily at the zebra-striped shadows and morning rays that peeked through the blinds and covered my bedroom wall. Lingering in my cozy bed, I pulled my flowered comforter up to my chin and nestled in, content to take full advantage of a late-morning summer snooze.

In just a couple more weeks, pool lounging and all-day adventures with friends would transition into crammed classrooms and late-night studying as a new school year, my eighth-grade year, would commence.

I rolled out of bed, threw on a pair of shorts and a t-shirt, and trotted downstairs to the kitchen for one of my go-to sugar-infused breakfast cereals to start my day.

Aware of the fleeting days of freedom, I intended to make the most of my time soaking up all the summer activities I could with my friends. My super social nature meant that coordinating quality time with friends was a top priority.

Since the option of driving was still a couple years away, I spent a lot of time with friends who lived within walking distance. On this particular Friday, I waited eagerly for my friends Kaitlyn and Gail to make the couple block trek to my house, each coming from opposite directions through various backyard short cuts. I looked forward to a low-key day of hanging out. No special agenda necessary. With friends around, my days felt full.

By early afternoon, Kaitlyn and Gail both arrived at my house. We convened in the living room, each of us selecting a spot on one of the matching brown and tan flowered couches to settle in and catch up on events that had taken place since we'd last seen each other. We had the house to ourselves, with the exception of my older brother, Sam, who had retreated to his bedroom upstairs. My dad was golfing with friends, and my mom was spending the day with my great-aunt Rita and my grandma Violet.

Kaitlyn and Gail had only been at my house for a short time when the shrill ring of our home phone interrupted our chat. Within just a few minutes, Sam came downstairs and approached our girl gathering. Still entrenched in our conversation and assuming he only intended to bug us, I ignored Sam's presence at first. I quickly snapped to full attention when, in a somber tone he said, "Gary just called. Dad had a heart attack on the golf course, and they rushed him to the hospital."

The blood drained out of my body. Swirling thoughts of fear, panic, and disbelief bounced around in my mind like fireflies trapped in a mason jar.

I darted upstairs as quickly as I could and locked myself in the hall bathroom. I sat in the cramped, dark room—with no time or need to turn on the light—and succumbed to an onslaught of emotions. Panicked and completely distraught, I did the only thing I knew to do. I sat on the closed lid of the toilet, laid my head on the bathroom counter, and through a stream of tears began praying more fervently than I had ever prayed. "God, *please* take care of my dad! Lord, *please* heal him and bring him home safely."

I had no concept of how long I spent locked in that dark bathroom alone and lost in my desperate pleas to God. But after I cried all the tears I could cry and prayed all the prayers I could pray, I felt a sense of peace. I reassured myself that God heard me, that my prayers made a difference, and that everything would be okay. With a natural propensity to see the bright side and believe the best, I reminded myself that people get rushed to the hospital all the time, and it works out just fine. This would be no different.

I finally went downstairs, with a splotchy face and swollen eyes, and rejoined my friends. With concern in their eyes and compassion in their tone, they both agreed to wait with me until I got an update while Sam headed to the hospital with a family friend. As we waited, I grasped for reassurance. "Everything will be okay," I said, as convincingly as I could for both my sake and theirs. "Soon enough," I predicted, "someone will call with the good news that they were able to take care of my dad at the hospital, and I can come visit him. Or better yet, he'll be on his way home!"

Then the doorbell rang.

I answered the door to see two of my parents' best friends, Jacob and Naomi, standing in front of me. I greeted them happily, grateful for their company while I waited for an update about my dad. I will never forget the look on Naomi's face—riddled with shock and grief—when she saw me. I looked at her with confusion in my eyes as I thought to myself, *Why is she so upset? Everything is going to be fine.*

She gazed intently at me with compassion in her eyes and asked in disbelief, "Hasn't anyone told you about your dad?"

I quickly responded, "Yes, of course! I know he's in the hospital. I'm still waiting for an update."

She immediately began crying and hugged me tightly. I don't know her exact words, but she proceeded to tell me the awful truth.

My dad was dead.

Instantly, I plummeted into a bad dream. All I could think was *no. No way could this be real.* This is not the outcome I anticipated. I was sure my dad was okay. I prayed! I knew God heard me! I believed that He would take care of my dad, and I trusted that it would all work out. There was no way that what she said could be true.

My friends, who quickly realized this situation had gone awry, left me alone with Jacob and Naomi. Not long after my friends left, my mom arrived home with an entourage of people. The scene I witnessed next is etched in my memory forever.

I heard my mom's wailing cry all the way inside my house. I can still hear it—a guttural cry that brings tears to my eyes just thinking about it. She made her way through our garage to the kitchen door entrance, the mid-afternoon sun shining from behind her so all I could see was her feeble outline. She could barely walk. Friends steadied her on either side, practically carrying her through the threshold.

When she entered the house, our eyes met. Her sobbing amplified as I melted into her embrace and succumbed to a suffocating sense of grief.

The rest of that day, and the days to follow for that matter, were a blur of emotional twists and turns. As the news of my dad's death spread that afternoon, my house gradually filled up with family friends, neighbors, church acquaintances, and relatives. I knew they were there to support us, but it was too much. All of this was too much. I needed to escape.

I shut myself in my upstairs bedroom and laid on my bed with my face buried. I bawled and bawled, unable to stop. Unable to believe that this was really happening. I heard the sound of my doorknob turning and someone entering my room but didn't bother to look up or stop crying. As my body convulsed in hysterical sobs, I felt a gentle hand on my back and heard the familiar voice of a family friend doing her best to console me. While I appreciated her compassion and the comforting gesture, I knew there wasn't anything anyone could say or do to soothe my anguishing, shattering heart.

My mind was a gushing firehose of thoughts about my dad: Our after-school card games of Spades, snuggling with him on the couch watching TV, his silly dad jokes and playful teasing. The way he coaxed me to dance along to one of his country tunes or joyfully belt out the chorus of a favorite song. When he put his arm around me and squeezed me close or wrapped me in his big bear hugs. The sense of love, safety, and affection that lingered in his presence.

I felt cheated. Robbed. Stunned. Utterly devastated.

I was only thirteen years old, my dad just a month shy of his forty-fourth birthday, and I couldn't conceivably grasp the thought of him being taken from me so early, so young. A series of questions played over and over in my mind. *Is he really gone? Am I really fatherless?*

Friday, August 16, 1991 became permanently seared in my memory. Life as I knew it would never be the same.

Putting on a Mask

I didn't know how to live my life without my dad, so I simply did what I had always done. I woke up early the next morning to go to soccer practice, just like any other Saturday in August. As I stepped out my front door and into my friend Lucy's car, it felt as if I stepped into an alternate universe. A haze of sorrow clung to me. I was a hollow shell of the person I had been just twenty-four hours ago, fragile and empty. The further I stepped away from my home, the more painfully aware I became that the world outside of my four walls carried on as if nothing had changed. I had to learn how to function with a shattered heart on the inside and a put-together persona on the outside.

The awkward tension set in like the dew on the morning grass as I arrived at practice and stepped onto the field. I casually greeted my teammates with a sideways glance, unable to meet their sympathetic stares. Several uncomfortable minutes of silence ensued while I preoccupied myself with getting my shin guards and cleats situated just right.

As practice began, I took my place in line in the middle of the field for our first set of drills. A few of us lingered in our designated positions, waiting for our turn to start passing down the field. As if taking cues from one another, a couple of the girls quickly muttered, "I'm sorry about your dad," before taking off toward the goal.

Aside from those few quick condolences, everyone else avoided the issue altogether and practice carried on as usual. While I appreciated both approaches—those who were kind enough to express sympathy, and the others for remaining silent and allowing me to ignore it—I instantly realized how uncomfortable my tragedy was, not just for me, but for others.

I did not want to be awkward. I didn't want to stand out. I wanted to be normal, like everyone else, so putting on a guise of "I'm fine" and going about my life as if everything were okay had become my new mission.

With the start of school quickly approaching, anxiety began to creep in like a gnarly weed that was smothering my peace. Fears plagued my thoughts. *What if people treated me differently? Or worse yet, what if a teacher or classmate who was unaware of my recent tragedy asked something about my dad? Would I be able to hold it together?*

Incessant worry plagued my thoughts as I contemplated how to manage all the unknowns and discomforts of being a fatherless teen.

> *I wanted to be normal, like everyone else, so putting on a guise of "I'm fine" and going about my life as if everything were okay had become my new mission.*

One night, about four months after my dad passed away, I went to a slumber party at my best friend Anastasia's house (we called her Stasi for short). Several of us girls sat around Stasi's room talking and sharing about what was going on in our lives.

In a vulnerable moment, I broke down and began to cry and confess that I missed my dad. My friends' consoling hugs and sympathetic comments were interrupted when one girl, with whom I wasn't as close, looked directly at me and coldly said, "That happened months ago. Shouldn't you be over it by now?"

Her words stung. I felt stupid. I felt ashamed. I wondered what was wrong with me that I still cried about my dad's death. And once again, I had confirmation that my emotions and this trauma made me different. It caused awkward moments and made me stand out from the crowd.

I desperately wanted to blend in and be like everyone else. And I certainly didn't want to be known as the crybaby who couldn't get over her dead father. I resolved to keep my feelings to myself as much as I could. I buttoned it up. Regardless of what I felt on the inside, I would keep my mask of "I'm fine" securely in place on the outside.

> *Regardless of what I felt on the inside, I would keep my mask of "I'm fine" securely in place on the outside.*

Solitary Sadness

I quickly learned that my dad's death, or the emotions surrounding it, wasn't something we discussed at home.

Sam—the self-proclaimed big brother bully—wasn't the warm-and-fuzzy-talk-about-your-feelings type. He had more important things to do than console his nagging little sister. At 17 years old and a junior in high school, Sam had already picked up some rebellious behaviors prior to my dad's death.

I distinctly remember a screaming match between the two of them not long before my dad died. My dad stood firm and fixed in our entryway at the bottom of the stairs, angrily reprimanding Sam over his most recent unsatisfactory life choice. Sam defiantly shouted back from a perched position halfway up the stairs, just out of reach. I watched anxiously from the safety of the living room only a few feet away, trying to stay as invisible as possible and silently wishing for the unnerving tension to dissolve.

I snuck away from the scene to retreat to our back deck, praying for peace between my dad and my brother.

Despite my brother's propensity to go out of his way to annoy me, I never liked seeing him get in trouble. Even when I was the butt of his jokes or the target of his torment, I juggled the desire for justice with the longing to be accepted. With each irritating interaction, I outwardly displayed disgust while inwardly craving his approval.

Sam's rebellion only intensified after my dad died. He spent most of his time away from home and when he was home, turbulence tended to follow.

Walking on Eggshells

I found myself trying to console the inconsolable as my mom wept uncontrollably on the stairway that led to her vacant upstairs bedroom, incoherently spewing her grief. What started as a few cocktails with her friends to unwind had once again spiraled into sobs and sadness. Sitting next to her in the dark stairwell, the eeriness of our empty, quiet home swept over me like an unwelcome icy breeze. With no words to say, only an arm to comfort her, my heart wrenched.

Watching my mom suffer and experience anguish so openly became all the motivation I needed to keep my feelings to myself. I rarely mentioned my dad for fear of invoking additional pain. And I certainly avoided sharing my own sadness with my mom because it would be cruel to add to her already consuming sorrow.

My mom seemed to me like a fragile, cracked vase, still functioning but on the verge of shattering into pieces if not handled delicately with extra care and caution.

Understandably so. She had lost the love of her life, her best friend and husband of twenty-two years. My mom and dad were teenage sweethearts and married right after high school. My mom was approaching 40 years old at the time of his death and had only known one adult life with my dad by her side. She didn't know how nor have any desire to be on her own or start over. Like a wounded animal broken but intent on survival, she limped her way through working full time, managing our household, and taking care of my brother and me.

Our fragmented family carried on, business as usual. Except nothing was usual about our home or our lives without my dad. I had a brother who took his new-found freedom to new limits, getting deeper into rebellion, farther away from our family, and leaving a trail of turmoil in his wake. I had a mother who, it often seemed, was a ticking time bomb of emotion.

So, I stuffed it down. Not only did I work harder at managing my feelings, but I also took on a new responsibility to hold it all together for our little broken family. I don't think I consciously thought I was bearing any kind of load, but I felt the internal pressure of not adding to our already tense lives. It was obvious to me that my mom couldn't handle any more stress, and my brother was certainly not helping the situation with his choices.

I resolved to be good. Stay the course. Focus on school and soccer. Make as few waves as possible to keep the peace in our home.

Unfixable

One of our first Christmases after my dad died, I went overboard buying presents for my mom. I couldn't bear the thought of her sitting with us Christmas morning only to receive a couple piddly kid gifts.

I scrounged together money I had earned from babysitting jobs and other odds-and-end chores, and splurged on her favorite perfume, some earrings, and other little gifts I knew she would appreciate.

I carefully wrapped each present with just the right festive paper, curling a ribbon on every package for an added touch. On Christmas morning, I excitedly waited for her to open her gifts. "You didn't have to do all this!" she exclaimed, stunned. "It's too much."

In that moment, I realized that no matter how hard I tried, whether it was with gifts or my good behavior, there was no way to fix this, fix her, fix us.

I saw the understanding in her eyes as she thanked me. But behind her appreciative smile, I could still see her brokenness. In that moment, I realized that no matter how hard I tried, whether it was with gifts or my good behavior, there was no way to fix this, fix her, fix us.

HAPPY²AMBER

My life growing up was not perfect, but to me it was pretty close. I have countless fond memories of family camping trips and vacations to the east coast, visits to my grandparents on Sundays after church, get-togethers with friends, and cozy evenings with my family sprawled out on our living room couches watching TV sitcoms like *Growing Pains* and *Family Ties*.

As a kid growing up in the 80s in a middle-class family, I felt like I had it all. I had two loving parents and an older brother whom I looked up to immensely, despite the fact that he had a self-prescribed mission to make me miserable (which he admits to this day).

Each of my parents contributed to my happy childhood and played a critical role in my life growing up. My mom was nurturing and creative and crafty, always coming up with unique or interesting games to play or things to do. She hand-sewed every costume I ever wore and made all my birthday cakes from scratch. Our days were never dull and the love she provided was tangible.

My dad was full of life and laughter. He had a sense of humor and a kind heart. He never met a stranger, friends with everyone. Detail-oriented and meticulous, he took care in knowing (and using) the exact number of screws required for a given project, such as building our deck or the storage unit in our garage. I saw my dad as affectionate and strong and capable. He held a special place in my little-girl heart.

I resemble my mom enough, with our similar smiles and dark curly hair, that in my early 30s I was once mistaken for her at a distant family member's funeral! I've often been told I have my dad's expressive eyes and friendly demeanor. There's no mistaking I'm their child, and I love both of my parents dearly; but it was no secret—I was daddy's girl.

Home Sweet Home

We lived in a nice tri-level house—not the newest or the biggest house, but just right—in suburban Ohio. Both of my parents grew up in our small town and so did many people who lived there. Our town was (is) the kind of tight-knit community where everyone knows your name—or at least the name of one of your relatives.

Our family pets livened up our peaceful home. Gabriel (Gabe for short) was our scraggly-haired rebellious but lovable Shih Tzu and Taneil, our orange-cheeked cranky and not-as-lovable cockatiel.

Gabe had an affinity for escaping our house to, quite literally, chase moving cars and wreak havoc in our neighborhood. Back in those days, we were on a first-name basis with our neighborhood dogcatcher. Maybe the proper term is animal control officer. Official titles aside, this woman, in her dutiful role patrolling the neighborhood, frequently showed up at our front door with Gabe in tow after one of his mayhem-inducing excursions. The dogcatcher often made idle threats about what would happen if we didn't keep Gabe inside, knowing full-well he would escape again and do it all over.

That misfit of a dog drove my dad crazy! Sadly, and ironically, Gabe's life of rebellion came to an end when he finally caught one of those cars he loved to chase. Getting hit by a car only a couple blocks from our house, while tragic, was a fitting end for our wild, free-spirited dog. While we all loved him, I would venture to say my dad was a bit relieved to be done with the drama that followed that dog like a dark cloud.

Taniel, well, she was about as cranky and unfriendly as a bird could get. Many birds sing beautiful tunes and bring melody and joy to those around them. Taniel was not one of those birds. If we put our hand anywhere near her, she squawked and pecked at us with her super sharp beak.

At any given point throughout the day, she screeched incessantly as if to let us know she was there and, for whatever reason, was not happy about it. Our only respite was a blanket over her cage that calmed and quieted her at night.

My brother's slew of hamsters spiced up our pet collection over the years. However, they did not seem to thrive in our environment, hence the hamster graveyards in the mulch bed on the side of our house and under the back deck.

Okay, so maybe it wasn't a pet paradise, but ours was a happy home.

My childhood memories are joyful ones, overflowing with love and laughter, peace and contentedness. Our family was whole and happy—quirky, annoying pets and all.

Growing Up

Life seemed about as good as it could get when I was in first grade. After Sunday school and church service, we went to my Grandma Eden and Grandpa Hugh's house.

My grandma greeted us with the sweet and savory aroma of cornbread baking and her infamous homemade chicken and dumplings, our family's favorite. Once our bellies were full, she spoiled us with treats from her special kitchen drawer overflowing with Hostess® cupcakes, Twinkies®, and candy galore.

Tragically, my grandma passed away on Christmas Eve when I was in second grade. Watching my dad go through the heartache of losing his mom was hard to bear. My heart broke watching him cry.

My grandma's funeral was my first face-to-face exposure to death. Everything about it seemed awful. The sadness of so many loved ones, the permanence of someone being stripped from your life, the emptiness that is left in the wake of someone so loved and cherished. There was a hole in our lives and our hearts after she was gone.

Following my Grandma Eden's passing, our after-church tradition transitioned to a gathering with my parents' best friends and their families at our favorite hole-in-the-wall breakfast diner.

Each week, we filed in the front door of the tiny, square, one-story cement building that was tucked away, barely noticeable from the road unless you knew it was there. A jingling bell on the heavy glass door notified the hostess of our arrival as she scurried to set up our usual spot in the back, scooching several long rectangular tables together to accommodate our large crew.

I loved the familiar feeling of stepping into our frequented eatery. Despite the lackluster decor with its muted brown carpet and matching mustard yellow countertops and vinyl chairs, the restaurant seemed to come to life each week when we arrived with our jovial crew. We always left with bellies bulging and hearts happy.

Firm Foundation

"Dad, do I really have to wake up early and be the only one to leave before the party's even over? Can't I just skip church this one time?" My attempts to forgo church for special occasions, like slumber parties, were always met with an emphatic "Not a chance."

My dad was a stickler about church. We did not miss.

Despite the early Sunday mornings and missing those last few hours with my friends after a sleepover, I loved my church life. I participated in all the things—youth group, choir, retreats, vacation Bible school, confirmation—and enjoyed every minute.

Church was more like a second home to me—so familiar, so comfortable. With its gray stone exterior, red-tiled roof, large peaks, and rooftop balcony, it felt more like a medieval castle than a church building. Wednesday nights, after our youth group gatherings or choir practices, we roamed free, exploring every nook and cranny. I knew every inch of that old building, every room, every secret closet.

Some of my favorite memories come from those years in church. Lock-ins with my youth group top the list.

Upon arriving at the deserted church in the late evening and dropping our sleeping bags and belongings in the largest Sunday school room near the back of the building, the festivities immediately began. Our brave youth group leader greeted us as we settled in. Brian had kind eyes, a joyful spirit, and a peaceful demeanor. With his quiet strength and enduring patience, he was the perfect guy to wrangle a dozen or so rambunctious teenagers through an entire night of feasting, fun, and fellowship.

The anticipation of an intentionally sleepless night "locked-in" our church building made it feel like a risky endeavor. Could we actually leave if we wanted? Yeah, sure. But the challenge was implied, the gauntlet thrown down.

Could you persevere through an entire night in a desolate, creepy old building? Do you have what it takes? And who would take the trophy as the sleepless champion? Not me. My heavy eyes typically got the best of me by the early morning hours, but there were always a few who conquered sleep and stuck it out, remaining vigilant through the whole night.

As the evening progressed, we rolled out the most popular games, like flashlight hide-and-seek and underground church. There was something thrilling (and a little spooky!) about walking around a seemingly ancient building, all the lights off, in the dead of night searching for a hiding friend or a hidden Bible. We told stories, laughed, prayed, and bonded, etching memories and positive experiences from church on my heart.

The Camp Crew

To know and understand what growing up in my family was like, I must introduce you to the Camp Crew. This unusual nickname was appropriately prescribed to a large group of my parents' lifelong friends because every year, for many years, they took an adult-only camping trip. These infamously wild summer soirees and the sometimes embarrassing, always hilarious happenings would be the butt of jokes and stories far beyond the conclusion of this beloved tradition.

The camping trips were how they attained their nickname, but the Camp Crew were (and still are) much, much more than just an unruly group of friends who liked to party at a campsite in their glory days. This fun-loving group of people was/is my family—or as we have referred to them all these years, my Camp Family. I consider my parents' friends to be my bonus parents and their kids, who are all very close in age to my brother and me, my bonus siblings.

From the time I was born, the Camp Crew was a consistent part of my life. We spent every single weekend together, with half a dozen families or more. Sometimes at our favorite hometown restaurant and bar, sometimes at someone's house, but always together, and always late into the night. As a kid, I felt so lucky to have this life. After all, every weekend was a party! Not just for my parents but for us kids, too.

Weekend Warriors

Friday night had finally arrived. At 12 years old, I had become accustomed to weekend nights packed with family fun—Camp Family fun. My excitement grew as my mom, dad, brother, and I piled into our dark gray Chevy minivan to head to our favorite local restaurant-and-bar hangout.

Just as I began to climb into the van to take my usual spot behind my dad, Sam clambered over me and plopped down. I did my best to hide my annoyance—*deep breaths*, I thought to myself. *He's just trying to get a reaction, as usual,* I reminded myself. I ignored him and took the other seat. Within just a few seconds of getting settled, he pushed me out of the way and said he wanted his seat back. "Ugh!" I exclaimed in utter exasperation. My anger bubbled over as a whining plea escaped my mouth, "Mom! Dad! Did you see what Sam just did?"

I stared out the window, silently seething as we slowly backed out of our driveway. *Why does he have to be such a jerk?* Holding back tears and allowing my anger to veil the incessant sting of rejection I felt from him, I tried to focus on the night ahead.

Within a few minutes, we arrived at our destination and pulled around to the parking lot on the backside of the building. We walked under the dark green awning with "Rick's Tavern" scripted in white letters and headed in through the creaking back door.

It took a few seconds for my eyes to adjust to the dim lighting and my lungs to adapt to the harsh cigarette smoke-filled air. I heard a popular Garth Brooks song blaring from the juke box, drowning out the chatter of scattered patrons grouped around square tables evenly dispersed throughout the narrow dining area.

My parents pointed out a long table tucked in a corner for us to occupy while they made their way to their friends who were perched at the bar. They ordered their first round of drinks for the night, and our weekend warrior routine began.

My mom and dad's friends arrived one by one. Our Camp brothers and sisters joined us at our table as their parents searched for an open stool at the long L-shaped bar. The small-town tavern became saturated with familiar faces and jubilant chatter.

The waitress made her way through the crowd to greet us kids by name. Forgoing the infamous pizza this time, I ordered one of my favorites—a fried chicken tenderloin sandwich and French fries. I felt so grown up, sitting at my own adult-free table, ordering food from a waitress who knew who I was, and having free reign to spend my evening with my friends.

We hurriedly scarfed down our food, stopped by for a quick check-in with our parents, primarily to grab some quarters for the game room, and then headed on our way to our night-time escapade.

Stepping through the doorway that separated the back half of the building (the bar) and the front half (the main dining area) was like entering an entirely different venue. Within just a few steps out of the doorway and into the skinny half-walled hallway that led to the front of the restaurant, suddenly darkness became glowing lights and loud music and cheerful chats dissipated into the soft murmuring of mannerly dinner conversations.

Parading through the restaurant like a gaggle of geese, we strolled toward our destination. I made a quick stop at the row of coolers lining the outer wall near the cash register, yanked open the glass door, and reached into the icebox to snatch a can of Mountain Dew® from the shelf. I flippantly shouted to a nearby waitress over my shoulder, "Put this on my tab!" and continued on my way.

We approached the front entrance of the building where the game room was tucked in a tiny nook about the size of a small bedroom. Two pinball machines sat side by side, accompanied by a two-seater head-to-head Ms. Pac-Man® arcade game. The snug gaming space didn't offer much, but we were content to settle in and feed the machines quarters as long as we could make them last.

The night carried on with multiple trips back and forth from the game room in the front to our table in the back. We invented games to play inside and outside, taking full advantage of the back parking lot to play The Floor is Lava®. We sang songs along with the blaring jukebox and laughed and mingled.

As the crowd died down, so did our energy. Heads and eyes heavy, we succumbed to exhaustion and sprawled out on booth seats and chairs, our heads resting on tables, whatever we could find to get some relief for our weary bodies as we waited for the night to conclude.

The lights came on, the music shut off, and our parents wrapped up their high-spirited conversations and said their goodbyes. As my mom, dad, brother, and I piled back into our family vehicle for the return trip to our house, I prayed silently for a safe drive home.

LOSING MY WAY

Take care, brethren, that there not be in any one of you an evil, unbelieving heart that falls away from the living God. (Hebrews 3:12 NASB)

3
LOST AMBER

Although I witnessed my parents' lifestyle and considered it a fun way to grow up, I was still adamant to not drink alcohol until I reached the legal age of 21. I had learned in church that following God meant following the rules, and I wanted to be the good girl I was raised to be.

After my dad died, that driving force to make it to church every week dissipated.

Teenage Rebellion

Why do we have to get up so early on one of my only days to sleep in? I thought to myself begrudgingly as I willed my tired body out of bed and rushed to make myself somewhat presentable for church.

My teenage years were for hanging out with friends and late-night parties, which meant early Sunday morning church services had become more of a burden than a blessing.

Sam, who moved out within what seemed like mere minutes after turning 18, stopped joining us on Sunday mornings altogether.

My mom and I entered the building, greeted by familiar friendly faces, and then headed in separate directions. She made her way through the oversized double wooden doors and down the mauve-carpeted aisle to her usual seat next to her friends on the right-hand side of the sanctuary, several rows from the front.

I climbed the winding stairwell toward the balcony to our youth group's self-designated section. As I scooched into the wooden pew next to a couple of my friends, overlooking our parents seated below, I couldn't help but notice how our group had dwindled significantly. A sudden surge of sadness mixed with jealousy emerged, as I acknowledged the absence of my missing friends, yet yearned for the day when, like them, I wouldn't have to endure early morning church services.

The booming music of a pipe organ filled the sanctuary and snapped me out of my wandering thoughts. The golden-robed choir members, tucked neatly and uniformly in the chancel, rose simultaneously to lead the congregation in worship.

I reached for the hymnal stowed in the wooden pocket fastened to the balcony wall directly in front of me and flipped through the delicate pages until I found the designated hymn. The familiar lyrics of "How Great Thou Art"[1] jumped off the pages as I joined in singing one of my all-time favorite hymns.

Preoccupation with my own selfish desires—wanting extra sleep or to be anywhere but there—melted away as I allowed the words flowing from my mouth to penetrate my soul.

Oh Lord, my God
When I, in awesome wonder
Consider all the worlds Thy hands have made
I see the stars, I hear the rolling thunder
Thy power throughout the universe displayed

The music traveled straight from my ears to my heart, and I felt a joy settle in that was not noticeable only minutes before. As if the melody had tiny hooks and wings, it attached itself to my innermost being and lifted and lightened my spirit. With an increasing joyfulness and completely out of tune, I joined in belting out the chorus:

---

1   Stuart K. Hine, translator, "How Great Thou Art," original lyrics by Carl Boberg, The Stuart Hine Trust, 1953.

Then sings my soul, my Savior God to Thee.
How great Thou art, how great Thou art!

Oh, if only I could feel that joy and peace the entire church service. As worship concluded, the sound of melodious music was replaced by the rustling raucous of a hundred or so congregation members settling into their seats. Pastor Daniel took his place at the pulpit and opened his Bible to begin teaching.

Here we go again, I thought. I could practically feel the pointy darts of condemnation shooting my way. It didn't matter what message he had planned for this morning, or that he had a kind manner, I knew that whatever he said would surely make me feel worse about myself rather than loved by God. Sometimes I wondered if that was intentional.

Was the goal of a sermon to guilt me into following God? If so, it wasn't working. The requirements of being a Christian seemed so unattainable and, quite frankly, anything but fun. I wondered if I would ever measure up. Did I even want to?

> *The requirements of being a Christian seemed so unattainable and, quite frankly, anything but fun. I wondered if I would ever measure up. Did I even want to?*

Did people actually avoid cussing? Refrain from getting drunk? Save sex for marriage? Maybe the goody-two-shoes of the world who had no friends or social life, but who wanted to be one of those?

As I gazed around at the adults filling the pews, I had a sudden overwhelming thought. *Of course, they're willing to follow these rules—they're old! They've lived their lives and had their fun.* The revelation struck me: I deserve to live it up while I'm young! I made a conscious decision, right then and there. *I'll come back to the boring life of following God when I'm old and have nothing better to do.*

My moral compass was gradually shifting, and the fear of missing out (FOMO) had officially set in. I was sure there were too many great things that I would miss by obeying God and living

23

a boring Christian life, so I began to compromise my beliefs for my own agenda.

I had once loved to learn stories from the Bible, strived to memorize scripture, and desired to live a wholesome life. As the months and years went on, I began to care more about fitting in with the popular crowd, being invited to the best parties, and getting drunk with my friends. What I once cherished now felt more like chains holding me in a cell of constraints. Had the message changed, or had I?

What I once cherished now felt more like chains holding me in a cell of constraints. Had the message changed, or had I?

Sadly, I had begun to believe the lie that being a Christian meant I had to give up anything and everything enjoyable to live a dull and dismal life. *Nope, I wouldn't get tricked into missing all the fun in life,* I thought. *I'm going to make the most of these years and live my best life doing what I want to do.*

Downward Spiral

The years following my dad's death were a slow progression into brokenness, a series of poor choices, unhealthy habits, toxic relationships, and crippling insecurity.

At age 15, only two short years after my dad died, curiosity won. I abandoned my previous vow of waiting until I was of legal age to drink, and I experimented with alcohol for the first time. I quickly fell in love with the sensation of being tipsy. Letting loose and feeling free—that was something I could get used to!

It didn't take long for my new-found pastime to catch on with my friends. We began drinking occasionally on the weekends as freshmen, intermittently incorporating alcohol into our recreational time. By my sophomore year, my social connections, coordinating parties, and drinking with friends became a top priority.

"Looks like my mom will be out of town again this weekend," I pointed out to a group of my best friends, Jasmine, Stasi, Rebecca, Brandi, and Olivia, as we nibbled on our soggy cafeteria pizza and fries during lunchtime. "Who should we invite over?"

My mom had a trip planned to visit her sister, Anne, a few hours away. These trips had become somewhat of a regular occurrence since my dad passed away. Getting some much-needed family time and support seemed like a reasonable thing for my mom to do, and it presented the perfect opportunity for my brother and me to take advantage of a parent-free house.

In fact, my house was often the weekend hangout. When my mom was home, I didn't have a curfew like most of my other friends, so staying at my house became a popular default. But, since she wasn't even home on many occasions, we had even more freedom to do whatever, go wherever, and have whoever else over.

My friends and I began brainstorming who we wanted to include for this upcoming get-together. We unanimously agreed—the more the merrier!

If socializing were a sport, I would have been the team captain. I mastered the skill of making friends with everyone, having as many friends as possible and, more importantly, being liked by as many people as possible—which mattered immensely to me. Fitting in and being liked was, in my opinion, the ultimate prize to be won.

Fortunately for me, most of my closest friends were very popular among our peers—cheerleaders, pretty, well-liked—so I became accustomed to being a part of the "in crowd" from an early age. Being one of the popular kids quenched my thirst for acceptance and satisfied my hunger for significance.

We settled the final details of our party plans and began spreading the word. Friday night. After the varsity football game. My house. BYOB.

My sleepy neighborhood came to life as cars filled my driveway and lined the street in front of my house. Eager partygoers unloaded from their cars and filed through my front door, beverages of choice in hand.

I greeted a wide range of guests, most of whom were from the large, tight-knit group of friends in my sophomore class. Sam, who had recently graduated, came home to join the festivities with some of his upperclassmen friends and other graduates as well.

Music blaring and drinks flowing, every room in our house spilled over with boisterous partyers. The night carried on with drinking games, mingling, and laughing. Intoxication increased with each passing minute.

As I trotted down our main stairway toward the kitchen, one of my close friends, Travis, stumbled from the living room into the entryway and toppled over at the bottom of the stairs on the tile right at my feet. Too tipsy to stand, Travis's inability to handle his new hobby was apparent. Those who witnessed his fall chortled as he fumbled around trying to stand up.

"Are you okay?" I asked, concerned, as I tried to help him to his feet. Aware that this was one of his first experiences with alcohol, I felt responsible for his well-being. Unable to make out his mumbling, I guided him to a nearby couch where he plopped face first for a drunken doze.

Suddenly, the jubilant sounds of socializing became hushed and panicked. "The cops are here!" someone shouted frantically.

Like a tree full of birds that scatter after being frightened by a loud noise, people began scuttering in all directions throughout my house, rushing for an exit or a hiding place. Several fled out the back sliding glass door and ran into the dark night to escape their presumed impending punishment.

My heart raced. *What do I do?* I crept down the flight of stairs to our walkout basement and took a sharp left into our rec room, which faced the front yard. Lights off, so as not to be noticed from the outside, I peered out one of the windows that was positioned at ground level, situated between overgrown evergreen bushes.

Yep, a police car lit up like a Christmas tree was parked right outside my house. Dread and anxiety flooded my body. The doorbell rang, and I felt a punch of panic in my stomach.

Sam was nowhere to be found, so I nervously made my way solo to the front door. I tentatively opened it just enough to reveal my face. A friendly, yet stern-looking, police officer greeted me as I gradually continued opening the door the rest of the way.

He informed me that the neighbors had called to complain about the noise level. "Where are your parents?" he inquired.

I answered guiltily, "My mom isn't here. She's out of town." I apologized for the noise, promising to quiet down.

"What about your dad?" he interjected.

"He doesn't live here," I sheepishly replied (it wasn't a *total* lie), hoping that was the end of the interrogation and a successful attempt at avoiding an awkward conversation about my dad.

The officer scolded me for being disrespectful to our neighbors and instructed me to conclude the get-together, quiet down, and go to bed. I quickly agreed, relieved that he didn't intend to investigate further.

"You understand," he added, "I'm going to have to call your mom to let her know what happened."

Ugh. I was afraid of that. So much for my good-girl façade. I guess she was bound to find out sooner or later.

The nerves leading up to seeing my mom on Sunday when she arrived home were much more intense than the conversation itself.

My mom was angry that we had a party, upset that we got in trouble with the police, and disappointed in and embarrassed by our behavior. We apologized, downplayed the actual events as much as possible, and promised not to do it again. Probably too emotionally exhausted to deal with us any further, she left it at that.

Whew. Disaster averted. *Next time*, I thought, *we'll have to be more careful.*

Swept Away

As I settled into my sophomore year and became acclimated with my new high school home, I quickly gained access to an even broader range of friends. A whole new world of opportunity presented itself as I immersed myself in a culture that fed my social cravings.

With a wide range of activities to partake in, I dove into as many as possible. Not only did I enjoy the perks of playing varsity soccer, but I also took on roles as an athletic trainer, a student council representative, and a yearbook club member, to name a few. All of which produced more opportunities for me to meet new people and gain even more connections. The more involved I could be, the better.

I took all honors classes and obsessed about getting good grades. I focused intently on athletics and my other extracurricular activities.

I thrived on knowing that I was doing well and that I was well-liked, my perfectionism at its peak. The more I achieved, the more significant I felt. The more known and liked I was, the more my value and self-worth were affirmed.

> I thrived on knowing that I was doing well and that I was well-liked, my perfectionism at its peak. The more I achieved, the more significant I felt. The more known and liked I was, the more my value and self-worth were affirmed.

While I was upholding my good girl image and enthusiastically carrying out my various responsibilities, I was simultaneously getting swept away into a lifestyle of partying, hanging out with upper classmen, and developing crushes on the older guys.

My friends and I spent numerous weekends at parties where alcohol was abundant and parental supervision was non-existent. What had started my freshman year as an occasional get together and some experimentation with alcohol gradually escalated with each passing year.

One afternoon in the early fall, just a couple months after beginning our sophomore year, my friends and I stood in a cluster in the commons after the final bell of the school day rang. Students rushed by in a hurry to exit the building and embark on their weekend festivities.

Lingering for a few extra minutes, we excitedly hashed out our plans for another one of our parentless parties scheduled that Saturday. We covered several of the most important factors—who would drive, where we would spend the night, and how we would get our alcohol.

My October birthday meant I was the oldest of most of my friends and therefore one of the first to have a drivers' license, making me the obvious choice to be the designated driver. My mom would, once again, be out of town for the weekend. So, my house was deemed the ideal after-party crash pad with no restrictions on where our collective group was going or how late we could stay out.

As for the alcohol, our friend Wyatt chimed in: "I have a connection. I've got it covered." Surprisingly, gaining access to alcohol as a 16-year-old was pretty easy to do.

Young Love

When Saturday evening arrived, my compact 1991 red Chevy Cavalier® reached near clown car status as we crammed as many people in as possible. As long as the doors shut and everyone could breathe, we deemed it a suitable ride.

As I drove into the dated neighborhood with rows of identical small one-story houses, a wave of nostalgia washed over me. Just down the street from our destination sat my grandma and grandpa's house where so many Sunday morning memories had taken place. Visiting this neighborhood had once been a family affair that felt sunny, simple, and safe.

Stepping out of my car and into the dark night, a swift pang of pain surfaced. Those memories seemed so distant. My life had distinctly shifted from a light-hearted joy and innocence to a pursuit of self-indulgence and short-lived gratification. A girl once drawn to wholesomeness now retracting to the shadows of selfishness, secrecy, and rebellion.

Abruptly pushing my memories and my conscience aside, I refocused on the festivities at hand and put a smile on my face as my friends and I piled into the crowded house. Despite being one of the only sober partyers, I had a great time, content to soak up the opportunity to socialize. As I mingled, my attention was drawn to an upperclassman whom I had seen around but did not personally know.

My life had distinctly shifted from a light-hearted joy and innocence to a pursuit of self-indulgence and short-lived gratification.

Leo was a senior—an athlete who was witty, popular, and cute—and he was flirting with *me*. Several instances throughout the night we crossed paths, pulled into playful conversations.

Immediately smitten with Leo, I could tell our attraction was mutual. However, this presented a major conflict, as we each already had a significant other. I had been casually dating Adam, a friend-turned boyfriend, for the past couple months. And Leo was in what I understood to be a serious relationship with Hannah, an acquaintance of mine a couple years younger than me.

As the night progressed, the flirtation increased and so did our denial of our current relationship statuses. The party began to die down, and we rounded up the crew who would finish the night at my house. Leo and a couple of his friends accepted our invitation to join us.

The night concluded with my first kiss with Leo, the beginning of many firsts with him. However, despite the high of this new infatuation, a dark cloud lingered. Sooner or later, we would have to face the consequences of our cheating.

I felt sick to my stomach over what I had done, and I could not rectify it fast enough. I already knew I liked Leo and had no doubt about pursuing a relationship with him. So, the very next morning, once all the overnight guests had left my house, I waited as patiently as I could for a reasonable time to call Adam without waking up his entire household.

I took a few deep breaths and rehearsed what I planned to say. I lifted the tan-colored receiver to my ear and pushed the buttons on the base of the blocky phone sitting on my mom's bedside dresser. I waited nervously for him to answer.

"Hello?" Adam's groggy voice on the other end of the line sent a shot of anxiety through my body.

After a quick greeting, I got straight to the point. "I need to talk to you about something," I said as I started to fumble over my words. *Get it over with*, I thought to myself. Careful to avoid divulging any incriminating details from the night before, I kept my message concise. "I'm sorry, but our relationship isn't working out. I think we need to break up," I finally blurted out.

Although he was surprised and disappointed, Adam acknowledged that if that's what I wanted, then he couldn't do much about it. He conceded, and the phone call ended, along with our relationship.

Relief washed over me like a cool shower on a hot summer day. I felt free. I considered myself exonerated of my crime since I was no longer attached.

Unfortunately, Leo's situation was not as simple. His relationship with Hannah was more serious than mine was with Adam. They had been together much longer.

Guilt gnawed at my insides. I knew what I did was terrible. As the person who always wanted people to like me, I was now faced with being the dreadful "other woman" who broke up a relationship. I knew it was wrong, but at the same time I knew I wanted to be with Leo. I justified that we both liked each other and wanted to be together, so it was okay. If I kept the focus on me and what I wanted, ignoring my conscience was much easier.

Weeks went by and Leo still had not broken up with Hannah. He continued to flirt with me and coincidentally ended up in the same places as me on many occasions. But I refused to repeat our mistake, despite his charming attempts. I was firm that if he wanted anything more than friends with me, he would have to end his relationship.

A couple of weeks before Christmas, Leo finally took the step and broke Hannah's heart. Ignoring the blame and the part I played in her misfortune, I gleefully rang in the New Year as Leo's new love interest.

> *If I kept the focus on me and what I wanted, ignoring my conscience was much easier.*

I felt amazing to be openly in a relationship with Leo. I reveled in the significance of being the girlfriend of someone who I not only adored and made me feel special, but who also elevated me to an even higher social status as a sophomore dating a popular senior.

Word travels fast in a small town, and the truth about how our relationship began surfaced. Well aware of Hannah's hurt and the disdain she had for me, I deflected and ignored. Unable to handle someone not liking me, even if it was deserved, I began to develop a reciprocal dislike for her. Rather than allowing the guilt to surface or taking ownership of my actions, I settled into a petty "mean girls" attitude, allowing her to be the butt of jokes and target of ridicule amongst my friends.

Other than the hurt and anger that came from those we left behind, Leo and I had no real repercussions or blemishes on our reputations for our behavior. Despite its scandalous beginnings, ours was a relationship that was widely accepted and admired by our peers.

I basked in my new identity as Leo's girlfriend. Our lighthearted, fun, flirtatious union rather quickly evolved into a deeper, more intimate one. I started recognizing and experiencing things with Leo that I never had before. Swept away in the rapids of teenage emotions, I couldn't imagine anything more fulfilling or more important than being loved by my boyfriend. The security, love, and affirmation I felt with Leo was a dream come true.

Swept away in the rapids of teenage emotions, I couldn't imagine anything more fulfilling or more important than being loved by my boyfriend.

4
SELFISH AMBER

Several areas of my life changed drastically in high school—some for the better and some definitely not.

My mom marrying Frank was a highlight of the summer before my junior year. After they dated for several months, and once I finally let my guard down about having an outsider in our lives, it became clear what a wonderful man he was and how happy he made my mom. It was such a blessing to have my stepdad and his two kids—Rose, a daughter just a year younger than me and a son, Ryan, three years younger—join our family.

The comfort of being a family unit under one roof with a mother, father, and siblings was something I valued more than I realized. Three years had gone by since my dad had passed away and while my dad was still dearly missed, Frank was a welcome addition to our family. He brought so much laughter and kindness and stability to our home and our lives. I was so relieved and grateful to see my mom thriving in her newfound happiness.

The Unwanted Truth

I lost track of time as I lay curled up in a ball in my favorite spot on our oversized couch, my eyes swollen and face splotchy from uncontrollably sobbing. The sound of the garage door opening jolted me out of my stupor of despair. My mom had just arrived home from work. The knot in my stomach tightened and the dread was almost unbearable as the realization sunk in.

I had to tell her.

After an eventful few months off from school, including my mom and stepdad's wedding, summer break concluded, and my junior year of high school arrived. The late summer sun poured into our large four-paneled living room window directly across from where I huddled on the couch, and the smell of freshly cut grass filled the air.

The events that led to this moment—me, drowning in a pool of tears and self-pity and fear on my favorite living room couch—would change the way I remember that smell and that season for years to come.

Just a few hours earlier, three of my close friends, Stasi, Olivia, Jasmine, and I somberly piled into Jasmine's car to set out for the answer I was desperately seeking but didn't really want to know. The gut feeling I had—what I *just knew* to be true. Could it actually be? Could I really be pregnant? I knew it sounded crazy. Just a few weeks earlier, I had lost my virginity.

Leo and I were in love (whatever love was to two immature, hormonal teenagers). I had boyfriends before Leo, but they were junior-high-type flings with no real substance. Crushes at best. I would categorize this as my first serious relationship. My first love. Everything about my experience with Leo was new and exciting. We fell for each other unexpectedly and deeply.

> *Could I really be pregnant? I knew it sounded crazy. Just a few weeks earlier, I had lost my virginity.*

Leo was a couple years older and more experienced. With him, I felt feelings that I'd never felt before. As our relationship progressed and our affections grew stronger, my previous standard of waiting until marriage slowly faded, and I began to rationalize that this previously set boundary could be broken for one exception and one exception only: being in love.

My moral code, my convictions, my beliefs dissipated. I made the conscious choice to go my own way, and it would cost me dearly.

My Choice

Surely, this couldn't be happening to me; not within just a few weeks of having sex for the first time! But my period was late, and birth control was not on my radar. I hadn't thought ahead enough to even consider what might come from taking my relationship to the "next level."

Being swept up in emotions and teenage love clouded my thinking, and it seemed that all rational thought escaped my decision-making process. I certainly hadn't considered how this one decision could and would affect the rest of my life. Whether I wanted to believe it or not, yes, this was happening to me.

I certainly hadn't considered how this one decision could and would affect the rest of my life. Whether I wanted to believe it or not, yes, this was happening to me.

When I told my friends my suspicions, they brushed it off and accused me of being paranoid. Still, they were the supportive, ride-or-die type besties, who stuck by my side no matter what. So, they agreed to go with me to the nearest facility to take a pregnancy test.

Looking back, I have no idea how I knew where to go. Unfortunately, I chose the wrong place. I guess I got what I was looking for—a pregnancy test. A positive one at that. I knew it.

Knowing what I know now—that there are pregnancy resource centers all around our area that not only offer free pregnancy testing but also free resources, classes, and counseling provided by people who genuinely care—I wish I would have visited one of those locations instead. I could have sat across from someone who talked me through my options, prayed with me, told me that I'm not alone and, even though it's inconvenient and scary, assured me that being a pregnant teen is not the end of the world.

Instead, I got a pamphlet that told me about abortion and how to schedule my appointment.

I think shock had set in. Even though I instinctively knew before I took the test that it was true, now it was real. Confirmed. Official. No turning back.

Everything around me faded into darkness. I was suddenly trapped in a haze of confusion, struggling to breathe. The word that best describes my emotional state in that moment is terrified.

As I typed that word, it struck me that I have always used that adjective—"terrified"—to describe how I felt in those moments when I first learned I was pregnant. I've never known why that specific word pops into my mind. For the sake of better understanding, I decided to look it up. The first definition that surfaced was this:

Terrified: 1) extremely frightened. 2) thrown into a state of intense fear or desperation.

Yes. I was most definitely terrified.

Terrified of what people would think about me. How would this affect my "good girl" reputation as an honor roll student, an athlete, and a Christian?

Terrified of losing everything I had dreamed for my present and future. What about my social life? What about college? Or my dreams of having a career?

As a selfish and self-centered teenager, I excelled at making everything about me and what I needed or wanted. I was sure that I did not want my life to be ruined by having a baby before even graduating high school.

As far as I was concerned, abortion was the only answer. I knew very little about what abortion was or what it involved, but somehow I knew it was an option. And I believed it would fix my "problem." The thing I kept telling myself was that it was legal and lots of people do it, so it can't be that bad. Right?

Wrong. But that's a lesson that would take me nearly two decades to learn.

My mom walked into our house after a day of teaching fourth graders at one of the local elementary schools. Just like any other day, she entered our kitchen through the garage and called out to say hello to me. She made her way around the corner to greet me where I lay curled up on the couch. As she passed through the archway that connected our main entryway to our living room, she caught sight of me and immediately realized something was terribly wrong.

"Amber, what is it? What's the matter?" she asked, exasperated.

Without hesitation, I blurted out, "I'm pregnant." My mom crumpled into a ball on our beige carpet in the middle of our living room floor and began weeping.

I barely gave her a chance to register what I had told her. She had a few seconds to process this bomb that I dropped when, through my own sobs and with as much authority as my 16-year-old self could muster, I declared, "I'm not keeping it. I'm having an abortion."

The wailing that came from my mother after I spoke those words pierced my soul. As if daggers were shooting directly into my heart, I could feel her disbelief—*stab!* Her disheartenment—*stab!* Her despair—*stab!*

Was she disappointed in me? Was she horrified and heartbroken about my actions and my choice? I can only assume so because there were no discussions, no questions, no further conversations. Only tears.

I don't remember how long we wept simultaneously in that room, a room in my childhood home where I had treasured so many bright memories, now tainted by this new dark stain. My mom and I were just a few feet from one another, lost in our emotional turmoil, feeling miles apart.

When I told Leo the news over the phone, I shared that I was pregnant and having an abortion in the same breath, giving him little opportunity to provide input. He sat on the other end of the line quietly, not much to say.

When he finally did speak, he simply explained, "I can't help pay for it. My family would be devastated if they ever found out."

"Okay," I said flatly. Money was the last thing I was worried about; I just wanted this problem to disappear. That brief exchange was the only discussion I recall having with Leo about the existence of our baby. The call ended, and the subject was closed.

It was settled. The decision was made. For the second time in just a few short years, my life and my future would be drastically altered.

My Way

I don't remember how much time had passed after I told my mom until the day of my abortion. A couple weeks? Maybe more? Maybe less?

But in that time, I lived in agonizing limbo.

I did not agonize about my decision; my mind was made up. Rather, I trudged day-by-day through the torment of living with this existing "problem," riddled with the fear of people finding out my secret, and longing for things to go back to normal.

I've heard that some women recall (and are even haunted by) the exact dates surrounding their pregnancy—the date of their abortion and/or their due date. I don't remember either.

I do know that I had my abortion sometime in August of 1994, and I can recall bits and pieces and a few significant events during that timeframe that help me pull together some details.

Despite this huge dramatic occurrence, I had to go about my life as usual with what felt like a looming bomb ready to drop at any moment. I recall having a few guarded conversations at school with the only three friends who knew my secret, the ones who accompanied me to get my pregnancy test.

We huddled in the corner of a classroom or at my locker or gathered at the lunch table—voices hushed and eyes darting around to make sure that no one overheard us and discovered the shameful truth.

Leo had just wrapped up his senior year and his family threw him a late-summer graduation/send-off to college party that happened to take place within a short time of us finding out the news of my pregnancy. This is one of the memories that stands out to me the most because of the peculiar stance I took at his party.

I started socially drinking at 15 years old, during my freshman year. So, by this time, beginning my junior year, having a few drinks at a party was perfectly normal, if not expected. However, at Leo's party, I refused to drink alcohol *because I was pregnant.*

Confusion, delusion, and denial persisted.

I thought it was perfectly acceptable to end the life growing inside my womb in a couple weeks' time but drinking alcohol that may adversely affect that same life was *not* acceptable.

I had been justifying that this decision was best for me, that it was okay because it was only a clump of cells, but somewhere deep down, I knew the truth. This was a baby. My baby.

I continued justifying, denying, and lying to myself in the days leading up to my appointment. My best friend Olivia's mom was the only adult I talked to, besides my own mom, about my situation.

> *I had been justifying that this decision was best for me, that it was okay because it was only a clump of cells, but somewhere deep down, I knew the truth. This was a baby. My baby.*

I spent countless hours at Olivia's house and had lots of interactions with her family. Her mom, Lola, was one of those moms who talked to us about anything and everything. She knew all about our lives, our relationships, and the latest gossip. She was easy to talk to and sincerely cared.

With my mom, I revealed my predicament and informed her of my plan to deal with it. With Lola, I had an open conversation. After confessing my distressing situation and sharing my decided solution, she lovingly responded, "Amber, I don't think abortion is the answer." She continued with a bit of urgency and concern by pointing out, "This is not what God would want for you."

To which I arrogantly, ignorantly, and selfishly replied, "I guess I will just have to deal with God later. This is what I need to do right now."

To this day, I'm grateful for Lola's courage and boldness to tell me the truth in love. I only wish I had listened.

The Point of No Return

The day of my abortion finally arrived. While I don't know the exact date, I do know that it was a Friday. I convinced my mom that, even though I would miss school for my abortion procedure—or as I told my school authorities, soccer coaches, and friends, for a procedure to remove a cyst from my ovaries—I still needed to make an appearance at the high school football game that evening.

Socializing at varsity football games was one of the highlights of our fall season, and I reasoned that it would be suspicious if I weren't there, that I needed to keep up appearances as the social butterfly I was known to be to avoid questions regarding my whereabouts.

At least that's what I told my mom—and myself. My pattern of unsound logic and justification to get what I wanted at all costs confirmed my overly self-centered way of thinking.

That morning, my mom and I drove in stoic silence to the abortion facility. After a twenty-five-minute trek that felt like two hours, we pulled into the parking lot of an inconspicuous brick building nestled just off the main road. The area was unfamiliar and the building one I had never seen nor knew existed.

We entered the threshold to a bland waiting room with chairs lining the small, rectangular room. Everything seemed so cold, so stale.

I didn't feel overly scared, but discomfort in the strange setting and nerves about the unknowns of what would happen began to set in. As I waited and focused on calming my nerves, I reminded myself this ordeal would be over soon. More than anything, I just wanted to put this behind me and to get on with my life.

I snapped out of my swirling thoughts when a woman peeked through a door and called my name. As I stood up, I shot a nervous, sideways glance at my mom, careful not to give away any emotions that would betray my confident, head-strong persona. Leaving my mom in the waiting room, I followed the woman through the door and down a narrow hallway for my intake meeting. I sat down across from her and anxiously awaited the routine pre-procedure questions, eager to keep the process moving.

Thankfully, the meeting was quick and methodical. However, one part of that brief encounter has always stood out to me. Not long into our questioning, the intake representative asked my age. "I'm 16," I answered matter-of-factly.

With a concerned expression, she responded, "Oh, sweetie, I'm so sorry." Tinges of awkwardness and embarrassment cracked my icy exterior, followed by confusion. *Weren't they there to help me? Wasn't what I was doing the best thing for me? Why would she be sorry?* Unable to reconcile these invasive thoughts, I quickly pushed them aside and focused on the plan.

After my intake meeting, the next thing I remember is lying on a table wearing nothing but a frumpy medical gown, my legs in stirrups. This was all new and extremely uncomfortable for me, as I had never even had my first appointment with an OB-GYN. The room felt empty and cold and stale, just like the waiting room and intake office. I don't remember seeing anything in it other than the table where I lay and a cart with a tray holding medical equipment.

Everything happened so fast. A nurse stood beside me, holding my hand as I waited nervously. When a man, whom I assumed was a doctor, entered the room, I don't recall any interaction with him aside from a quick and formal introduction. Wasting no time, he carried on with what he was there to do—as if completing a banking transaction, minus the typical pleasantries of a friendly customer service representative.

Silent tears rolled down my cheeks and my legs shook involuntarily, as if my physical being intuitively knew what my numbed emotions were incapable of acknowledging. Unsure and a little embarrassed about why my body was betraying me, I looked to the nurse for reassurance, "I don't know why this is happening," I said, motioning to my face and legs.

"Don't worry," she quickly responded. "The medication they gave you causes the tears and shaking." Whether she was telling me the truth or not, I readily received her answer, feeling comforted that it wasn't my own feelings causing these reactions.

Then, sudden pangs of discomfort, pressure, and an unnerving sound of suction jolted me out of my thoughts. I immediately became aware of how uncomfortable and unnatural everything was—the matching stoniness of the room and the abortionist, the awkward and exposed position in which I laid, the way my body leaked tears and shook without my permission, the unsettling noise and invasiveness of the suction tool. I desperately wanted it all to be over—to desert that place and delete that memory for good.

Thankfully, within minutes, the procedure was done. Afterward, I spent a short time in a recovery room with juice and a snack, surrounded by other young women who had presumably just experienced the same thing.

I soon left with my mom to drive home in the same stoicism and silence in which we had come—though now the heaviness of my problem had lifted. Relief flooded my mind and body. The nightmare was over. I finally felt like I could breathe again.

Numbness and denial set in.

Safely tucking this experience in a deep dark closet of secrets, I rejoiced that I would never have to think about my pregnancy again, and no one would ever know the shameful truth.

Problem solved.

> *Safely tucking this experience in a deep dark closet of secrets, I rejoiced that I would never have to think about my pregnancy again, and no one would ever know the shameful truth.*

Web of Lies

I have never been a good liar. I may have mustered a few little white lies or exaggerations here and there, but I am naturally a truth teller, a rule follower. What I soon discovered after my abortion was that lying, deceiving, and covering up would be my new normal.

When I found out I was pregnant, the most dominant concern I had was "What will people think of me if they find out I'm pregnant?" And the most dominant concern I had after my abortion was "What will people think of me if they find out I had an abortion?"

But now that fear of what people would think was a thousand times worse because my pregnancy wasn't a problem I could solve. Abortion, along with the shame and trauma that accompanied it, was now a permanent part of my past, present, and future.

I believed the lie that abortion would make everything better. However, within mere minutes of my procedure, I clearly had something bigger, more shameful to conceal. Desperation set in as

> *Abortion, along with the shame and trauma that accompanied it, was now a permanent part of my past, present, and future.*

I realized I had to keep my secret at all costs. No one could know the awful truth about me.

At that point, Leo, my three best friends, Olivia's mom, my mom, and my stepdad were the only people who knew. I was determined to keep it that way.

A few awkward encounters occurred right after my procedure where I was forced to blatantly lie. Those who thought I had had surgery to remove a cyst from my ovaries genuinely cared and wanted to know how I was doing.

The phone woke me from my nap on the couch. My mom's best friend and a Camp Crew bonus parent, Cory, called to check on me. She worked in the medical field and, out of genuine curiosity, asked which hospital I had my procedure done, as well as a couple of other innocent questions about how it went.

Still half asleep, I stumbled my way through the conversation, giving very vague, made-up answers—partly because I was groggy from the events of the day, but mostly because I didn't know them. Back then, I didn't have access to pocket-sized computers or quick Google® searches to research every possible detail about a given procedure.

Later I told my mom about that conversation with Cory and how I thought I did a decent job of answering her questions and covering up the truth. My mom informed me that I did *not*.

She confessed that she told Cory about my abortion because my answers didn't add up. Lying was clearly not my strength. And now, unfortunately, we had added another name to the list of people who knew the terrible truth about me.

I had a couple other encounters—one with a friend who rushed up to me on the sidelines of one of my soccer games as I was sitting out (being the rule follower that I was, I complied to post-procedure regulations of forgoing physical activity for two weeks) to ask how I was doing. She inquisitively asked if she could see my scar and wanted to know more about my surgery. I awkwardly brushed off the inquiry and rushed away, pretending to be preoccupied with watching my team warm up for the game.

Pangs of guilt and worry gnawed my insides as I desperately tried to avoid, deny, and hide the truth.

At a family event, my aunt Anne, who is a nurse, had several questions about the procedure that I, again, had no idea how to answer. Guilt and shame trickled deeper into my conscious as I felt forced to carry on a charade of deception around those I loved.

My secret tormented me. Over the years, vicious rumors spread and confrontations about the truth of my past threatened to unravel my sham of virtue. I lived in a perpetual state of defensiveness and deception, desperate to uphold my image of morality, all the while hoping my shameful deed would disappear if I just buried it deep enough.

I never really considered the sticky mess that would evolve from that solitary lie. But the lies compounded, one after another, and the web kept expanding. The shame of my actions and the stress of keeping my secret left me feeling bound and restricted, consumed by a desperation to maintain an unblemished reputation. The more I spun this falsehood fantasy, the more entangled I became in my own web of deceit and disgrace.

LOSING MYSELF

Whereas she who lives for pleasure and self-indulgence is spiritually dead even while she still lives.
(1 Timothy 5:6 AMP)

5
BROKEN AMBER

I continued dating Leo for almost a year after my abortion. During my junior year of high school, he went off to college and despite our best efforts to stay connected, feelings faded (his more than mine, if I recall correctly), and the relationship ultimately ended the summer before my senior year.

I was wounded and jaded after Leo. Not only did I think we were in love and that love was forever, but I had also given him a part of me that I could never get back—my virginity.

> *Not only did I think we were in love and that love was forever, but I had also given him a part of me that I could never get back—my virginity.*

We also harbored this huge secret about my abortion but were now no longer guarding it safely together. I was even more concerned about people learning the truth about me, worried that he would be less motivated to protect my privacy or carelessly share my shameful secret with others.

In my woundedness and rejection my walls began to go up, and I resolved that I would not fall for someone in that way again. I would not allow myself to get hurt or be rejected.

Immediately after my breakup with Leo, I rebounded into a fleeting fling with Adam once again. Adam was a good friend, a familiar comfort, and safe place for the affection and attention

I needed while nursing the wounds from my failed relationship with Leo.

But my feelings for Adam were superficial and self-seeking and didn't last long. After our futile attempt at reconnecting dissolved, I casually went on dates with other guys but had no real desire to be tied down.

More than dating, I enjoyed being surrounded by friends, many of whom were the opposite sex. I maintained a higher-than-average ratio of close guy friends. While my relationships with them were strictly platonic (perhaps a few were a bit flirtatious but harmless nonetheless), they seemed to fill a void that my girlfriends couldn't fill.

My male friends treated me differently than they treated other girls—they made me feel special, respected, and protected. I cherished the connections we had and welcomed the sense of security, comfort, and affirmation those friendships brought to my life.

Reaching the Top

Arriving at our senior year, we had reached what my friends and I considered the pinnacle of our high school career. We reveled in our high-ranking status and made the most of every social opportunity.

Achievements and social standing at an all-time high, I found my identity and self-worth in such things as being in the National Honor Society, captain of the varsity soccer team, elected to student council, and voted onto Homecoming Court. I wore my social, athletic, and academic accomplishments like badges of honor. The more decorated I was, the more significant I felt.

I wore my social, athletic, and academic accomplishments like badges of honor. The more decorated I was, the more significant I felt.

Beyond doing what needed to be done for school and sports, my default setting was all fun, all the time. My sights were constantly set on whatever exciting engagement was ahead on the social calendar.

Huddled in the crowded stands of our high school gym, I bounced back and forth from cheering on the varsity basketball team and chatting with my friends. I noticed a few glances in my direction several rows away from my friend Jordan and some of the guys sitting with him but didn't think much about it.

That night, a large group of friends gathered at my best friend Stasi's house for one of our typical weekend get-togethers. Jordan approached me with a sly grin on his face. "I know someone who likes you," he taunted.

Jordan proceeded to tell me that Carter, who was a sophomore at the time, had a crush on me. I had never dated anyone younger than me, but I was immediately intrigued by the idea of being pursued by him.

Carter was a popular underclassman—athletic, charismatic, and good-looking. Almost too good-looking. The type of guy who seemed to have girls giving him extra attention wherever he went.

Always insecure about my looks, I found that fact to be super intimidating. Of all my friends, I was definitely not the prettiest. *Why would he be interested in me?* I wondered.

I gave Jordan permission to pass along my phone number, and Carter and I began to get to know one another over lengthy, late-night conversations. Still unsure if I really wanted to settle down with someone or even open myself up to all that comes with being in a relationship, I dragged my feet when it came to committing to Carter. However, I eventually succumbed to his charm, and within a few months, we became an official couple.

While I was attracted to Carter's good looks, charisma, and sense of humor, what drew me to him most was how openly he adored me. From the very beginning, he professed his strong affection for me and made me feel special—just the kind of affirmation I craved.

I felt like I had the upper hand in our relationship. Carter seemed to be more infatuated with me than I was with him, and I found comfort in being in control of my emotions.

Our relationship progressed rapidly. What started off as a fun-loving attraction turned into a deeper, more committed endeavor.

My relationship with Leo led me to the deduction that having sex was okay within the confines of a committed, loving relationship. That's how I justified my choices with Leo, and that's also how I justified becoming sexually active with Carter. He was the first person I cared deeply for since Leo. We loved each other. We were committed. Physical intimacy was the obvious next step.

Or so I thought.

From my experience, from what my friends were experiencing, and based on what seemed socially accepted, even expected, that's how I understood relationships to play out. Having sex was a part of the deal. When you give all you have—physically and emotionally—you gain the maximum measure of adoration and love your significant other has to offer. At least that's how my friends and I saw it. Teenagers have it all figured out, right? I certainly believed we did.

Besides, plenty of people I knew were having casual sex and didn't even uphold the prerequisite I had for being in a monogamous relationship. When I compared myself to others, which I incessantly did, I concluded that I was much more virtuous.

Sex was still a really big deal to me, and I didn't take that proverbial next step lightly. Checking all the boxes that qualified my relationship for intimacy made me feel justified in my choice to take things with Carter to the next level.

I was like a toddler riding a race-car amusement park ride with a fake steering wheel and pedals. I had the illusion of being in control, but rather than an easy-going kiddy ride, I found myself on a full-scale relational rollercoaster packed with unexpected twists and turns, ups and downs.

A Fractured Bond

Another rumor floated through the hallways at school and landed at our lunch table as the focal point of conversation. "Do you think it's true? Have you talked to Carter?" Jasmine inquired. The sensitivity and compassion in her voice softened the sting of her question.

"I don't know what to believe. There are so many jealous girls out there who would say anything to break us up," I replied. "Carter assured me it was all lies. He would never cheat on me. He loves me too much," I rationalized, more for myself than for the others.

Giving Carter the benefit of the doubt and assuming that his love for me trumped all possible missteps became the lens through which I chose to view our many obstacles. Insecurity, a seed that was already deeply rooted in me, began to sprout and overtake my thoughts. *Was I pretty enough for him? What if he doesn't want me anymore?*

My best defense was to play it cool. As long as he cared a little more than I did, I was in the driver's seat. As long as he loved me more than I loved him, I could rest securely behind my perceived safety belt of control.

But our relationship became tumultuous as, surprisingly, Carter became increasingly jealous and suspicious of my actions. He constantly accused me of liking or flirting with other guys, or God-forbid, cheating, which required me to plead my innocence on a regular basis.

The drama became too much, our fighting too frequent, and I broke things off with Carter. The first of many break-ups.

For close to seven years of cycling on-and-off, Carter and I battled through hurts, hurdles, and heartbreaks. With each passing year, more discrepancies surfaced, more mistrust piled on, and more damage ensued.

When we were off, Carter and I were never fully off. Our break-ups were short-lived. We never truly separated because we stayed in touch, often continued to hook up, and inevitably got back together in a short amount of time.

I was the initiator of our breakups, usually because of my unsettled feelings about our connection or lack of drive to persist through the emotional obstacles; however, my willpower to stand by my decision continually faltered. Carter persistently and charmingly pushed to reunite whenever we were apart.

Even when he wasn't actively pursuing me, I knew the door was always open if I had a sudden change of heart or a lonely spell. His consistent drive to get back together partnered with my propensity to hope for the best and longing to love and be loved led us back into each other's arms more times than I can count. Like a moth to a flame, I couldn't resist the lure of getting back with him all the while knowing that one or both of us would walk away with a new burn.

After graduating high school, I started college in the fall of 1996, moving across Ohio nearly three hours away from home. I started my freshman year committed to Carter, convinced we could make it work.

However, it didn't take long for more rumors to circulate about his infidelity, and it became even more challenging to trust him from afar. Our on-again-off-again cycle recommenced, and I began to embrace the idea of single life as a college student.

What had once been only Carter's bogus suspicions became a reality as I sought out substitutions in his intermittent absences. Living a new life of independence away at college, I justified my interactions with other guys during the times that Carter and I weren't officially together. Being hours away from Carter gave me the freedom to explore my options (as did he), and gain attention and affirmation from those suitors who were conveniently in proximity.

Still holding strong to my moral standard of not sleeping with someone unless in a committed relationship, I rationalized that my actions were innocent and defensible. I reasoned that flirting with and kissing guys was harmless, oblivious to the irreparable damage done with each act, not only to me personally but also to the fidelity of my relationship with Carter.

> *I reasoned that flirting with and kissing guys was harmless, oblivious to the irreparable damage done with each act, not only to me personally but also to the fidelity of my relationship with Carter.*

Each time Carter and I got back together, a new list of offenses would have to be rehashed and reviewed, leading to fresh new wounds or seeds of doubt and insecurity about our trustworthiness and commitment to one another. While our relationship was tumultuous and often-times hurtful, I opted for clinging to the comfortability of being with Carter rather than facing the unknowns of being alone.

I chose to block out the negative and home in on the high points, unable to deny my feelings for him or the unexplainable attachment I had to him. Not to mention with our teenage hormone thermostat set on high, our strong chemistry was a persistent pull. However, our relationship went beyond physical attraction. Carter was fun to be with, and we cared deeply for one another. But we were simply young and immature and made poor, hurtful choices far too often. Each time I went back to Carter, I justified my choice by focusing on the fullness I felt from being loved by him, however flawed that love was.

> *Like a fish needing water to breathe, it's as if I would suffocate without sufficient affirmation, affection, and adoration from a significant other.*

Like a fish needing water to breathe, I felt like I would suffocate without sufficient affirmation, affection, and adoration from a significant other.

For years, Carter fulfilled that need in me, despite our blemished connection, and I heedlessly consumed every bit of his love and devotion whenever he offered it.

Betrayal

Recently graduated from college and back home full-time, I lounged on my bed in my room at my mom and stepdad's house. They moved just after I graduated from high school so that my younger stepbrother and stepsister could finish high school in their current school district. I only lived in the new house a few short months before moving off to college, so it didn't yet fully feel like home. At least not the way my childhood home felt.

This house was just a twenty-minute drive from my hometown, but it might as well have been two hours. My whole world had been within a five-mile radius most of my life. This new part-time residence felt so far from my friends and everything I knew. Coming back home during summer breaks was not the same.

The phone rang and I snatched the receiver from my nightstand. "Hello?"

The familiar voice of my friend Olivia along with a couple other girls who were apparently tagging along for a group call, filled my ear with hurried greetings. Then Olivia said in a sober tone, "We have something to tell you that we think you need to know."

"Okayyy," I said nervously.

"Carter hooked up with Rebecca," Olivia said unemotionally. "And it wasn't just a one-time thing."

My body went numb, and my mind went blank. Panic, disbelief, and anguish poured over me from my head to my toes. After several attempts to deny the possibility of one of my best friends and my perpetual on-again-off-again boyfriend doing something so inconceivable, I finally accepted the proof that was provided.

This was not another vicious rumor. This was truth. A truth that wrecked me to my core.

I hung up the phone and began sobbing uncontrollably, my face buried in my pillow. My thoughts swirled with replays of every time the three of us had hung out together, every conversation in which I confided in Rebecca about my relationship, every loving word Carter had ever said to me. Everything I knew to be true about love and friendship, trust and loyalty, crumbled into a meaningless pile of dust that was blown away in a sudden gust of wind.

Carter and I had faced quite a few ups and downs over the previous five years. Our relationship was anything but perfect. We overcame many obstacles and hurtful incidents and forgave each other countless times. But *this* was unforgivable.

Little pins and needles of anger and hurt stabbed my heart. Humiliation violently simmered and began to boil over, scalding my ego. *How could I be so stupid? How could I believe that Carter actually loved me?* Every kind word he had ever spoken to me, every loving encounter, all of it was now erased—null and void.

I dealt with Carter the only way I knew how—through rage and hatred. I didn't have the satisfaction of a face-to-face or even phone conversation with him because he was away in basic training for the military. Instead, I wrote an explicit letter—using language that would make a sailor blush—telling him exactly how I felt, how disgusted I was with him, and how hurt I was. I concluded my letter with a pledge to cut him out of my life, once and for all.

Irreparable Damage

Confronting my broken heart with regard to Rebecca was a different experience altogether. The anguish I felt over her betrayal was other-worldly. She was like a sister to me. We had been inseparable since junior high. The hurt was suffocating. The heartache unbearable.

I pulled into the driveway of Rebecca's childhood home. Sadness settled in my spirit as I took in the view of what had felt like a second home over the years. A friendship so carefully forged through countless precious memories now melted into a heap of ashes after being burned by betrayal.

The knots in my stomach were so intense that I was sure you could physically see them if you looked close enough. I methodically walked the winding path to the charming, covered porch and took the couple steps up to her front door, simultaneously trying to calm my nerves and will my body to stop shaking.

Rebecca knew I was coming over to talk, but I didn't tell her about what or why. I needed to hear the truth directly from her, to see and read her reaction in real-time, face to face. Most importantly, I wanted to know *how* and *why* she could do such a thing.

Keeping rhythm with my pounding heart, thoughts pulsed incessantly in my mind like the booming base of a car stereo system. *How would she react? Would she deny what I already knew to be true? What possible explanation could she give to justify her actions?*

Rebecca welcomed me at the front door with a smile. Unable to return her cheerful greeting, I mumbled a half-hearted hello and kept my eyes glued to my feet as I followed her upstairs to her bedroom for a private chat. I could sense the tension building as she picked up on my unusually somber demeanor.

We entered her bedroom, and I found a place to steady myself as she closed the door. Unable to hold it in for more than a few torturous seconds and battling the urge to throw up on her plush, baby blue carpet, I blurted out a quick recap of the information I had learned about her and Carter.

Through tears, she confessed and apologized. *There it is!* I thought, triumphantly. *She admitted it.* Relief and righteousness arose in my spirit. Finally, after hours of agonizing over what would happen and how this would go, I had the confession, I had the truth, and I had an apology.

However, much to my dismay, she had no real reason or justification for *why*. No excuses. No explanations. Just a grievous apology accompanied by remorse that I couldn't be sure was less related to what she had done and more connected to being caught.

The satisfaction of achieving my mission was quickly smothered by a sense of anguish as I plummeted into a pit of hurt and hopelessness. Nothing Rebecca said made me feel any better. No amount of her tears could wash away the blemish of betrayal. No number of apologies or pleas for forgiveness could undo the damage. In that moment, I realized there was nothing she could say to make me understand how she could carry out such deliberate disloyalty and be willing to destroy a lifelong friendship.

After meeting with Rebecca and hearing the truth from her, my heart was even more shattered than before. I wanted to be hateful. I wanted to scream and yell and throw things. But the pain and sadness devoured every ounce of fight I had in me. I left her house in a haze of hurt, leaving our friendship and a piece of my heart behind.

False Forgiveness

After months of feeding the bitterness and unforgiveness that ran through my veins like venom, something happened that suddenly changed my perspective: September 11, 2001.

Most people old enough to remember the day our country was attacked by terrorists have stories of where they were and how that day impacted their lives. I could say a lot about the events of that day, the loss suffered by so many, and how it impacted me personally, but that's a story for another day.

I bring it up because it was that event that prompted me to reunite with Carter. A sense of "life is too short, and we should cling to those we love" overcame me, and I resigned to forgive the past.

Triggered by this traumatic event and possibly still fueled by the need to be loved and the inability to let go, I took Carter back. However, the damage was too extensive. My injuries still lingered beneath the surface; my insecurity never fully resolved. Our relationship was seemingly irreparable. Our efforts to reunite were futile and in less than a year of attempting to start fresh, we inevitably broke up. This time for the last time.

It didn't take long after my final breakup with Carter to rekindle my friendship with Rebecca. Once he was out of the picture, the past hurts that had created a barrier between my friend and me seemed to have lost their significance.

Besides, Rebecca and I had so much history and our lives were so intertwined that it was almost impossible to avoid her for too long. Not to mention she had been one of my best friends for years. I hated being apart from her, and I missed her dearly. We gradually worked our way back to a close connection and all was forgiven.

At least that's what I told myself and what I portrayed with my well put-together exterior and happy-go-lucky demeanor. I really did love her and wanted to be friends, and I truly believed I had forgiven her. I desperately wanted things to be back to normal and to forget all the unpleasantness we had been through. I wanted my best friend back.

But while I hid behind my protective walls of "I'm fine-We're fine-Everything is fine," fragments of unforgiveness still festered like termites tearing apart the beams holding together my mending emotions. In the closed off rooms of my heart, I was still tormented by the past, unable to fully let go of the pain and betrayal, riddled with insecurity.

Spending time with Rebecca only reminded me how inferior I felt—that she was prettier than me, more fun to be around than me, more appealing than me. Feelings of bitterness and jealousy still lingered beneath the surface and leaked out in backhanded comments or gossip about her past sins. Ensuring she wasn't off the hook for her dishonorable behavior or gaining sympathy from others made me feel better about myself and our reconciliation. As much as I wanted everything back to what it once was, my unresolved hidden hurts compromised the integrity of our refurbished friendship.

6
DESPERATE AMBER

My head pounded, my body groggy as I woke up from a restless partial night's sleep. I shifted carefully so as not to disturb the friend lying next to me in my bed—who after far too many drinks the night before, had been upgraded to more-than-friend status.

I emerged from my bedroom and made my way to the living room to find others who had crashed at my apartment after our late night of partying. My friend Parker, who was still half asleep and bleary-eyed, began trying to piece together the events of our alcohol-induced festivities.

"What a crazy night!" he reflected. "I remember everything up until that third round of Jager® bombs. Who drove us back to your apar—" He stopped mid-sentence when he heard someone stirring in my bedroom and looked at me quizzically for an explanation.

"It's Gavin," I whispered, as I looked at him intently with eyes wide and eyebrows raised, answering his unspoken question with just one look.

Knowing that my overnight guest was a long-time friend, Parker blurted out, "Geez, Amber, you'll make out with anyone!"

I shushed him quickly, for fear he would be heard. The accusation stung, but he wasn't too far off base. I had a reputation for getting overly flirtatious when alcohol was involved, and the night before was no exception.

In fact, as a perk of my single status, I maintained a lineup of go-to guys who met the requirements of providing me adequate attention and affection when called upon. Some of whom were just friends who transitioned to more than friends after a few drinks—like the situation with Gavin. Others were guys on whom I had ongoing crushes and/or who had crushes on me, and we kept things between us light and noncommittal.

If one of my regulars was not around on a particular occasion when I was tipsy and in need of affection, it was easy enough to find a stand-in for the night. I managed my emotional cravings by surrounding myself with and constantly looking out for those men whom I knew would give me what I needed—to feel seen, to feel special.

The pattern went something like this: Go out with friends on the weekends, drink heavily, search for a guy who gives me attention—either one I already know or find a new one—become extremely flirtatious, end the night with a make-out session with the suitor of choice. Rinse and repeat.

I justified that since I didn't have sex with these guys, what I was doing was innocent and harmless. I was the conductor of each nightly performance, orchestrating every encounter to gain what I wanted, nothing more, nothing less.

But as I masqueraded as a confident woman in control of my emotions, my soul was slowly eroding, and I sunk deeper into insecurity. On the outside I held it all together. But internally, my desperation for affirmation was a rapidly expanding chasm of self-doubt and loneliness. I battled a continual feeling of inadequacy—painfully aware that I was not the most attractive or most sought-after of my friends—which often led to compromise, settling for the one who would make me feel desirable, even if I didn't really desire him.

> But as I masqueraded as a confident woman in control of my emotions, my soul was slowly eroding, and I sunk deeper into insecurity.

Each time I experienced the sting of rejection or was overlooked for another girl, I either resorted to seeking affirmation from whomever would give it or ended the night alone, dejected and disappointed. I depended on the attention of men to quench the insatiable thirst for affection, to feel good enough, to feel loved.

Gradually, the boundaries I prided myself on having regarding my sexual encounters began to topple like a house of cards in a slight breeze. My need to be filled, need to be accepted, need to be loved superseded my morals. It was only a matter of time before that lifestyle would lead me to a junkyard of regrets.

Roommates and Besties

My first roommate after college, Lynn, was as close as a sister to me. We grew up playing soccer together and were good friends all through high school. Although, it wasn't until after graduation that our friendship deepened. She was and still is my person.

The person who knows everything about you—the good, bad, and ugly—and loves you anyway. The one with whom you can double over laughing or bawl your eyes out together without any regard for how you look. The one with whom you can hang out every day and never get tired of each other's company or go weeks without talking and pick up right where you left off without missing a beat. One of the first people with whom you want to share good news or the shoulder on which you would seek out to cry in a tragedy. Lynn is that person to me.

Our adventure as roommates began about a year after I graduated from college and not long after my devastating debacle with Carter and Rebecca.

"I have a crazy idea," Lynn said during one of our afternoon phone chats. "What if we move out and get our own apartment together?"

The idea had never even crossed my mind. I lived comfortably at my mom and stepdad's house. I had just started my first real job working for the marketing department of a large bank in our downtown metropolitan area. Living day-by-day, doing what I wanted, and saving money, I had never contemplated my next steps.

Excited, yet a little intimidated by the undertaking, I agreed. "How fun would it be to live together?!" I squealed as the anticipation of this new adventure began to resonate.

We immediately started our apartment search and within a few months we had a moving truck, and several family members lined up to help us make the move.

I will never forget that day in February. In true unpredictable Ohio weather, nearly a foot of snow caked the ground and thick flurries persisted as if taunting and challenging our well-thought-out moving-day plans.

Unwilling to surrender to the snowfall and delay our move, we forged ahead as scheduled. I arrived at the U-Haul® dealer early that Saturday morning to pick up our reserved box truck, half expecting them to tell me I was crazy and to go home. But I was delighted and admittedly a little nervous to get the keys to our truck and head on my way on the snowy streets.

I had never driven a giant truck like that before, let alone in near-blizzard conditions, but there was a first time for everything! The year I got my driver's license, we had one of the worst winters of my lifetime, so I learned my driving skills in intense conditions. I wasn't one to let a little snow hold me back.

Our family members who trudged back and forth through piles of snow to move our meager furniture—out of the truck, up from the parking lot, around the building, down the sidewalk that was nestled along the snow-covered pond, and up a tall flight of stairs through the entrance of our apartment—deserve a medal for their dedication to helping us as we forged ahead on that blizzardy moving day.

Living with Lynn felt like my first true grown-up experience away from home. Sure, I had gone away to college and lived in various dorms and even had an apartment for a couple of years with two of my besties, Stasi and Eden. But our homemaking skills were dismal at best. My ramen noodle, Kraft Mac & Cheese®, Tuna Helper®, and fast-food diet was certainly lacking, and I'm not sure our apartment would qualify as clean by any standard.

Yes, Stasi, Eden, and I were on our own while at college, but not in a way that felt like adulthood or would be a sustainable long-term living arrangement. Our priorities consisted of doing the bare minimum schoolwork to get by, socializing as much as possible, and sleeping off hangovers so that we could do it all again.

Our apartment was merely a homebase for facilitating those goals, not necessarily a home we were fostering.

With Lynn, who was far more domestically inclined than me, not to mention a year older and wiser, I gained a newfound enjoyment in homemaking—home-cooked meals that consisted of more than a box of processed carbohydrates, deep cleaning that left surfaces sparkling and smelling fresh.

After a long week of adulting Monday through Friday, I looked forward to our Friday night routine. As I opened the door and began the ascent up the fifteen or so stairs to our main living area, the sharp scent of Clorox® and the sound of Tim McGraw's country twang saturated our snug apartment.

Lynn usually made it home from work before me, and she faithfully kicked off our weekly cleaning ritual. Arrangements were made and the night's plans set. Once the apartment sufficiently sparkled from top to bottom, we ate a delicious baked spaghetti dinner and then settled in with a couple of cocktails as our friends arrived for a pre-outing get together. We drank, laughed, and played games as we geared up for a night out on the town.

An Old Friend

With several years of being single under my belt since Carter, I had mastered the skill of interacting with men on a very surfacy level. I enjoyed the attention—the flirting and even their pursuit. Still, I had no desire to take things any further. When it came to men and my feelings, I felt like I was in control. Until David.

Our small town buzzed with gossip of an old friend coming back home after getting married and moving out of state. Rumors rumbled like distant thunder about David's difficult separation from his wife and how he would be moving in with his parents until he could get back on his feet.

Not long after David arrived home and settled in at his parents' house, a mutual friend, Brody, mentioned that he was interested in connecting with me.

David and I were friends in high school but not super close. He was a couple years older than me, and we spent plenty of time hanging out in the same circles of friends. Always the life of the party, the center of attention, David was fun to be around. With a bit of a rebellious side, he was also one of those guys whose appeal was usually accompanied by a few warning bells, albeit muffled by his charisma and charm.

After nearly a decade of being disconnected from David and well before we used social media to keep tabs on each other, I was eager to reconnect. I genuinely wanted to support him through what seemed to be a really difficult time. I passed along my phone number and after a couple quick chats, David and I hashed out a plan to go out and catch up one Friday night.

As I put on the last of my makeup and finished getting ready for my night out with David, a train thundered through our sleepy neighborhood, shaking the lamp on my nightstand. Glancing around my bedroom, I reflected on how much had changed in the last couple years.

Less than two years after Lynn and I moved into our apartment, Lynn's parents had to make an unexpected move for her dad's job. Their old nineteenth century home had sentimental meaning as it had been passed down from Lynn's grandparents. Not quite ready to let it fall into the hands of strangers, Lynn offered to buy their home.

Our journey as roommates abruptly shifted from apartment life to homeownership for Lynn and to home improvement projects for both of us. We eagerly began painting and prepping Lynn's new old house to make it our own. The adorable old-fashioned home was full of character and nestled on a corner lot just a couple blocks from our town's quaint little downtown area.

I grabbed my jacket out of the closet and tried to shake my nervous thoughts. *What would it be like to hang out with David one-on-one? I'm not nearly as interesting or outgoing as he is. What if he gets bored?*

A loud knock jostled me out of my rabbit trail of insecurities, and I refocused my attention on the present moment. Carefully trotting down the narrow staircase, I made my way through the family room to our front entrance.

As I swung open the door, David's familiar friendly smile and bright eyes melted away my uncertainty. I fell into his welcoming embrace and surrendered to a feeling of comfort and friendship.

David and I enjoyed a casual night at a local bar playing pool and catching up over a few drinks. We reminisced and laughed and covered as many of the highlights as we could from our past ten years apart.

David also opened up about the terrible separation he endured from his wife. His woundedness and anger seeped through as he shared the events that led to what he described as the shocking rock-bottom in his marriage and the ultimate decision to move back home. My heart ached for him.

After several hours, David dropped me off at my house with a casual, "We should hang out again sometime."

"Sure!"

I had a great time with David, as I expected I would. He was easy to be around, a good guy, and an old friend. A little quirky at times with a much bigger personality than mine but fun to be around, nonetheless. Plus, with all he was going through, I wanted to be there for him.

Falling Fast

Our "sometime soon" plans to hang out again came much sooner than I had anticipated. David reached out and asked me to go to a local amusement park the very next weekend.

About a day or two before David and I were scheduled to head out for a fun-filled day of rollercoasters and junk food, I chatted with Brody about my upcoming outing. Brody, who was a mutual friend but one of David's close friends, expressed his opinion about our plans. "You know this is a date, right?" he asked matter-of-factly.

I scoffed and then I laughed at his ridiculous claim, and I told him he was wrong. "We're just friends," I reminded him.

He responded with a smug, "Well, not if he can help it."

I went into that day with Brody's words tumbling in the back of my mind. I still had only friendship intentions with David. He was a great guy, but I didn't think about him romantically. Moreover, he was obviously heartbroken and bitter about his separation and clearly not in a proper emotional state to date someone. I just wanted to be a good friend and help him get acclimated back to life at home during such a difficult time.

As the day progressed though, I started to notice a flirtation taking place. It didn't take David long to make it clear he was interested in me, and I slowly began to let my guard down. I allowed the irresistible pull of being pursued, being liked, to draw me into David's world, ignoring the faint traces of warning bells that jingled in my head.

Within just a couple weeks, our friendship transformed into a full-blown relationship, and we spent every possible minute together. I fell for David so quickly and unexpectedly that my head was spinning. I had never developed such deep feelings for someone in such a short amount of time.

David held back nothing. He was openly infatuated with me, professing his love and affection for me every chance he got. I cherished every minute of it, savoring every doting word. He made me feel so special and so loved—treasured even. Any control I once had over my emotions completely vanished.

The connection I had with David was almost tormenting. I longed for him in a way I had never longed for another man. If we weren't together, I could only think about the next time I would see him. When we were together, I was entrenched in him and his life. I felt a fullness with him I hadn't experienced before, and I was oblivious to the world around me.

Once the one who couldn't resist being with as many friends as possible or attending every social event, I could now take it or leave it. My only requirement for contentedness was to be with David. My heart increasingly craved closeness and intimacy with David, and I completely surrendered to my feelings for him.

Not once did the word *adultery* ever cross my mind—our relationship wasn't scandalous and it wasn't a secret, not even from his estranged wife, so what was the harm?

Trouble in Paradise

Several months into our high-speed relationship, once the euphoria of being together began to level out, some of the imperfections of our connection began to surface. An uneasiness bristled inside of me.

The anger and hatred in David's voice spewed out as he complained, once again, of his not quite ex-wife's recent behavior. "This will all be better once your divorce is final," I reassured him. "Have you made any progress since the last time you checked in about your next steps?" I asked. "You know I can help you with paperwork or whatever you need to get this resolved," I offered, trying not to sound too eager.

My concern for his well-being, coupled with my own selfish desire for him to have a clean break from his wife once and for all for our relationship's sake, fueled my motivation to help.

"No, no. I wouldn't want you to have to do that. I'll get it taken care of this week," he promised.

How many times have we circled this topic? I thought to myself. The fact that David tended to be a lot of talk with little action in various areas of his life had become an ongoing frustration for me.

Over the course of the past six months, a myriad of David's unfavorable behaviors and habits had surfaced. Blinded by infatuation in the beginning, I overlooked many of the warning signs. But as we became closer and the more I grew to care about him, the more I recognized the destructive patterns and the more I desired for him to make positive changes in his life.

Those once distant jingling warning bells had become incessant, clanging cymbals. Determined to ignore them, I clung to my faltering fantasy of a life with David.

In the beginning of our relationship, David went out of his way to avoid doing things around me that I disapproved of, and he continually expressed a desire to change. His need to please me was evident. However, several months into our relationship, I noticed he seemed less concerned with covering up his undesirable actions and more combative when I lovingly confronted him.

"I'm a grown man. I can do what I want," he retorted. "Why do you want to change me?" His words pricked my heart, as I felt the sting of irritation and indifference in his voice.

He seems so distant lately and like he no longer cares how I feel. What did I do to make him suddenly so disinterested in me? Worry and angst consumed my thoughts.

I was drowning in a sea of conflict. Like a Ping-Pong® ball endlessly bouncing back and forth from one emotion to the next—frustration and joy, disapproval and elation, contentedness and insecurity—never landing in a stable or peaceful place.

Several days had passed without a word from David. He had been ignoring my phone calls, or even worse, having his parents relay dodgy messages about being away at work or unable to talk.

Our interactions over the past few weeks replayed in my mind: His distant, distracted demeanor. The change in how he looked at me and talked to me as if I were a random acquaintance rather than his love interest of the last six months.

The waterfall of compliments and words of affirmation that typically flowed when I was with David had all but dried up. He had even developed well thought-out, almost believable excuses that prevented us from being physically intimate.

I no longer felt pretty enough or interesting enough or lovable enough to hold David's attention or affection. A feeling of being unloved and undesirable became a dense, sticky spider web that snared my soul and entangled my mind in debilitating self-doubt.

A feeling of being unloved and undesirable became a dense, sticky spider web that snared my soul and entangled my mind in debilitating self-doubt.

A mixture of panic, insecurity, and anguish seared my insides like venom running through my veins. Worry and helplessness set in as I became desperate to track down David and get to the bottom of his unusual and hurtful behavior.

The Other Woman

On Friday night with almost a week of no word from David, Lynn pleaded with me to stick with our plans to go to a costume party at one of our favorite bars downtown.

"You'll feel better once you're out!" she encouraged me. "You need to get your mind off of David, or you'll make yourself crazy."

Battling tears and a ceaseless sick feeling in my stomach, I reluctantly agreed. I halfheartedly donned my costume with a green grass skirt flowing around my waist, a multicolored Hawaiian lei draped on my neck, a pink and white flower tucked behind my ear, and an unconvincing smile pasted on my face.

Several hours and multiple drinks into our evening, the distractions of the crowded venue and loud music faded, and thoughts of David bombarded me once again. I couldn't stand the torture of not knowing what was going on. *Why was he ignoring me? What had I done wrong? When would I hear from him again?* My insides churned with the anguish of the unknowns.

Throwing my pride out the window, I convinced Lynn to ditch the party and go to David's house with me to confront him. As we pulled onto the docile street and parked in front of David's parents' modest one-story brick home, Lynn asked again for about the fifth time since we began our short five-minute car ride, "Are you sure you want to do this?"

"I have to," I insisted. "I feel like I'm losing my mind. I need to know what's going on."

Aware of the late hour, we approached the front door quietly and knocked softly so as not to disturb David's parents. David's mom, Cindy, slowly opened the door and peeked to see who was there. I could see David's dad, John, hovering not far behind her. When Cindy saw me, she swung the door open the rest of the way and lovingly embraced me.

Since David lived at home with his parents and we spent almost every waking (and sleeping) minute together, I had become quite close to his family. His mom and dad were both always loving and kind to me, despite the awkward nature of our relationship. They regularly expressed that they loved how happy I made him, especially considering the hurt and sadness that he endured from his separation.

Lynn and I took a couple steps into the house as John shut the door behind us. I nervously tried to find the words to ask about David when I suddenly noticed the compassion and distress in their eyes. They shared knowing glances and after what felt like an eternity, Cindy finally spoke.

"David's not here, sweetie." She paused, as if unsure of whether to keep going. "He has been with Rachel all week. I'm so sorry."

All the air left my lungs, and my legs became noodles. I crumpled to a nearby couch, unable to stand. Was I hearing this correctly? The thought itself sounded so ludicrous in my head that I couldn't possibly say it out loud. But the reality of my situation flashed in my mind like an obnoxiously buzzing neon sign. *My boyfriend was cheating on me with his wife.*

Through tearful sobs, I hugged and thanked Cindy and John for loving me enough to tell me the truth. Lynn and I quickly said our goodbyes and exited the way we came in.

Lynn drove us home as I stared out the window at the blurry streetlights in a state of sheer devastation, my heart broken. I felt used, rejected, and utterly stupid. *How could I have believed that David really loved me? How was I so foolish to fall so hard for someone whose heart clearly belonged to someone else?*

Learning to Let Go

My relationship with David didn't end there. Once his secret was out in the open, we finally talked. Our circumstances complicated even further as he confessed his uncertainty about getting back together with his wife and professed his love for me. He wavered back and forth between his feelings for Rachel and for me, torn by the hurt he had endured with her and the comfort he had found with me.

Even in the heartache, even after the weeks of torment and feeling unloved, even after such devastating betrayal, engulfed in desperation and selfishness, a part of me still wanted David to choose me.

And he did. After several weeks of emotional tug-of-war with David, we got back together.

The faintly jingling warning bells in the distance that had progressed into clanging cymbals were now blasting bombs that crashed and exploded right in front of me, forewarning me about the self-destructive path ahead. But I was blinded and deafened by my infatuation with David and the desire to be loved.

I couldn't let go. I was shackled to David. And I was addicted to finding any hint of how elated I felt to be loved by him, even if those feelings were now stained with insecurity and instability, betrayal and heartache.

The faintly jingling warning bells in the distance that had progressed into clanging cymbals were now blasting bombs that crashed and exploded right in front of me, forewarning me about the self-destructive path ahead.

After several more months on a toxic emotional roller coaster with David, our relationship ended. Not long after we broke up for good, he went back to his wife.

No matter how angry I wanted to be at him, no matter how hard I wanted to fight for him and beg him to stay with me, I realized that I couldn't. I couldn't do that because I loved him, and I ultimately wanted what was best for him.

That's always what I had wanted for him. As much as the rejection hurt, being mad at David for wanting to be reunited with his wife and to repair his broken family was not an option. What he chose was a good thing. It was the right thing.

It just so happened to be the thing that shattered my heart into a million broken pieces and left me feeling even more insecure,

The roots of rejection and abandonment had burrowed so deeply that it felt unfeasible for them to ever come out.

more undesirable, and more damaged than I ever had. The roots of rejection and abandonment had burrowed so deeply that it felt unfeasible for them to ever come out.

7
RECKLESS AMBER

During the timeframe that I dealt with the back and forth and ups and downs with David, a few big changes took place in Lynn's life, leading to major changes in mine as well.

In the spring of 2004, Lynn and her boyfriend, Carl, got married. While I was elated for Lynn and for her future with Carl, sadly, it meant that our days as roomies had come to an end.

In May of that same year, I bought my first house and began a brand-new adventure of being an independent homeowner. My new home was conveniently located only a mile from Lynn and Carl and less than two miles from my mom and stepdad, who had recently moved back to our hometown after my stepbrother graduated high school. Thankfully, I didn't have far to go for a comforting meal at my mom's or for some girl time with Lynn.

For the first time in my life, approaching my mid 20s, I was on my own. I slid into living alone with much more ease than I had anticipated. I quickly began to appreciate the solitude and soaked up the freedom of designing my days to suit my desires. I thoroughly enjoyed taking on the responsibility of homeownership and thrived in my newfound independence.

Downward Spiral

While I flourished in my career, my role as a homeowner, and my personal life with the exception of boyfriends, of course, my self-worth and self-confidence continued to rapidly decline. This was less noticeable from the outside, as I had long since mastered the skill of masking my internal turmoil.

But inside, something had shifted in me after David. The brokenness I felt developed an even deeper root, and I tunneled into a darker place than I had ever been.

Each rejection seemed to compound the last and push me further and further into a pit of insecurity, self-doubt, and loneliness. I desperately wanted to be loved, but I didn't know what love really looked like.

I fell back into my pattern of drowning my feelings in drunken weekend outings and seeking attention in all the wrong ways. My drinking and my desire to be loved severely impaired my decision-making process and my ability to say "no." I found myself on more than one occasion compromising my gradually eroding standards only to deeply regret it later.

I desperately wanted to be loved, but I didn't know what love really looked like.

As my self-worth decreased, my need to numb and ignore the pain increased. Social drinking, late night parties, and barhopping had been a staple in my life for close to a decade. This easy-going, party girl, weekend warrior lifestyle was my escape.

However, the deeper the woundedness I felt, the more dramatic my nights became. What started off as a free-spirited, joyful buzz inevitably ended in drunken despair. Unable—or unwilling—to stop drinking before the point of inebriation, I became increasingly irresponsible and reckless.

Lynn and I recently recalled the time I took my reckless abandon too far—one of my wake-up calls.

Wandering Amber

My friends, Lynn, Jess, Cammy, and I bounced and laughed as we belted out the chorus to Bon Jovi's "Living on a Prayer" on the packed dance floor. The song faded out and we paused, anxiously awaiting the DJ's next selection. Song after song, we demonstrated our enthusiastic approval for each hit that blared through the speakers with relentless jumping, dancing, and singing.

As the last song in a string of upbeat tunes concluded, so did our dancing. Breathless, with arms linked, we formed a train and pulled one another through the crowd. We filed away from the dance floor and toward the rest of our friends stationed at the bar, ready for a much-needed break and another drink.

As we each claimed an open spot and joined in the conversation with the rest of our group, another round of shots appeared in front of us. I downed mine without a second thought about my already unstable legs, fuzzy head, and slurred words.

As the minutes passed, the sound of chattering conversations around me faded like a freight train traveling off into the distance. I backed away from the group and slumped into a stool, an irresistible urge to isolate began to overtake my previous happy-go-lucky demeanor.

As if an internal switch suddenly turned off, I came down from my high of dancing, drinking, and laughing with friends and sunk into quicksand of sadness, loneliness, and despair. Desperate to escape the crowd and the suffocating feelings, I slipped away from my friends, staggered to the front entrance of the bustling night club, and stumbled out the door into the dark night.

As if on drunken autopilot, I took off my high-heeled shoes, slung my purse over my shoulder, and trudged through the parked cars toward the street to begin the trek home.

Even though I knew people would worry about me, something about walking down dark streets in the middle of the night and sneaking away from my friends made me feel like I could breathe again.

But the breath of fresh air was short-lived as feelings of purposelessness, sadness, and self-pity covered me like an unwanted heavy blanket in the humid summer night air.

My recent breakup with David left me feeling broken and unloved. I had started dating other guys, but my emotional thermostat seemed to be permanently stuck on cold. I could not feel.

About half a mile into my walk, not even one fourth of the way to my destination, my bare feet began to ache as much as my heart. My cell phone rang, and I fumbled through my purse to find it.

I flipped open the receiver, pressed the green call button, and held the small device to my ear. "Hello?"

"Where are you?!" Lynn bellowed from the other end of the line, sounds of loud music and chatter booming in the background.

"I'm walking home," I said matter-of-factly.

"Well, I figured that when I couldn't find you," she answered, a bit exasperated. Lynn was accustomed to my habit of disappearing in the middle of a gathering to meander the streets, sometimes with a destination in mind, sometimes just to get out and clear my head. My bizarre late-night pastime was so well-known that Lynn had begun jokingly referring to me as "Wandering Amber."

"You could have at least told someone! We would have taken you home," she scolded.

Just then, headlights pierced the dark night, and I looked over my shoulder to see a car approaching from behind. A gray, four-door sedan slowed down and pulled up beside me. A friendly-looking man, clean-cut and maybe in his early 40s, called out through the rolled down passenger window, "Do you need a ride?"

Beginning to regret my choice to walk, I quickly evaluated my aching feet, unsteady legs, spinning head, and the long distance yet to go. "Sure!" I replied, eager to accept his offer.

"Don't you *dare* get into that car!" Lynn's screeching voice pierced my ear. I almost forgot she was still on the phone.

I hesitated for a moment and then in my most sober-sounding voice possible explained to the kind stranger that my friend didn't approve. He reassured me that he meant no harm and only wanted to help. He told me about his family and the kind of guy he was. I wholeheartedly believed him.

"Lynn, he's a nice guy. He has three kids! It's fine," I reasoned. This wouldn't be the first time I hitched a ride with a random stranger in the middle of the night. I didn't see what the big deal was.

With Lynn's panicked protest persisting in my ear, I opened the car door and slid into the passenger seat. "Do not hang up the phone with me until you're home," she conceded.

"Okay. You're being silly, but fine," I agreed just to appease her. I felt a tinge of guilt because I could tell how distressed she was over the situation. But my intoxicated state shielded me from feeling any real remorse or taking any responsibility for my actions.

I nonchalantly made small talk with the nice stranger while Lynn continued to mutter her disapproval over the phone. In less than 10 minutes, we turned onto my street, I pointed to my house, and he pulled into the driveway. I thanked my pseudo-taxi driver, closed the car door behind me, stumbled to my door, and waved as he drove away.

Feeling justified in my choice, I threw in a quick, "I told you it would be fine" to Lynn.

Rather than brushing it off as she normally did when I pulled similar stunts in the past, an unmistakable anger and concern permeated her tone, "What you just did was not okay. I was scared to death."

To emphasize the seriousness of the matter, she added, "And now this random guy knows where you live and that you live alone. Did you think of that?"

"Oh. I'm really sorry."

No, I didn't think of that. We ended our phone call, and feelings of guilt and fear set in. I suddenly felt terrible for causing my friend so much stress, not to mention feeling extremely vulnerable knowing that I, in fact, did live alone as a single woman and now there was a mysterious man who could come back at any moment.

I tossed my purse and shoes on the floor of my bedroom and climbed into bed for what ended up being a restless night of worry, regret, and loneliness.

Dating Dilemma

A couple of years after my relationship with David had crashed and burned, I was still stuck in a half-hearted dating cycle but starting to hope and be open to the possibility of finding my Prince

Charming. Now in my late 20s, I was increasingly aware of the taunting ticking clock as I wished for a husband.

My friend, Jasmine, had a coworker whom she wanted me to meet. She gave him my phone number, and we set up a time to get together. My first blind date.

In all my years of being single, I had plenty of guys with whom I dated or hung out, but all of them had been familiar in some way. In my small town, everybody knew everybody. For the most part, my pool of prospects typically came from people I knew from school, sports, or another family or friend connection.

This guy was a complete stranger from a totally different town over an hour away. With the exception of Jasmine, nobody knew him. And even at that, he was merely a coworker whom she claimed "seemed like a nice guy."

I knew very little about him, and none of my friends knew who he was. Because of that, he was appropriately given the nickname "Stranger" and was jokingly referred to by that name whenever I discussed him with my friends.

Stranger and I had long chats on the phone getting to know each other over the course of several weeks with a few dates sprinkled here and there.

Everything about dating Stranger felt new to me. He wasn't another one of my high school friends-turned-make-out-buddy after a night of drinking. We went on actual dates. He wasn't young or immature and didn't have obvious baggage to ignore. He had a career, lived on his own, and seemed to have his act together. What we were doing felt more grown-up than most of my past experiences.

One date night as I pulled into the parking lot of our go-to Italian bistro, I parked and paused for a few minutes to calm my nerves. Not only was Stranger a few years older than me, but he had a good job, a nice house, and was established and confident. He was attractive and he knew it—sure of himself in a slightly arrogant, yet appealing way. His confidence intimidated me.

I felt pressure to be likable. I was painfully aware that although I was well-known and liked in my town with lots of friends who would vouch for my character and likability, all that was meaningless for someone like him—a stranger. We were starting from scratch, and I needed to prove myself worthy of getting to know.

Somehow, I had to make him see me as someone interesting enough, smart enough, pretty enough to want to date. All the while, I was unconvinced that any of that was actually true.

Stalling, still sitting in my car, my insecurity bubbled. *Who am I if I'm not the friendly, popular girl from my small town? Do I have anything worthwhile to offer?* Often, I doubted that I did.

> *Somehow, I had to make him see me as someone interesting enough, smart enough, pretty enough to want to date. All the while, I was unconvinced that any of that was actually true.*

I took a couple deep breaths, put on a mask of confidence, and hoped for the best as I stepped through the large double doors to another self-doubting rendezvous.

Compromise

Stranger and I continued to date for several more weeks, evolving into hanging out at my house from time to time. He worked in my hometown but lived over an hour away, so it made sense to stop by my house after work.

One evening when we were watching a movie snuggled up in my living room, the familiar routine began. We started kissing, and Stranger pressed to take things further.

"I'm not ready," I resisted as I had done quite a few times before.

He persisted with his ongoing argument: "Don't you like me?" he continued, unfazed by my response.

My thoughts raced. Everything about dating in this way was new to me. I came from such a long line of dysfunctional interactions with men that I didn't know what normal was at this point.

I did know, however, that having sex was still a big deal to me, and I didn't do that with just anyone. Yes, I had long since passed my moral threshold. Admittedly, I had even made mistakes and taken some interactions a lot farther than I would have liked. But sleeping with someone was far from a casual occurrence for me.

When I thought of that level of intimacy, I thought of love. Or at least the potential of being in love. *I do not want to have sex with him,* I thought in a panic. *I don't love him.* I wasn't sure how much I even *liked* him.

I continued to squirm and push him away, trying to refocus on the movie. Openly disgruntled, he shifted and turned his attention to the screen in front of us, distancing himself from me. Hurt by his reaction and feeling unsure how to mend the situation, I continued watching the movie in silence, self-consciousness swirling inside me.

Toward the end of the night, however, he picked up where he had left off with round two, as if unwilling to accept defeat. We kissed and I, once again, resisted his advances. He huffed in frustration and paused to look at me. "What's the big deal, anyway?" he asked accusingly as if there was something wrong with me.

Feeling stupid and a little babyish, I thought to myself, *What is the big deal? Why am I such a prude about sex?*

I started rationalizing with myself that this is what adult dating looks like: *You go on dates with guys, and you have sex with them. That's normal, right?* Everything promoted in our culture and shown on TV and movies would suggest that to be true. I knew plenty of people who wouldn't hesitate to have sex in a similar situation.

Furthermore, hadn't I already passed the point of saving myself for marriage? What would it matter if I added one more guy to my list?

I finished the internal dialogue with myself and reluctantly relented. *Fine. I guess this is how dating works as an adult. I might as well get used to it.* I succumbed to the pressure, I believed the lies about dating and about myself, and I gave away another piece of my soul.

Stranger and I probably only dated a month or so after that. Even though my feelings for him were lackluster at best, after having sex with him, I felt as if I had to make it work to justify my actions. But it was obvious that neither of us had much of a spark for the other. We were going through the motions.

> *I succumbed to the pressure, I believed the lies about dating and about myself, and I gave away another piece of my soul.*

I felt used. I felt stupid. Most of all, I was angry at myself for letting things go that far.

I had finally gotten up the nerve to have a chat with Stranger about how this dating relationship wasn't working, but he suddenly stopped returning my calls. I had never been so happy for a guy to *not* call me back! I felt relieved but also a little baffled by his lack of maturity and respect. At least I had been willing to do the adult thing and have a conversation.

Oh well. Another failed attempt at a relationship, another notch in my belt, another blemish on my character, and another reason to feel like I would never find *the* one.

INVITED

Bless the Lord, O my soul,
and forget not all his benefits,
who forgives all your iniquity,
who heals all your diseases,
who redeems your life from the pit,
who crowns you with steadfast love and mercy,
who satisfies you with good
so that your youth is renewed like the eagle's.
(Psalm 103:2-5 ESV)

8
HYPOCRITICAL AMBER

A couple of years after Lynn got married, she invited me to go to the church she and Carl had been attending. I accepted.

At 28 years old, I had not been to church—except for the obligatory Christmas Eve and Easter services—in over a decade. On a wintry January morning, I excitedly stepped into my first regularly scheduled Sunday church service as an adult, my heart open and my mind set on revisiting my relationship with God.

Sitting in a cushioned chair just a few rows from the stage, waves of worship music swept me away in a familiar feeling of belonging. Peace and love sprinkled over me, trickled into my mind, seeped to my soul, and filled my heart to overflowing.

The fog lifted. The despair dissipated. After so many years of searching, trying to fill a void in all the wrong ways, desperately seeking love and falling short over and over again, I suddenly saw clearly: *this* is what was missing. God is what—rather Whom—I had needed. *He* was the missing piece of my life!

> *I suddenly saw clearly: this is what was missing. God is what—rather Whom—I had needed.*

I felt overwhelmed with relief and a sense of home. Despite all my mistakes, my ugly past, my intentional rebellion against God, I felt His affection and acceptance that Sunday morning. His tangible love lavished over me as I began to grasp, possibly for the first time, that He was not holding a grudge against me. He was not sitting in a heavenly courtroom ready to slam His gavel and angrily dole out punishment to me.

Rather, my Heavenly Father was comforting me. He was even delighting in me! He was rejoicing that I was willingly taking a step toward Him even though I spent so much of my life turning away. I was the Prodigal Daughter—after years of straying, wandering, and lost in selfishness, rebellion and brokenness, I was finally returning to His loving, open arms.[1]

A Slow Climb Out of the Pit

I wish I could say that upon my return to church and, more importantly, to God I was suddenly whipped into shape and living whole-heartedly for the Lord. On the contrary, it was a slow and methodical process with lots of slip-ups and backsliding along the way.

While this revelation of God's acceptance and love began to penetrate the walls around my hardened heart, I still had a plethora of selfish desires, unhealthy habits, and harmful thought patterns to correct—not to mention trauma from which to heal.

Kind of like a giant cruise ship changing course, my turnaround didn't happen in an instant. My course correction took place bit-by-bit, habit-by-habit, thought-pattern-by-thought-pattern.

I began attending church sporadically at first but soon became a regular Sunday morning attendee. Every single week, tears streamed down my face during worship as truth and peace pierced my soul.

With each passing week, the cold, depleted, hollow feeling inside of me filled with a soothing warmth. I didn't understand how or why, but I felt the tangible refreshment of the Lord. He patiently and affectionately wooed me back to Him, week after week.

Within a few months of attending church, I enrolled in my first women's Bible study. My hunger for the Lord grew as I began to take a deep dive into who God really is and who He says that I am.

---

1   Luke 15:11-32

Getting to Know God

I had grown up in church and knew a lot of information *about* God but didn't really know God personally. What I discovered through studying the Bible—with a brand-new perspective and surrounded by other women who were earnestly seeking truth[2]—is that not only did I know very little about God as my Heavenly Father, but I knew even less about what it looked like to be in a relationship with Him and live my life like I believed what He said was true.

While I knew that Jesus was God's Son whom He sent to die for us on the cross, that if we believed in Him, we would have eternal life,[3] I didn't actually *know* Jesus.

I lacked relationship. I didn't truly know the Father, I didn't know Jesus, and I had very little information or knowledge about who the Holy Spirit is. I had a long way to go and a lot to learn.

A hunger and even a desperation for the Lord bubbled up inside me. I dove into Bible study after Bible study. I attended as many women's ministry and church events as possible and surrounded myself with others who wanted the same thing or were living a life I desired. I couldn't quench the incessant thirst for more of Him, so I continued to seek out every opportunity to learn, grow, and connect with God.

Living a Double Life

"I'm sorry. I can't go out tonight. I have…church," I responded sheepishly to a friend who wanted to meet up for drinks. I couldn't even bring myself to say the whole truth—that I was attending a Bible study that evening. My friends knew that I had been going to church lately but admitting that I was in a Bible study group made me sound like some kind of Bible-thumping Christian.

Why was I so hesitant to share the whole story? Why did I feel a sense of embarrassment about being the type of Christian who was openly pursuing a relationship with Jesus?

---

2   1 John 5:20
3   John 3:16

I became aware of the negative, almost derogatory, perception I previously had of Christians—at least the ones who openly professed their faith and lived like Christians. In my view, they were lame. As far as I was concerned, they weren't part of the cool crowd.

After all, they were missing out on all the things that I believed were important to having an enjoyable life—drinking, parties, crude humor, pop culture, sex…basically anything normal. As my perception of Christianity began to change and I contemplated a new way of living, I faced the nagging worry once again: "What would people think of me?"

As I took tentative steps toward God and my new life, I began to realize how conflicting it was to openly be a Christian. Not just to *say* you're a Christian, but to actually *live* it.

I started to recognize a double standard that so many self-proclaimed Christians lived by—the unspoken false understanding that you can go to church on Sundays (or not), say you believe in God, even claim to accept the truth about Jesus as the Savior, but then go on living your life like you always have, the way you want.

Up until this point, that is how I lived most of my life. If you were to ask me, I certainly would have claimed to be a Christian. But to anyone looking in from the outside, no evidence existed to back up that claim. I looked and acted just like everyone else around me, living for and by the world's standards. I was beginning to understand now that that kind of lifestyle completely contradicts what the Bible says it looks like to be a Christian.

Do not love the world or the things in the world. If anyone loves the world, the love of the Father is not in him. For all that is in the world—the desires of the flesh and the desires of the eyes and pride of life—is not from the Father but is from the world. (1 John 2:15-16 ESV)

Even after coming back to church and back to God, I found myself living a double life—a typical weekend of drunkenness followed by a Sunday morning in church, engaging in premarital sex with my current boyfriend one night followed by a group Bible study the next.

I had to ask myself: *Did I really value what God values? Was I actually living the way Christ commanded me to live? If I truly believed that Jesus died for my sins and claimed that He was the Lord of my life, then wouldn't my life demonstrate that truth? Jesus said, "If you love me, you will keep my commands"* (John 14:15 ESV).

> *If I truly believed that Jesus died for my sins and claimed that He was the Lord of my life, then wouldn't my life demonstrate that truth?*

Out with the Old, in with the New

"Oops, I'm sorry, Amber. I know you're religious now." Another stinging remark seared my pride as my friend Michael apologized for making a derogatory comment in front of me. A few smirks and snickers followed from some of the others engaged in our conversation.

My face flushed with embarrassment. "Oh, it's no big deal!"

As I coolly brushed off his comment, heat traveled from my face to my belly in a ripple of dejection. That was just one of many recent occurrences that forced me to see that I no longer fit in. I stood out from the people who were closest to me and whom I loved dearly.

That lifestyle and those relationships were all I knew. The thought of leaving any of it behind caused a sense of dread and loneliness to weigh me down like an anchor tethered to my ankle. I still loved my friends, and they still loved me, but our lives were seemingly going in different directions.

Once again, I felt the discomfort that I felt as a teenager who wanted so desperately to blend in and be accepted. Faced with a choice, I had to answer the glaring question: Whose approval mattered most to me—people's or God's?

For am I now seeking the approval of man, or of God? Or am I trying to please man? If I were still trying to please man, I would not be a servant of Christ. (Galatians 1:10 ESV)

I can't shake the image of a familiar cartoon meme with a young girl standing in front of Jesus, clutching her little baby blue stuffed teddy bear tightly to her chest.

Jesus is standing in front of her, holding His hand out, asking her to give Him the bear. But she is peering up at Him with doubt and skepticism, unwilling to release her precious toy.

What the little girl cannot see is that while she is clinging tightly to her teddy bear, reluctant to release her treasure, Jesus is holding a teddy bear behind His back just like hers but much larger. He won't reveal it to her, or hand it over, until she releases what she is holding. The little girl does not understand that what she is grasping onto is merely a fraction of what He has for her.

9
SURRENDERED AMBER

On June 19, 2007, nearly eighteen months after returning to church and pursuing a relationship with God, I prayed a prayer that changed my life.

I walked into the sanctuary on this Father's Day Sunday and took my regular seat near the front, eager to worship the Lord and glean from my pastor Charlie's teaching.

"God loves you too much not to do everything He can to try to bring you back," Charlie began. His words pierced my heart like darts of truth breaking through my hardened exterior. Charlie repeated that phrase several times. Each time a new truth dart hit its mark, it was as if it released a salve that soothed and filled the fractured pieces of my heart.

I might as well have been the only one in the room because I knew that what Charlie was saying was meant for me. Every word resonated deep in my being. Each truth brought more profound revelation of my Heavenly Father's love for me.

Overcome with emotion, I had an overwhelming desire to let God have His way in me once and for all.

Charlie closed the service with an invitation to join him in a prayer to surrender all to the Lord. I eagerly accepted. With my hands open in my lap, I repeated the prayer silently to myself and meant every word with all my heart. *I'm done living life my way. Lord, please lead me. Please take the reins of my life. I surrender all to You.*

Charlie closed his message with a bold prediction: "Those of you who truly meant what you prayed are in for a life change."

As I left the building, feeling uplifted and excited about the prayer, I had a lingering skepticism about what it could really mean for me and where I was headed next. I had been on a journey now for over a year, gradually inviting the Lord in, but I knew I was still holding back.

While I genuinely desired God and the peace and joy and fulfillment that He promised, there were still areas of my life where I struggled with repetitive sin, not to mention all my past mistakes that made me feel damaged and ashamed. Plaguing thoughts ran through my mind. *Could I really change? Are God's promises really for me? How could He fully accept me after all I have done?*

As soon as I got into my car and turned on the ignition, confirmation that God knew me and heard my prayers blared through the car speakers. A final dart of truth penetrated my heart through a familiar song ringing out on the radio. I immediately burst into tears, consumed with emotion. The song was one I had played over and over for the past couple months as my personal prayer to God.

On my knees, I'll ask
Last chance for one last dance

'Cause with you; I'd withstand
All of hell to hold your hand
I'd give it all; I'd give for us
Give anything, but I won't give up

'Cause you know, you know, you know
That I love you
I have loved you all along
And I miss you
Been far away, for far too long[1]

---

1   Nickelback, "Far Away," lyrics by Chad Kroeger, Ryan Peake, Mike Kroeger, and Daniel Adair, *The Best of Nickelback, Vol. 1,* Roadrunner Records, Inc., 2006.

Although it's a secular song about a love story between two people who were estranged, to me it represented my deep repentance for straying from God and my hopeful plea to the Lord for one more chance.

Just as I had prayed only minutes earlier inside the church—that I no longer wanted to do things my way; I wanted to surrender all to God and His way—this song expressed my hopeful longing for Him to be back in my life.

The song ends with what I perceived as God's response to my prayer, one that I replayed over and over again, in which He reassured me that He has loved me all along, He had forgiven me, and that He would never let me go.

Those lyrics were nourishment for my dry and weary soul. Tears of joy streamed down my face as I sat alone in my car in the deserted church parking lot.

I don't believe that God ever left me; however, I certainly turned away from Him. In my sin, I separated myself from God, so any distance between God and me was my own doing.

> *Behold, the Lord's hand is not so short that it cannot save; Nor is His ear so dull that it cannot hear. But your wrongdoings have caused a separation between you and your God, and your sins have hidden His face from you so that He does not hear. (Isaiah 59:1-2 NASB)*

I knew that repentance was the way back; that it was my responsibility to confess my sins, turn away from those things that separated me from God, and turn back to Him.

> *So having overlooked the times of ignorance, God is now proclaiming to mankind that all people everywhere are to repent. (Acts 17:30 NASB)*

The incredible part about my personal song-prayer and the revelation that came from it is that God never tired of waiting for my return! Not just that, but He gave His one and only Son to pay the price for my sins. And He *did* forgive me.

Who is a God like you, who pardons sin and forgives transgression
of the remnant of his inheritance? You do not stay angry forever
but delight to show mercy. (Micah 7:18 NIV)

I clung to the symbolic words of that song as a reminder on that impactful Father's Day Sunday of what my Heavenly Father felt about me and how He had forgiven me and vowed to hold onto me and never let go. I felt comforted by that truth.[2]

I ran from God for so many years of my life, feeling ashamed, damaged, unworthy. I struggled to make significant adjustments in the way I lived for fear of missing out or being rejected or lacking belief that I could really change. But those days and those old ways were quickly fading. My pastor was right: By praying that prayer and truly meaning it, I was in for a life change.

Goodbye FOMO

Just a few months after my life-changing prayer and parking lot revelation, I sat in the airport with about fifteen other group members as we chatted excitedly about our upcoming trip to Jamaica—my very first mission trip.

Acutely aware of my insecurity about being in a "church" group in public, I quickly brushed off my worries of how we were perceived by those around us. Not too long before, I would have scoffed at a group like ours, presuming they were doing something uninteresting and unfun, something far less exciting than my own travels.

My concerns about other people and their perceptions of me continually dissolved as I experienced some of the most authentically fulfilling, vitalizing, and significant moments of my life in Jamaica.

Singing worship songs on a bus full of believers broke the chains of image management and brought a sense of childlike joy and freedom I didn't know existed.

Witnessing unfathomable living conditions and caring for children and the elderly in need both shattered my heart and filled it to overflowing in a way that can't be explained. Deep dives into

---

2   Deuteronomy 31:8

scripture and heartfelt prayers with our group each evening opened my heart and mind to a broader understanding of God's word, to living with Him and for Him in an authentic way, and to helping me gain a closer connection with other believers.

Friendships and bonds blossomed as we laughed together and cried together. We worked tirelessly, praised God fervently, and grew in our faith exponentially. The fruit of our week together not only left a lasting mark on the lives of those we loved and served, but it forever changed my relationship with the Lord. I'm confident that I gained far more from that mission trip than I could have possibly given.

However, sometimes old habits are hard to break. A couple weeks after my trip to Jamaica, I went out for drinks with some friends at one of our go-to venues. In my typical overly tipsy fashion, I danced, laughed, and flirted my way through the night.

I almost bumped right into another girl as I stumbled out of the bathroom. Legs unsteady and head woozy, I took a moment to stabilize myself and focus when I suddenly realized the familiar person standing in front of me was my new friend Marissa, whom I had just met on our mission trip. We squealed excitedly, hugged, and took a few moments to catch up before heading back to our friends.

As I walked away, I felt a jolting angst in my spirit and an unexpected flood of embarrassment and guilt. *What was I doing here? Hadn't I just had a life-changing, soul-altering experience in Jamaica? Why was I still acting as if my joy and fulfillment comes from a night of partying?*

My worlds were colliding and like oil and water, they didn't mix. The lifestyle I had maintained for more than a decade did not mesh well with the new one I was trying to establish. Late nights of binge drinking with friends, chasing attention from guys, saying, watching, and doing what I wanted, when I wanted—none of it lined up with what I was learning to be a genuine life of following Jesus.

I began to recognize that the angst, the unease that I felt that night, was a nudge from the Holy Spirit. A reminder of all I had been learning and experiencing with Him—a clear distinction between the life I knew and had been living versus the one now attainable in Christ, a life that I desired.

> *For the desires of the flesh are against the Spirit, and the desires of the Spirit are against the flesh, for these are opposed to each other, to keep you from doing the things you want to do. (Galatians 5:17 ESV)*

Just as I did when I was a teenager, just like the little girl and her teddy bear, I was clinging to my way, focused on what I would have to give up rather than what I would gain.

> *Just as I did when I was a teenager, just like the little girl and her teddy bear, I was clinging to my way, focused on what I would have to give up rather than what I would gain.*

I knew that I wanted Jesus in my life. I believed what I was learning about Him was true. I wanted to believe He was worth it. Yet, the amount of sacrifice I faced seemed daunting. My social status. My recreation. Even some of my friends. Why was it so hard to let go?

I didn't know where or how to begin. My whole life looked one way based on what I previously believed and valued. I knew that if I really believed and valued Jesus and His truth, that had to change—in a drastic way.

> *Then Jesus told His disciples, "If anyone wants to come after Me, he must deny himself, take up his cross, and follow Me. For whoever wants to save his life will lose it; but whoever loses his life for My sake will find it. For what good will it do a person if he gains the whole world, but forfeits his soul? Or what will a person give in exchange for his soul? (Matthew 16:24-26 NASB)*

The selfishness in me wanted to fixate on all that I would miss, all that I would have to give up to follow Christ. But I was beginning to see that what the world has to offer is a cut-rate imitation of what God provides. Far too often I settled for cheap fast food when a gourmet meal from a five-star restaurant was right in front of me.

I began to embrace the truth that God has so much more for me if I would just be willing to let go of what I was holding onto and accept His extended hand. I get to choose to walk with Him, to surrender to Him, to trust Him. When I do, He will give me more than I can ask or imagine!

But I was beginning to see that what the world has to offer is a cut-rate imitation of what God provides.

Now to Him who is able to do far more abundantly beyond all that we ask or think, according to the power that works within us. (Ephesians 3:20 NASB)

Embracing Change

"Thanks for the invite, but I'm staying in tonight." I hit send on the text message response to my friend Jacob and snuggled up on my couch with my favorite cozy blanket for a solo night of rom-coms and ice cream. The fact that this was the third Saturday in a row of laying low, hanging out alone at home, didn't diminish the sense of contentment that permeated my soul.

For the past few months, nights out had become less frequent as I focused more intently on seeking a relationship with Jesus, as well as some much-needed time getting to know myself and what I really wanted.

I became increasingly aware of the choices I made, the words I spoke, and the things I did and how they affected me and others.

Now that I had taken some time to pause, to pull back from what I had always known and always done, I began to desire more for my life. I became increasingly aware of the choices I made, the words I spoke, and the things I did and how they affected me and others. My resolve solidified, and I could feel the shift taking place in my spirit. My heart's desires were different.

I genuinely wanted to live a more wholesome life—not because it was the right thing to do or because someone from a church pulpit was telling me I should, but because the satisfaction I found in my relationship with Jesus far exceeded anything else I had ever wanted or needed.

For the first time in my life, I began to truly feel and recognize the realness of God in my life—not just as some authority figure in heaven casting down judgments when I misbehaved, but an actual loving Heavenly Father who cared about me, His daughter, and every detail of my life.

I was experiencing what the Bible says in Ezekiel 36:26, "I will give you a new heart and put a new spirit in you; I will remove from you your heart of stone and give you a heart of flesh."[3]

With that revelation and a new heart came an authentic peace and joy. Not the self-medicating, numbing, attention-seeking, temporary void-filling I was accustomed to but a genuine fullness that I had not yet experienced as an adult.

When I felt pangs of sadness or battled a fear of missing out, God reminded me of the bonds I had been making with other believers, the unforgettable adventures, the joy-filled experiences, the undeniable changes taking place in my heart and my mind, the confidence and strength that came from knowing my value and my worth came from Him.

I began to embrace His way and consequently reaped the benefits of living my life for Him and with Him rather than tangled up in my own messy, self-indulgent way.

Late nights in a bar, waking up the next morning physically and emotionally depleted with a list of regrets on replay were gradually replaced with mission trips, women's ministry events, and church gatherings saturated with worship, genuine connections, laughter, and a joy and fulfillment that lasted well beyond the next day.

Turmoil that came from broken, dysfunctional relationships and chasing after affirmation from men, a constant sense of insecurity and rejection was increasingly exchanged for a contentedness, fullness, and intimacy that emanated from a relationship with the Lord.

Discarding my previous beliefs about myself and leaving my old life behind became a joy, not a burden. As I began to accept my identity as a beloved daughter, as I sought an authentic, intimate

---

3 NIV

relationship with my Father in heaven, I was lavished with more love and acceptance than I had ever known.

See what great love the Father has lavished on us, that we should be called children of God! And that is what we are! (1 John 3:1 NIV)

I was getting a taste of the authentic good life. Gradually, I began to realize there was so much more to life than weekend partying, attention from men, selfish desires, and living for myself.

I had a new understanding of my relationship with God, a deeper love for Him, and I wanted a life with Him more than I wanted any of those other things. I was no longer simply memorizing a list of dos and don'ts; I was immersed in a relationship with my Lord and Savior.

The more I got to know Jesus, the more I wanted to live *for* Him—not out of obligation or a fear of getting in trouble, but because I loved Him. Likewise, I was gradually grasping how wide and high and deep His love is for me.[4]

What I thought I wanted all my life, the things I thought would make me happy, consistently left me empty, many times, jaded, hurt, and rejected. As the truth of God's design for me and plan for my life sunk in, I became less and less content with my own design and plan for my life.

My soul was a worn and tattered bucket, perforated and punctured. Every time I filled it up with what the world had to offer, it leaked, incapable of remaining full. My thirst for someone or something to fill me up or make me feel good about myself left me with an emptiness I couldn't explain.

That is, until Christ came along and patiently began patching every hole and sealing every crack and filling me with His love and truth.

And our own completeness is now found in him. We are completely filled with God as Christ's fullness overflows within us.

---

4   Ephesians 3:18

He is the Head of every kingdom and authority in the universe!
(Colossians 2:10 TPT)

The more I got to know God, the more I allowed His unconditional love to fill me up. The more secure I became in my identity in Christ, the more confident and content I became in who I was and the choices I made. Those things that I thought I would miss, the entertainment and inclusion that I thought I couldn't live without, slowly faded like the setting sun on the life I was leaving behind.

As the debris and rubble of the old way cleared away and I embraced the change that was taking place in my heart and in my life, a desire that had been deeply buried, almost forgotten, began to emerge. For the first time in a long time, I allowed myself to dream about my future husband and prayed for God to bring him into my life.

10
HOPEFUL AMBER

In the early 2000s, the poker game Texas hold'em rose in popularity in our area, and my family and friends occasionally gathered to play. I grew up playing cards and loved games, so this new pastime became a fast favorite.

Sam invited me to join a weekly Texas hold'em poker league with some of his friends. I eagerly accepted. I was the only woman in a group of about twenty guys, but that ratio didn't intimidate me. Moreover, I was confident in my poker skills. During our first season, I took second place in the league and reveled in my status as a formidable female opponent.

As I began enjoying my new pastime, I also got to know some of the guys during our weekly league games. I began to hang out on the weekends with my brother and several of his friends from the league—joining in on a wide variety of activities from mud volleyball tournaments to daytime cookouts to late nights at a local bar—all of which typically included drinking plenty of alcohol.

At the time, I was still in a wicked game of tug-of-war between the new life I wanted to live with Jesus and my deeply ingrained past lifestyle. I was still entrenched in what was familiar but gradually working toward the change I desired.

Gambling on Love

While I'm not proud of many of the choices I made while balancing on the sea-saw of my old life and launching fully into a life surrendered to Christ, I'm eternally grateful for this season because it's how the Lord led me to my husband!

One night, while out at a local bar listening to live music with the regular crew, Rob—one of my brother's friends who became one of my poker league buddies—and I quietly stood back from the crowd, acknowledging the rowdiness that ensued in front of us. As I gazed in a trance-like, half-tipsy state at the scene unfolding around me, I had one of my many epiphanies since my new journey with Jesus. I looked at our friends who were belligerently drunk, observed the partying crowd around us, examined the wild atmosphere we were in, and I made a mental note: *This is not who I am anymore, and this is not what I want.*

> *This is not who I am anymore, and this is not what I want.*

I glanced at Rob standing next to me with his calm and friendly demeanor, his adorable smile, and gorgeous blue eyes, and recognized for the first time that I was drawn to him. I pushed aside the lies that told me he wasn't my type because he wasn't the typical "fixer-upper" I was usually attracted to. I allowed the truth to settle in and, instinctively, I knew that he was the kind of guy I needed. Not just that, but the kind of guy I would be lucky to be with!

Like the revelation I had in junior high when I wore my first pair of prescription glasses and could see the distinction between leaves on trees for the first time, I was suddenly seeing Rob with a new clarity. I realized what a great catch he really was.

I had already observed the obvious—that he was handsome and athletic (which made him even more attractive in my opinion) and kind and fun to be around. I had also been learning the past few months through our one-off conversations and from those close to him how responsible, loyal, and dependable he was, not to mention the bonus of having a stable job and a nice house.

Ever since my turnaround moment with Jesus, I had been veering away from the old ways and pursuing the new. With those pursuits came a hope for my future and strong desires to find a husband and start a family. I worried that I waited too long, that I wasted too much time living life for myself. At nearly 30 years old, I feared that the door to those dreams would close, and my opportunity would be lost. Despite my doubts and fears about what might not be, I fervently prayed for months for God to bring me the man He had for me, the man with whom I could live this new life I hoped for.

Like a black light that switched on to illuminate a hidden message, I could suddenly see that Rob was the kind of guy I had been praying for; and he was standing right in front of me.

Before my fleeting moment of sanity and courage disappeared, I turned to him and as casually as I could extended an invitation: "We should hang out without these other guys sometime."

He agreed. We had our first date about a week later and, just like that, our happily-ever-after began.

I think it's sweet now to hear Rob describe how he patiently waited for his chance with me while other guys, as he puts it, "crashed and burned" after hitting on me. He claims he owes his victory of winning me over to his superior slow-play strategy but will admit in the same breath that he was too shy and much less bold than the others when it came to talking to women. He half-jokingly touts his patience and willingness to wait to make a move as his winning tactic. Maybe it worked, because I was the one who ultimately initiated our first date.

Comfortable Connection

Several months into our dating relationship, I casually lounged on Rob's living room sofa while he finished taking his dogs outside and locked up his house before we headed out for the night. Dressed in green and geared up for a celebration of one of the wildest party holidays of the year, St. Patrick's Day, Rob and I hopped into his car and headed to a nearby sandwich shop to grab a bite to eat before meeting a group of friends at a popular downtown bar.

As we finished our submarine sandwiches and chatted about the festivities ahead, our excited energy noticeably fizzled. Neither of us wanting to disappoint the other, we danced around our reservations about the impending evening events, casting little hints and hoping for a bite.

"It already feels so late. Am I getting too old for this?" I asked half-jokingly.

"Yeah, it's been a long time since we've gone out for a night like this," he said. "Seems like a lot of hassle with the crowds and the late night."

"Do you still want to go?" I asked, trying not to sound too obvious that I secretly hoped he didn't.

"Do you?"

After a few seconds of inquisitive, playful stares—the scandalous thought of skipping out on our plans lingered while we tried to decipher what each other really wanted so as not to be the one to let down the other—we both concurred that our original party plans had lost their appeal.

On the contrary, the lure of a quiet house, alone on a cozy couch was extremely inviting. As I snuggled with Rob under a warm blanket on the love seat in his living room, content in this peaceful place, both physically and relationally, I couldn't help but count my blessings.

How had I gotten so lucky to find a guy with whom I fit so well? With Rob, everything seemed so natural, so easy. There were no pretenses to uphold or any drama to overcome. The butterflies that fluttered in my belly when I was with him felt wholesome, and a joyful anticipation stirred in my heart.

I savored the simplicity and authenticity of our connection. I marveled at what an incredibly great boyfriend, and human being for that matter, Rob was. I began to allow myself to, ever so cautiously, dream of a future with this man whom I was beginning to believe God had lovingly and intentionally brought into my life.

Making a U-Turn

Rob and I quickly realized how much we had in common and how much we liked being together. I enjoyed the flirtatious interactions, long conversations, and frequent time spent with each other in the early months of our relationship. Spending time with

Rob became one of my favorite things to do. Our connection felt effortless; we were like puzzle pieces that just fit together.

My heart swelled as Rob enthusiastically joined right in with my frequent family gatherings and game nights, not to mention the many get-togethers with my friends. Having him by my side—a constant, devoted companion—felt good. It felt right.

Even the most mundane of tasks—cooking a meal or running an errand to the hardware store—seemed more fun and meaningful with him. I felt a sense of peace flood my soul as I sunk into a pool of contentedness, authenticity, and joy with Rob that I had never experienced with any other boyfriend. I loved spending my days with Rob and felt increasingly drawn to him with each date, each conversation, each interaction.

As our relationship progressed, so did our connection. Within several months of dating, our feelings for one another deepened drastically and we crossed the threshold of simply liking each other to professing our love for one another. I was excited about the direction our relationship was heading and the connection we had, as I knew there was something special about what we were experiencing. At least, that's how I felt.

However, swirling feelings of insecurity began to cause angst to stir in me. Still stuck in my old mindset of what relationships were supposed to look like, I worried that Rob's feelings for me were not as strong as mine were for him because we had not yet become physically intimate.

Unable to keep the tormenting thoughts to myself any longer, I confessed my concerns one evening while we were lounging on the couch. "Is something wrong? Sometimes it feels like you're holding back, like you don't have the same feelings for me that I have for you."

"Of course not! What would make you think that?" he responded.

I carried on, more motivated by finding out his true feelings than worrying about the awkward nature of the conversation. "Well, if you have the feelings you say you have for me, then I guess I don't understand why we haven't had sex yet." Feeling extremely vulnerable in my confession, I shyly glanced away as I waited for his response.

"That's not it at all!" he exclaimed. "It's actually the opposite. I care so much about you that I don't want you to feel rushed into something you're not ready for. You're worth the wait."

My heart could have burst. I can honestly say that was a first for me! I felt so valued and loved without any expectations of sex in return.

Many things about dating Rob were a pleasant change from my past relationships. He was an oasis after years of wandering in a desert of brokenness and distorted love.

After an open discussion about our genuine feelings for one another and a hope for a future together—and after my misguided prompting—we eventually took what I presumed to be the natural next step in our relationship and became sexually involved.

Despite my new-found Christianity, I was still blinded by the cultural norms. That was all I had known; the only instruction manual to a relationship that I had ever read or followed. To me, a world didn't exist where two people in love who were dating *didn't* have sex. Sexual intimacy in relationships was not only the norm and fully accepted, but it was also expected.

"I care so much about you that I don't want you to feel rushed into something you're not ready for. You're worth the wait."

Though, this time it didn't take long for me to start feeling unsettled. I had been on a trajectory toward Christ and living a life that honored Him for quite a few months now. My heart and my desires had started to mirror His more and more, and I had an overwhelming sense of how much I was grieving the Holy Spirit by my actions. I felt a sense of guilt for my sin, a knowing and discomfort surrounding my actions that I had not experienced in the past when my heart was closed off to the Lord.

I knew, based on God's word, that His design for sex is within the confines of marriage.[1] I also knew that despite my past mistakes and pattern of sexual sin that I didn't have to live like the world tells me to live anymore. That previous lifestyle left me damaged,

1   Hebrews 13:5

broken, and alone. I no longer wanted to turn away from God but run toward Him!

I knew that by choosing to have premarital sex, not only was I opening a door to depravity in my life and my relationship with Rob, but I was also creating a wedge between the Lord and me, which is the last thing I wanted.

For this is the will of God, your sanctification: that you abstain from sexual immorality; that each one of you know how to control his own body in holiness and honor" (1 Thessalonians 4:3-4 ESV)

I began praying about how I could possibly turn this self-destructive situation around. I knew what I would be asking of Rob was seemingly impossible and could even be perceived as irrational by the world's standards. But I wanted to please God more than anything else.

Several months passed as I agonized over how to handle this touchy subject and how Rob would react. I loved him so much, yet I had been pulling away and avoiding intimacy with him because of the overwhelming guilt I felt.

Despite my internal struggle about the sexual side of our relationship, everything else between us was wonderful. Dating Rob was a breath of fresh air after years of suffocating in toxic relational fumes. As far as I was concerned, I had hit the jackpot of boyfriends.

We began talking about and preparing for our future, and after almost a year together, Rob asked me to marry him. Ecstatic about the prospect of spending the rest of my life with this incredible man, I eagerly said yes.

What seemed like the perfect opportunity had finally arrived. As Rob and I snuggled on my couch one lazy Saturday afternoon, basking in our new engagement and making plans for our life together, I trudged up as much nerve as I possibly could to tell him what was on my mind. With a nervous but resolute voice, I explained how conflicted I had been about having sex while wanting to please the Lord and follow His way. "Would you be willing to wait to have sex again until after we are married?" I asked with a hesitant, yet hopeful plea.

Holding my breath, I prayed for a positive response but prepared myself for the worst. To my shock and delight, he answered with a resounding and compassionate, "Of course!"

Turns out, Rob thought something was wrong because he had noticed I was avoiding being intimate with him. He was relieved that it was because of my unsettled spirit and not related to my feelings for him.

Rob was also on a new journey with God, as he had begun regularly attending church with me for the first time in his adult life. While he admittedly was still new in his faith and his relationship with the Lord, he was still actively pursuing a life of following Christ and wanted to do the right thing as well.

A hundred-pound weight dropped from my shoulders and my heart buoyantly lifted knowing I would now carry out a wholesome relationship with my future husband and honor God.

We had a year-long engagement that quite often tested our self-control and our commitment to this new vow of celibacy. I can honestly say that was one of the most rewarding decisions I have ever made. The fact that Rob and I made it together, choosing to honor God and His way above our own selfish desires, strength-

> *Despite the lies the enemy tells us, it's never too late to turn away from our sin and turn to God.*

ened our love for one another and for the Lord. I know God was pleased with both of us for choosing His way, and I truly believe our marriage and our bond as husband and wife has been blessed because of our obedience.

One of the biggest lessons I learned is that, despite the lies the enemy tells us, it's never too late to turn away from our sin and turn to God. There is hope and He will make a way! Nothing is impossible with God[2]—not even refraining from sex.

---

2   Matthew 19:26

FINDING HEALING

*Heal me, Lord, and I will be healed; save me and I will be
saved, for you are the one I praise.
(Jeremiah 17:14)*

11

UNFORGIVABLE AMBER

During my first mission trip to Jamaica in 2007, months before I had started dating Rob, the Lord encountered me in a multitude of ways, teaching me a sacrificial love for others and allowing me to see, probably for the first time, what it looked and felt like to let go of my own selfish desires.

As I served a community of people who, despite overwhelming poverty and unthinkable conditions, still loved and worshiped the Lord with all their hearts, my own heart softened. Immersed in that profound experience and far removed from the distractions and norms of home, the cares of the world dissipated, and my priorities began to shift.

I felt a tug to step out of what I thought my life should look like, to intentionally tune into God's design for my future. I began contemplating how to align my life with His will.

As I was getting to know one of my roommates, Lilah, from our church group, I discovered that she worked at a pregnancy resource center (PRC). Unfamiliar with this type of organization, I was immediately captivated as I learned of their mission to support families with unexpected pregnancies, demonstrating the love of Christ.

I inundated Lilah with countless questions, fascinated by this ministry. She shared that her place of employment was just one of thousands of PRCs scattered across the United States serving families. She described the free resources offered—a multitude of material items, including diapers, formula, clothes, and large supplies like cribs and car seats, as well as counseling, parenting classes, miscarriage care, and more.

"You should come check it out! Maybe you could become a volunteer," Lilah suggested.

What a wonderful mission! I thought to myself. I contemplated how fulfilling it would be to get involved with an organization like that. The invitation had been extended, the seed planted.

Once we arrived home from our trip, I kept in contact with Lilah and followed her journey at the PRC for months, continuing to feel drawn to it. Nearly three years later, after quite a few changes in my personal life, including meeting and marrying Rob, and after many nudges from the Lord, I finally took the leap to become a volunteer at the pregnancy center where Lilah worked.

Facing the Truth

Eager to start my new journey of serving others, I showed up on the first day of the two-week volunteer training with bright eyes and an excited heart. I entered the double doors leading into the modest meeting room and immediately felt at ease in the peaceful atmosphere adorned with lovely floral paintings, shelves lined with books, and tables and chairs neatly positioned in a U-shape facing the podium with a TV monitor in the front. I selected my seat and settled into my chair.

Throughout our training, we learned how to talk to pregnant clients about their options, including parenting, adoption, and abortion. Even though abortions were not offered at the pregnancy center, they took care to inform individuals about the various abortion procedures and potential side effects so that each woman leaves the appointment informed and empowered to make the choice that is best for her and her baby.

It never dawned on me that we would discuss abortion at the pregnancy center, so I felt off-guard. Up until that point, I had never faced my abortion. Nor did I fully understand it. Until recent years, I had believed the lie that my pregnancy at 16 years old was just a clump of tissue, not an actual baby.

I always told myself that because abortion was legal, it must be okay. I spent nearly my whole young adult life in denial—hiding my secret, living in shame, and completely ignoring it. I had fooled myself into thinking I had done the right thing for me.

Though, deep down, even at the time that I followed through with that choice, I knew something wasn't right. In my gut, I knew it wasn't what God wanted for me. But I was too selfish and scared at that time to explore why.

In the years after coming back to church, I began to grasp God's word about the sanctity of human life. Scriptures like Psalm 139 in which God tells us that He knit us together in our mother's womb[1] began to dismantle the walls of deceit I had constructed to protect myself from the truth of what I chose.

A creeping sense of guilt and shame trickled into my heart and my conscience. Underlying feelings of insecurity and unworthiness stained my self-image once again. Simply at the mention of the word "abortion," I felt as if someone were yanking a knot tighter in my gut. Still, my secret remained tucked deep in a drawer in my heart—carefully covered, concealed, and contained.

> Simply at the mention of the word "abortion," I felt as if someone was yanking a knot tighter in my gut.

How would anyone, especially those in the church, ever accept me if they knew the truth? I felt alone and ashamed, convinced I was the only one sitting in a Sunday morning service guilty of such an unforgivable sin.

There I sat, in volunteer training, alongside a dozen other men and women with a desire to help others, as I came face-to-face with reality. A reality that I could no longer turn away from, ignore, or tuck away.

As we read through scientific literature and discussed fetal development, I learned that at six weeks gestation, at the time of

---

1   Psalm 139:13

my abortion, my sweet baby already had arms, legs, ears, and eyes that had begun to form, not to mention noticeable fingers!

Her nervous system, thyroid gland, spinal cord, lungs, liver, stomach, kidneys, and intestines were all identifiable.

And, my baby's heart, which was the first of her organs to form, had a regular heartbeat that could be seen and heard on an ultrasound.

My stomach churned and tears threatened to spill from my eyes as I began to see a clear image of my child, the one that I once believed was merely a random clump of cells aimlessly floating around in my uterus.

Training continued with video testimonials from abortionists who had performed thousands of abortions as they methodically described each medical procedure. I sat in sheer horror as an animated video demonstrated a D&E abortion procedure,[2] performed between thirteen and twenty-four weeks,[3] in which the fetus[4] is pulled apart one piece at a time and then, once outside the womb, reassembled like putting a puzzle together to ensure no body parts were accidentally left in the uterus. I felt lightheaded and nauseous as shock set in. My entire body stiffened, and my insides felt as heavy as lead as the next video explained a first trimester abortion procedure—the one I had undergone. I watched the animation of a tiny superpowered vacuum-like tool suction a fetus from her mother's uterus.

Memories flooded my mind. The sound of the suction replayed in my ears and the feeling of my shaking legs and quiet tears resurfaced. The realization of what I had done hit me like a crashing

---

2 "D&E Abortion," What Is Abortion?, accessed June 9, 2025, abortionprocedures.com.

3 "Fetal Development," Cleveland Clinic, March 19, 2024, my.clevelandclinic.org/health/articles/7247-fetal-development-stages-of-growth.

4 "The bearing or hatching of young, a bringing forth, pregnancy, childbearing, offspring" according to Douglas Harper, "Fetus (n.)," Online Etymology Dictionary, accessed February 19, 2025, etymonline.com/word/fetus.

See also "children (of a parent)" according to Kevin D. Mahoney, "Latin Search Results for: Fetus," Latdict - Latin Dictionary and Grammar Resources, accessed February 19, 2025, latin-dictionary.net/search/latin/fetus.

wave, and a waterfall of pent-up emotion streamed down my face as I choked back sobs.

The unequivocal truth that I had a precious life in my womb—my child's life—and I chose to end that life was unbearable.

For the first time, I was bombarded with the unnerving reality that when I was a terrified teenager, thinking only of myself and my circumstances, the decision I made was, in fact, *not* just about me. The decision couldn't possibly be made only based on what was best for me because there was an entirely separate human life at stake. And that life—my baby—not only couldn't defend herself but, sadly, also could not depend on the one person who should have loved and protected her no matter what—her mother.

> *The unequivocal truth that I had a precious life in my womb—my child's life—and I chose to end that life was unbearable.*

Forgiven and Set Free

I had no idea when I signed up to volunteer at a pregnancy center that it would be so directly related to my past trauma, my future family, and my present healing. At the time of my training, Rob and I had been married nearly a year and recently decided we were ready to start our family.

After training ended one afternoon, still flailing in a hurricane of emotions, I spent hours lying in my bed bawling. My insides felt like they had gone through a paper shredder, ripped and torn apart, much like the dreadful death my baby endured when she was, quite literally, torn from my womb.

I was completely broken, overcome with grief and sadness over the death of my child. The heaviness of my choice buried me in a blizzard of burdens—guilt, shame, and remorse over my part in the tragedy.

The immensity of this truth felt like a looming thirty-foot cement wall in front of me, a barricade around a castle preventing trespassers from entering in. I now petitioned with God because I wanted to start a family and have a baby on *my* time and *my* terms. I became painfully aware of the lengths of my selfishness and the ludicrousness of my request. I felt like an intruder wanting to enter the castle with no credentials and blocked by the giant barricade of my transgressions.

How could I possibly expect God to allow me to have children after what I had done?

I didn't feel worthy to have a second chance at having a child. As I learned more about potential side effects of abortion, I worried that I may not even be able to get pregnant again or carry a baby to term. If that were true, wouldn't I deserve that punishment for my actions?

As a terrified 16-year-old, I laid curled up and sobbing on the couch of my childhood home, desperate to fix a problem and determined to ignore God. Selfishness and fear ruled my heart.

Sixteen years later to the exact month, as a heartbroken 32-year-old, I laid in a ball in my bed in a new home that I hoped to fill with my future children, aware of a problem I couldn't solve, desperate for God to fix my shattered heart, and hoping *He* wouldn't ignore *me*.

Repentance and sorrow poured from my soul.

Flooded with tears of grief and remorse and engulfed in an ocean of heartache, I endured condemning thoughts churning in my mind like a lurking sea monster. *What had I done? How could I recover from this? Could God really forgive me?*

Drowning in one of the most gut-wrenching, humbling moments of my life, I did the only thing I could do. Through sobs and gushing tears, I released every bit of my abortion to the Lord—the sorrow, the shame, the guilt, the rebellion, and the sin—and I begged for His forgiveness.

God met me right there in my swamp of brokenness. Not with a condemning iron fist or to dole out punishment but with the reminder that Jesus died on the cross for me. His shed blood covered every single sin—past, present, and future—so that I could be free.

In him we have redemption through his blood, the forgiveness of our trespasses, according to the riches of his grace, which he lavished upon us, in all wisdom and insight. (Ephesians 1:7-8 ESV)

I latched onto His life preserver of truth and clung to His rescuing redemptive love.

The cement wall crumbled to the ground and the castle gates opened. Access to His truth, His freedom, His forgiveness, His love—granted. By God's mercy and grace alone, I found healing and forgiveness, forever set free from the shackles of shame for my abortion.

For you, O Lord, are good and forgiving, abounding in steadfast love to all who call upon you. (Psalm 86:5 ESV)

With a new understanding of the tragedy of my abortion and after reconciling my sin with the Lord, I felt a prompting to also confess my secret to Rob. I had not intentionally hidden this discriminating detail of my past from him. The truth is that my abortion was buried so deep that it wasn't something I ever thought to bring up or deemed relevant enough to share. Until it suddenly, glaringly was.

While I had received God's forgiveness for my transgression, I still had to face the consequences of my actions. I didn't know for sure what the future would hold for my dream of a family with Rob, or how he would feel about me once I was honest with him about what I had done.

Knowing I would be unable to hide my swollen eyes and splotchy face from my afternoon sob session, I wasted no time when Rob got home from work. After a quick greeting, I guided him to the couch for a chat.

"There's something I need to tell you," I began. I quickly explained the decision I made as a 16-year-old and my recent heartbreak as I faced the truth for the first time.

"I'm so sorry you went through that," Rob responded with sympathy. I watched intently as he processed what I had told him, trying to read the unfazed expression on his face and gain insight into his true feelings about the bombshell I had just dropped.

While I still had the courage, I carried on with the whole truth. "I don't know what this means…if I will be able to get pregnant again…if we will be able to have kids. What if that was my one and only chance to be a mom?" I confessed through sobs. "I'm so sorry. Can you ever forgive me?"

Rob hugged me tightly as I cried. "Of course I forgive you. Everything will be okay." I melted into his arms, the searing pain in my heart soothed by his compassionate embrace and uncondi-tional love. I was overcome with gratitude that he received my confession with a heart of love and compassion and without judgment. He shared in my grief for the loss of my child, and we agreed that, together, we would trust the Lord's plan for our future.

> *The shackles of shame broke off me, and the truth flooded my soul: I am loved. I am forgiven. I am a child of God.*

The profoundness of God's forgiveness in light of my past sin became more of a reality than ever when I faced my abortion head-on. After so many years of hiding my past, running from my transgressions, believing the lie that I had committed the unfor-givable sin, my Heavenly Father met me in my moment of despair and lavished me with His love, His mercy, and His grace.

In that moment of repentance, as I bared my soul, acknowl-edged my deepest regrets, and petitioned for my innermost desires at the foot of the cross, the shackles of shame broke off me, and the truth flooded my soul:

I am loved. I am forgiven. I am a child of God.[5]

Within just a few months of this cleansing confession session, I became pregnant.

Necessary Heartache

One of the requirements of becoming a volunteer at the preg-nancy resource center is for anyone with a past abortion to go through the center's abortion recovery program. Eager to carry out my healing journey and to step into my role as a volunteer, I began the eleven-week Bible study, Forgiven and Set Free.[6] My faithful

---

5   1 John 3:1
6   Abortion recovery programs are best done in a group with other post-abortive women with a leader who is also post-abortive. Find a group that fits your needs at H3Helpline h3helpline.org, call or text 866-721-7881.

facilitator, Nina, the Director of the Abortion Recovery Ministry and eventually a mentor and dear friend, walked me through each week's lesson with compassion, insight, and dedication.

I entered into the study with a solid faith foundation, a heart that had already begun to heal, and an established understanding of God's forgiveness for my past sin. Still, the study and the weeks of reflection, introspection, and digging into God's word for His truth and guidance gave me a deeper understanding of my experience and the many ways this one incident poisoned the rest of my life.

I was shocked to discover that much of the lifestyle I led was consistent with what many other women experience after an abortion. I had never considered that the effects of my trauma likely contributed to my emotional and behavioral turmoil—deep-seated shame, feelings of rejection and unworthiness, binge drinking, promiscuity, the need to numb and seek affection at all costs.[7]

I was grateful for a better understanding of why I behaved and felt the way I did, yet I sensed a righteous anger stirring, once again, about the lie I was told that abortion is so simple, so meaningless. Merely a choice that fixes a problem rather than a life-altering act that creates a festering wound from which to heal.

Nina patiently prayed with me, encouraged me, and provided wisdom. I walked away from that study not only with a vaster head knowledge of abortion trauma and how it affects women, but also a greater grasp on my personal experience, the emotions attached to it, the decisions I made, and life I led afterward. I had a newfound freedom, confidence, and peace.

6b Linda Cochrane, *Forgiven and Set Free: A Bible Study for Women Seeking Healing after Abortion* (Grand Rapids, MI: Baker Books, 2022).

7   Willy Pedersen, "Childbirth, Abortion and Subsequent Substance Use in Young Women: A Population-Based Longitudinal Study," *Addiction* 102, no. 12 (November 19, 2007): 1971–78, doi.org/10.1111/j.1360-0443.2007.02040.x.

    Priscilla K Coleman, Vincent M Rue, and Catherine T Coyle, "Induced Abortion and Intimate Relationship Quality in the Chicago Health and Social Life Survey," *Public Health* 123, no. 4 (March 26, 2009): 331–38, doi.org/10.1016/j.puhe.2009.01.005.

    "Post Abortion Syndrome," Johnson County Right to Life, accessed April 1, 2025, jcrtl.org/post-abortion-syndrome.html, an excerpt originally published by the Elliot Institute.

At the end of the program, participants are offered an opportunity to hold a memorial service for their lost children. The service allows mothers to give dignity and honor to their children and openly grieve their loss, as would be expected with the death of any loved one.

Tragically, aborted children have fallen through the cracks, treated as disposable and discarded into the garbage after a procedure, their parents never given a proper opportunity to acknowledge the human being—their child—who was lost.

Despite Nina's recommendation, I declined to have a memorial service at the end of my program. "Thanks, but I don't think that it's necessary for me," I assured her, convinced my healing was complete and I was ready to move on.

However, years later, after having both of my children, I began to reconsider the notion of memorializing my first baby.

My heart felt like it was shattering all over again as I finally began to recognize the depth of devastation my choice caused.

As I lovingly rocked my second-born son before bed one evening, an undeniable ache suddenly gripped my heart. Unexpected tears streamed down my face as I silently grieved the baby that I never got to hold. What had once been more of a conceptual loss, now felt so tangible, so real. The two sweet, precious children whom I was raising provided an all-too-clear image of the one I had lost. My heart felt like it was shattering all over again as I finally began to recognize the depth of devastation my choice caused.

Reluctant to face such a deeply buried pain but overcome with a longing to properly mourn my baby and find closure, once and for all, I reached out to Nina to set up my baby's memorial service.

On May 18, 2014, Rob accompanied me to the quaint chapel at the pregnancy center for the service. Soft music played as Nina recited scripture and read a devotional. Through tears, I shared a few words about my sweet baby girl (during the Bible study, God had graciously revealed her gender to me), how sorry I was, and how dearly she was loved and missed. I had the opportunity to name her, acknowledge her, and properly mourn her death.

Nina concluded the service by pressing play on one final poem.

Father God, when is my mommy going to be here?

The words jolted me. The voice of a sweet child asking about his mother seared my soul. But as I listened to the dialogue unfold between this child—my child—and God, the scathing shards of guilt, shame, and pain from my shattered heart began to dissipate. Unable to hold back sobs, my emotions spilled out as I grasped the final captivating truth conveyed in the poem.

Father God, why has my mother never held me in her arms before?
She never had the chance to do so, my child.
Why did she never have the chance, Father God?
I don't remember, my child.[8]

With those closing words came a gushing wave of forgiveness and freedom that flooded my body from my head to my toes, washing and soothing every scalding wound from my abortion.

The thought of my child, safe in the loving arms of her Heavenly Father joyfully anticipating my arrival, brought a warmth that filled my heart to overflowing. The fact that God had fully forgiven and forgotten my transgressions released me from the heavy burdens of guilt and shame that had been weighing me down.

For I will be merciful toward their iniquities, and I will remember their sins no more. (Hebrews 8:12 ESV)

Rob and I thanked Nina and left the memorial service, arms linked and hearts full. I praised the Lord for inundating me with His love and mercy and for giving me closure that I didn't even know I needed.

---

8   Jeremiah 31:34, Hebrews 8:12, Della Baker Hutto, "A Child's Conversation with His Heavenly Father," March 1994.

Walking Toward Freedom

In order to receive healing from my abortion, I had to revisit a wound that had long since been buried. At 16 years old, I placed a BAND-AID® on that wound, convinced it was sufficiently covered, and I carried on with my life. However, an adhesive bandage is temporary protection for an exposed injury and never meant to permanently mend what festers beneath the surface.

That dressing, while effective in my youth to help me shield my trauma and even soothe some of the pain, could not last forever. As I desired a life of freedom, those old wounds with temporary bandages no longer served me well.

Over the years, I had wrapped my wounds in a barricade of protection—like layer after layer of elastic bandages covering aching, festering injuries hidden under my carefully bound barrier of defense, denial, and survival. That deep-seated abortion wound was the first to seep through the worn and dilapidated dressing. Eventually, the self-assembled swath began to lose its integrity and no longer served its initial purpose to repress and protect.

After that first breakthrough, the Lord started to pull back the BAND-AID®, bringing light to areas of my life that needed healing, thoughts and habits that needed correction, and wounds that could no longer be protected by old bandages. The dressings began to disintegrate, God's healing light started to penetrate wounds and restore my soul, and I launched into a journey of understanding what it truly meant to be free.

12
SOBER AMBER

I rolled over, reaching to silence my buzzing phone alarm and winced as the pain of my pounding headache surfaced. As I willed myself to wake up, snapshots from the night before scrolled through my thoughts like a highlight reel of my friend Christy's birthday celebration.

My mind flashed with memories: Rob and I with a group of fifteen friends shuttled on a party bus to a downtown destination; lots of drinks, dancing, and laughs; dinner in a nice restaurant; more drinks, including shots and a variety of toasts and cheers for the birthday girl; more dancing, more laughs, more celebrating; followed by stumbles, slurred conversations, and fuzzy, out-of-focus interactions.

There I lay, sprawled out across the seats of an empty party bus parked outside the final venue of the celebratory birthday tour, too inebriated and too sick to join the group for the rest of the festivities. My protective husband sat dutifully by my side, bored on the lonely bus but undaunted by my unfavorable conduct. The party concluded and the rest of the group joined us for the ride home.

Only a few short hours after arriving home, I laid in bed trying to shake the memories from my mind, scolding myself. *Ugh. Why did I overdo it last night?* Our kids were toddlers now and social engagements like this were infrequent. On this rare night out—with our boys safe at home with a babysitter—I had allowed a night of letting loose and my old habit of drinking in excess in the name of fun to get the best of me. The excitement of being around long-time friends for a fun night out clouded my judgment.

I felt the frustration of knowing I had lost control. I knew this wasn't who I was anymore, nor was it who I wanted to be. Not only did I make a fool of myself, but now I suffered the physical ramifications as every inch of my body seemed to ache in protest. I did my best to ignore my hurting body and my throbbing head as I rolled out of bed and pulled myself together for church.

After Rob and I dropped off our boys at their kids' ministry classrooms, we headed toward the sanctuary. As we navigated through the crowd of churchgoers, we passed one of Christy's friends who had been out with us the night before.

I sheepishly said hello, barely making eye contact, and quickly moved on. My face burned with embarrassment and my heart seared with guilt as the flashes of drunken debauchery flooded my mind once again.

Here I was at church, claiming to love and follow Jesus, to have a transformed life in Christ, yet I knew that my excessive drinking the night before did not reflect that truth. Last night, I looked and acted just as I had looked and acted all those years without Jesus in my life.

Back then, I was able to stuff the guilt, ignore the shame, and deny the effects of my drunken behavior on my soul. But I was no longer oblivious to the truth. I didn't want to deny or deflect anymore so I could get my way. I wanted *His* way because I had no doubt it was better!

And do not get drunk on wine, for that is debauchery, but be filled with the spirit. (Ephesians 5:18 ESV)

I recognized that God did not bring me out of that pit and make me a new creation in Christ just to keep living my old life, stuck in the same murky mess of self-indulgence and regrets.

For the grace of God has appeared that offers salvation to all people. It teaches us to say "No" to ungodliness and worldly passions, and to live self-controlled, upright, and godly lives in this present age. (Titus 2:11-12 NIV)

I knew I had lost control the night before. I knew that I had let my worldly passions take over. And I knew, without a doubt, that was the last time I ever wanted it to happen. The dense fog of delusion dissipated around me, and I could finally see clearly what was and was not fun.

Refusing to wallow in guilt or beat myself up for messing up and for inadvertently choosing things that hurt me rather than helped me, I focused my attention on my Savior and Redeemer.

I spent that morning in church asking God for His forgiveness and praising Him for the blood of Jesus that washed away all my sins—past, present, and future—this time with an emphasis on the present. I thanked the Lord for His mercy and grace. With a decided heart, I made a vow to myself and to God: That would be the last time I let my drinking get out of control.

Would You Give It Up for Me?

Over the course of the following years, I partook in a couple of drinks on occasion while socializing but successfully refrained from getting drunk. My priorities had shifted, my resolve strengthened. I felt clear-headed and content, knowing that with the help of the Holy Spirit I had conquered the temptation of losing control with alcohol.

So, imagine my surprise when I felt a nudge from the Lord in early 2016 to give up alcohol completely. Not to cut back but to have no. more. drinks. Period.

I started my typical justification process, bargaining with God. After all, the Bible says not to get drunk.[1] It doesn't say we can't have *any* alcohol. *But, Lord, I don't even get drunk! I barely even*

---

1   Ephesians 5:18

drink. Of all the people I know and hang out with, I drink the least by far. Surely, having a few drinks here and there is harmless.

Justify and deny.

This is when the Lord began to remind me about all that alcohol had represented in my life. The mistakes and regrets that came after too many drinks. The crutch that it was for me during times of sadness. How I used it to self-medicate, to numb, to forget. The occasions I had relied on it to be my source of entertainment and joy. I began to feel the Lord asking me a couple of jarring questions: "What good comes from you drinking?" and "What are you getting from alcohol that you can't get from Me?"

Then, only in God's perfect timing (a God-incidence), I *just so happened* to watch a message a friend shared on social media, and she *just so happened* to talk about how the Lord had asked her to give up drinking alcohol.

My body tingled from my head to my toes with confirmation as she disclosed almost the identical dialogue I had with God on this very subject. Then she shared the simple question He had asked her that went something like this, "Would you give it up for Me just because I'm asking?"

That question pierced my heart like a needle. *Was I hovering over the line, trying to see how much I could get away with and still be in God's good graces? Was having a few drinks more important to me than pleasing God? Even if I wasn't necessarily sinning by having a drink once in a while, what were my motives? Where was my heart with regard to alcohol?*

I knew what I had to do. I decided right then and there that I was done with alcohol. For good. For God.

"Don't you think that's a little extreme?" Rob's less than enthusiastic response stung a bit when I told him of my latest revelation, but I had prepared myself for the pushback, knowing it would seem drastic. He confessed that friends had even asked him lately how he felt that I had changed so much from when we first met, pointing out, "She used to be fun."

Even though Rob assured me he didn't share their sentiment, my heart stung with rejection. My early fears when I first became a Christ-follower of being considered uncool and unfun resurfaced.

Yet, I knew I heard clearly from the Lord and prayed that He would lead me through these unknown waters and protect my heart and my marriage. I knew that if God was prompting me to make this change, there must be a reason.

What I soon learned is that alcohol still had much more of a grip on me than I thought. While I wasn't addicted to the substance or its effect on me anymore, a giant flood light suddenly appeared and exposed all the hidden areas where alcohol was still deeply entrenched.

Drinking was a large part of my life from the time I was a kid. Every bit of my social life seemed connected to alcohol—get-togethers with friends, vacations with family, holidays, cookouts, summer days on a restaurant patio or hanging out by a friend's pool. Rough times, good times, and everything in between—limitless excuses to drink were woven into all occasions. Like a favorite, cozy armchair that I could sink into and fit just right, drinking was my comfortable go-to for relaxation, respite, entertainment, and consolation.

I began having an identity crisis. I didn't know how to be a person who didn't drink because for most of my life, that's who I was.

Critical thoughts raced. *Who am I if I'm not the fun, social girl I've always been? What will people think of me if I'm not drinking? I've already been deemed the "religious girl," do I really have to add "prude-who-doesn't-drink" to my ever-increasing list of lame Christian characteristics?*

I battled thoughts and feelings of not wanting to be different, of wanting to fit in, and of feeling like this change was just too big. It seemed like an unrealistic expectation, impossible to implement.

> *I didn't know how to be a person who didn't drink because for most of my life, that's who I was.*

However, God showed me the truth and set me free! God liberated me from the shackles of social drinking. I began to bask in the contentedness of being the only person drinking water at a social event. I embraced the nickname "Uber® Amber" as the sober driver who took everyone home on special occasions.

Not only did I feel healthy, clear-headed, and free, but I also had the opportunity to demonstrate how the Lord was transforming me. I could still have a good time *and* represent the Lord well.

At my high school reunion or a friend's birthday celebration or holiday gatherings, I didn't sit in the corner with a pouty face, making sobriety look miserable. I danced, laughed, socialized, and exuded joy—which, in turn, prompted many conversations that usually started with someone approaching me in disbelief to say things like, "You're not drinking? I could never be in this environment without being drunk!" or "Are you sober? You look like you're having a good time. I would have never known!"

Having grown up in an environment where alcohol was prevalent, I was also painstakingly aware that everything I did at home was being observed by the inquisitive eyes of my little ones.

Despite his initial apprehension, Rob observed the positive changes that had been taking place in my life and supported my choice. While he didn't feel led to make the same drastic changes I made, he did cut back on his drinking and began to consider his choices more carefully, especially around our children.

We both agreed that God had blessed us with a responsibility to guide our sweet boys and set an example for them, and we wholeheartedly wanted to represent Him and His will well within our four walls and beyond.

Amongst friends, families, and even strangers with my supportive husband by my side, I had opportunity after opportunity to testify to God's grace and show that my joy and fulfillment comes from *Him* not from alcohol.[2] I became increasingly aware of God's goodness—how His plans and His ways,[3] while they may not always make sense to me, are for my good. He is trustworthy, and He is so worth the challenges and changes that are necessary to fully surrender to Him.

> *I became increasingly aware of God's goodness—how His plans and His ways, while they may not always make sense to me, are for my good.*

2 Ephesians 5:18
3 Isaiah 55:8

What I also learned is that the enemy hates when we start discovering and living out God's truth. If we become a Christian but still live our old lives, maintain our destructive habits, think and act the same, we are no threat to the enemy.

I had two major triumphs in my new healing journey with the Lord so far: freedom from the shackles of shame from my abortion and freedom from the chains of addiction and destruction from decades of alcohol overuse.

Bit by bit, the devil was losing his grip on me. His old tricks no longer worked, so it came as no surprise that he looked for new ways to keep me from fully walking out God's plan for my life. The enemy is relentless.

Be sober-minded; be watchful. Your adversary the devil prowls around like a roaring lion, seeking someone to devour. (1 Peter 5:8 ESV)

13
DISTRACTED AMBER

Both of my pregnancies in 2011 and 2012 were deemed high-risk due to marginal cord insertion (MCI), an abnormality in which the umbilical cord attaches to the edge of the placenta rather than middle.

This is problematic because the sides of the placenta are much weaker and have less tissue compared to the central area of the placenta. With this condition, there is a chance that the baby may not receive enough nutrients and oxygen.

During my pregnancy with my first son, the doctors had assessed that he was at risk for intrauterine growth restriction, a common risk of MCI. I had to get weekly ultrasounds to carefully monitor his development.

This diagnosis added tension to my already taut nerves from the unknowns of carrying my first pregnancy. However, I looked forward to each ultrasound appointment and savored those special check-ins when I got to see my child growing and developing before my eyes.

Throughout my pregnancy, I was in awe of the miracle of the life growing inside me. Not only did I see my sweet boy week after week on the screen and in printed black and white images, but I also *felt* him—little kicks, sudden shifts in position, pressure on certain internal organs where he rested.

I often reflected on the sugarcoated lie I once swallowed that convinced me a fetus in the womb was not yet a life, that what took place in a woman's body during pregnancy was nothing more than a clump of cells floating around aimlessly rather than a human being at the beginning stages of his development.

What I experienced first-hand debunked that myth outright, and I knew I couldn't possibly be the only one to have discovered this truth. After all, ultrasounds had been around for years, so what happens inside a mother's womb during pregnancy was no longer a mystery.

Righteous anger simmered as I considered the widespread and frequently distributed falsehood that so many women accept about their own bodies and their own children: that the person inside of the womb somehow has less value than the one on the outside of the womb, and for some unknown reason, that child is not worthy of the right that every other human being has—the right to life.

As the child inside me grew, so did a passion for protecting babies and their mothers from this dangerous and devastating lie and attack on motherhood.

Ready or Not

Despite the nerves and uncertainty with my pregnancy, I felt at peace and trusted the Lord to protect my baby and guide the doctors. I continued to pray and seek God's wisdom and comfort throughout the process, knowing that it was all in His hands.

A few days before my baby shower, at close to 33 weeks pregnant,[1] I arrived at the medical facility for another one of my routine weekly ultrasounds. During the visit, the doctor expressed minor concerns about my baby's progress. This was not completely new information—we had been aware that he was small, and his growth was a potential issue, hence the close monitoring. However, on this occasion, the conversation was a bit more somber, and I sensed the seriousness in his tone.

---

1   "Fetal Development," Cleveland Clinic, March 19, 2024, my.clevelandclinic.org/health/articles/7247-fetal-development-stages-of-growth.

The doctor gave me a steroid shot, which he informed me would spur the baby's growth. I was also instructed to go on bed rest until further notice with an added prescription to "eat a lot more." The primary goal: Help baby grow.

While the thought of being confined to a resting position for the remainder of my pregnancy was distressing and disappointing, within the second half of the doctor's orders was a silver lining that seemed easily achievable.

Anyone who knows me knows that I love to eat. As a matter of fact, my eating habits have been somewhat of a family joke since I was little. I recall once at about nine years old at our usual restaurant after church with family and friends announcing to my parents what I intended to order from the menu. My dad, shocked and half in protest exclaimed, "That's what *I'm* getting!"

I looked at him with a blank stare and retorted, "So?" Laughter broke out around me as I failed to see the humor in being a young girl who thought it completely acceptable to eat the same portions as an adult man.

I left the appointment and immediately shared the news with Rob, relaying the heaviness I felt and my uncertainty about how I would comply with the orders. He reassured me that everything would be okay, and we would get through this. We both concluded we were confident that the rest of my pregnancy would carry out as planned and all would go well, by God's grace.

On a phone call with Lynn later that day, I updated her about my appointment. "Did they mention anything about you delivering the baby early?" she asked. She went on to explain that one of the primary reasons for a steroid shot is to help the baby's lungs develop for an early delivery. "You're going to have your baby soon!" she insisted. Having gone through a premature delivery six years prior with her oldest daughter, Lynn felt confident in her assessment of my situation.

"What? No!" I protested. "I'm sure the doctor would have mentioned something if that was the plan." I brushed off her remarks and did my best to push them out of my mind. I was not ready to have my baby. It wasn't time!

I carried on with the weekend plans, doing my best to rest while still partaking in my baby shower festivities that Sunday afternoon. On Monday morning, I received a call from my OB-GYN. She told me not to panic, that everything would be fine, but that I needed to gather my belongings and make my way to the hospital. "You're having your baby today," she declared.

My body froze as I sat stunned and stiffened like a statue on our living room couch. I did not expect this, despite Lynn's prediction. How did I not know this would happen? Fear festered in my thoughts as I contemplated the complications of having a baby so early. *What will happen to him? Will he be okay?* A slew of "what ifs" raced through my mind.

I deliberately snatched up every nagging, fearful thought and surrendered each one to the Lord. I knew that spiraling into a state of fear was not the answer. I prayed and petitioned for God's help.

Jesus, please help me. Take these thoughts from me and replace them with Your truth and Your peace.

One of my favorite Bible verses immediately popped into my mind, comforting me and calming my nerves:

Do not be anxious about anything, but in everything by prayer and supplication with thanksgiving let your requests be made known to God. And the peace of God, which surpasses all understanding, will guard your hearts and your minds in Christ Jesus. (Philippians 4:6-7 ESV)

My first son was born that day, nearly seven weeks premature, weighing four pounds, five ounces.

Groggy and drained from my c-section, and eyes bleary from a mixture of joy and stress-filled tears, I held my baby close and told him I loved him, completely in awe of this new life that came from my body. Within a couple of minutes, my tiny blessing was bustled away to the Neonatal Intensive Care Unit (NICU), and I was rolled off to recovery.

The doctors prepared us for what they said could be a long stay. They explained that a premature baby typically needed to be cared for in the NICU for approximately the same length of time that he would have been in the womb—so in our son's case, about seven weeks.

However, our baby boy thrived during his time in the hospital and defied the standards. He never required oxygen or other medical intervention, with the exception of a feeding tube. Just like when he was in my womb, the primary goal was to help him grow.

We were filled with hope as we saw him progress, and we pressed on with our goal of helping him learn to eat without the tube and grow to a safe weight. The days were long and the travel back and forth to the hospital wore on us, but our positivity and prayers persisted.

On a chilly Sunday morning almost two weeks into our whirlwind introduction to parenthood, Rob and I sat in our Easter church service, bodies weary, hearts heavy. While our son's progress was better than expected and he was doing well in the hospital, it felt unnatural and disheartening to be apart from him.

The reality of his battle for growth and our struggle to stay strong loomed like a dark cloud. We longed for the skies to clear and this ordeal to be over, to be home together. I snuggled up under the comfort of Rob's arm as sadness set in and tears threatened to spill from my eyes.

As we spent the morning celebrating the resurrection of our Lord Jesus Christ, I clung to the truth that He is our Savior, the hope of the world, the Lord of our lives. He never leaves us or forsakes us.

The Lord himself goes before you and will be with you; he will never leave you nor forsake you. Do not be afraid; do not be discouraged. (Deuteronomy 31:8 NIV)

I silently petitioned for God's healing touch and a surge of growth and strength for our sweet son. I praised the Lord for His goodness, for the gift of being a mom, and for the life He had created. I was reminded that God personally and purposefully knit our baby boy together in my womb[2] and that He had plans to prosper him, not to harm him.[3]

Music filled the room like a sweet aroma. Worship and praise spilled from my lips and filled my heart, and I surrendered feelings of helplessness and sorrow, allowing the only One who could help to take the reins of my thoughts and emotions and our situation.

Thanks to our son's fighter spirit, phenomenal nurses, and God's grace, our baby boy was

Despite the rocky beginning and the bumpy road of parenting, of one thing I was certain: being a mom was one of the biggest blessings I could ever receive.

released from the hospital with a clean bill of health just sixteen days after he was born; three days after our Easter church service, and more than four weeks earlier than estimated.

Grateful to be out of such a stressful situation and settle in with our new little family of three, Rob and I carefully, excitedly bundled up our first-born and took him home.

The weeks and months following were filled with challenges, uncertainty, learning, growth, joy, love, and lots of prayer. Despite the rocky beginning and the bumpy road of parenting, of one thing I was certain: being a mom was one of the biggest blessings I could ever receive.

Medical Mayhem

After my son's birth, my personal season of medical mayhem began to ensue. Within a couple of months of recovering from my c-section, I started experiencing waves of abdominal pain. In August of 2011, I had a bout of abdominal pain so severe and persistent that all I could do was lay awake the entire night, writhing and counting down the minutes until my doctor's office opened the next morning.

I had never been so desperate for morning to come, and as soon as the office opened, I called to plead for the first available appointment. Thankfully, my doctor could see me right away. Not

2   Psalm 139:13
3   Jeremiah 29:11

wanting to burden Rob with what I assumed was a virus that had simply gotten the best of me, I assured him I would be fine and convinced him to go to work while his mom took care of our baby and I set out for the doctor's office, promising to keep him updated.

Upon arriving at my appointment and meeting with my family doctor, I endured several minutes of questions and poking and prodding around my abdomen, accompanied by my involuntary groans and jolts of discomfort. Not long after my exam, the doctor admitted me to the hospital and after some tests scheduled an emergency appendectomy that day.

While emergency surgery was not my first choice of how to spend my day or the next six weeks of recovery, I was grateful for an immediate solution and definitive resolution to my health issues.

The Saga Continues

Only three short months after my appendix surgery, I lay awake during a restless night, baffled at finding myself in yet another health predicament. My body was a wrung-out washcloth, drained and depleted after a long night of suffering and sleeplessness.

But the morning rays of sun brought a renewed resolve as some of the squeezing, throbbing, and nauseating pain in my gut and back had dwindled slightly (or had I just gotten used to it?), and I knew I was closer to getting help (or so I hoped).

Just three weeks before, I suffered the same kind of pain, landing me at the local hospital's emergency room in the middle of the night. After hours of waiting, with Rob by my side and multiple inconclusive test results, we headed home with a prescription for pain meds and defeated spirits.

Facing all of this in such a short time since my appendectomy, I felt inundated with a continual onslaught of medical issues, the current one seemingly having no solution. I floundered in feelings of vulnerability and discouragement.

Intent on not repeating the previous futile (and expensive) ER visit, I endured the night of suffering to schedule a regular sick visit with my family doctor. I understood that, as the manager with sole responsibility for running his store, Rob didn't have the luxury of simply calling off work for the day. So, I reassured him that I had it all under control, shooed him off to work, and called to secure an early morning appointment the moment the doctor's office opened.

Not realizing how depleted I was from such an exhausting night of agony, I scrounged up as much energy as I could, cringed my way through the remnants of pain and discomfort, and gathered my seven-month-old and his belongings to drop him off at my mom's house.

Several times, I questioned whether I should ask for help, but I didn't want to be a burden and was convinced that if I could just make it to my doctor's office, all would be well. I left my son at my mom's and began the three-and-a-half-mile drive to the hospital where my doctor's office resided. During the eight-minute ride, my sight faded in and out of blackness as I felt the familiar sensation of my body on the verge of fainting. About halfway to my destination, I pulled over on the side of the road to regain my composure.

I hastily parked my small SUV in front of a nearby house and thrust the driver's side car door open, allowing my body to hang out like a rag doll, my face within inches of the snowy street. I gratefully gulped up the wintry November air and willed my body to comply as I tried to make the rest of the short trek to safety. *Only a few more minutes and I will be there.* I reassured myself. *Lord, help me!*

I finally arrived at the hospital and trudged my way through the slushy parking lot. I sluggishly navigated past the lobby attendants toward the elevator, nausea and dizziness threatening to overtake me. The elevator ride was a welcome rest as I leaned against the wall, waiting for the climb to the fourth floor.

After I emerged from the elevator and rounded a corner, I could see the door of my doctor's office just thirty yards down the hall, the finish line finally in view. A new sense of hope flooded me as I slowly and steadily completed the last stretch of this grueling journey.

Like a marathon runner at the end of a race, I staggered through the office door and crumpled on the floor in front of the check-in window, completely indifferent to how I looked or what people thought of my dramatic entrance. Back against the wall, head resting on my bent knees, and my body clammy from fever and sweat, I allowed relief to flood my body and waited for help. *Praise God, I made it.*

Within minutes, I was sprawled out on the table in my doctor's office, rehashing my symptoms. She promptly called for a nurse to load me into a wheelchair and admit me to the ER. Hindsight, I could have avoided a sleepless night of agony and grueling journey to the hospital that morning if I had just gone straight there.

Déjà vu set in as I faced a friendly but bewildered nurse and answered the same slew of questions about my symptoms that I had answered a few weeks prior. This time, however, they decided to run a more extensive test on my gallbladder, as it was the most logical culprit of my pain (and the one I had suggested from the beginning, based on my unsophisticated internet research).

After undergoing a lengthy test, we discovered that my gallbladder was only functioning at 8%, explaining the waves of pain and nausea.

Upon receiving the news of my gallbladder, the nurse made a snide remark about my less-than-adequate ability to appropriately describe my symptoms. The explanations I provided during my ER visits apparently did not match what they expected. I made a mental note to add symptom-describing to my list of skills to develop.

With a new diagnosis and a new surgery scheduled, I let relief wash over me, grateful for a solution to yet another medical mystery.

Facing a Familiar Fear

A few months after my cholecystectomy, to our great joy, Rob and I found out that I was pregnant again. However, the traumatic experience of our first child's premature birth left us feeling a mixture of excitement and nervous reservation.

Due to my previous high-risk pregnancy, and the fact that I would be thirty-five at the time of my due date in January 2012, my doctor placed me under special watch from the start of my pregnancy.

To our shock, we soon learned that, once again, the baby's umbilical cord was inserted in the wrong place in the placenta. When the doctor discovered MCI with my first pregnancy, he commented about how rarely he had encountered it. When he discovered it with my second pregnancy, he marveled that in nearly three decades of doing his job, he had never seen this condition occur twice with the same mother.

Despite the diagnosis and extra precautions, our second baby grew perfectly, and my pregnancy progressed smoothly. Rob and I both had a sense of peace and optimism about this pregnancy and trusted the Lord to take care of us and the baby. I required fewer ultrasounds and needed less monitoring this time, providing Rob and me added reassurance that all was going well.

Two days after Christmas of 2012, three weeks before my due date, I began experiencing discomfort in my lower abdomen while getting ready for work. Dismissing the pain that came and went, and writing it off as cramps, I finished getting ready and then drove to my mom's house to drop off my son before heading to my office at a software company just a couple miles from her neighborhood.

While at my mom's house, the cramping continued. As I sat on her couch, belly bulging, waiting for the most recent wave of pain to subside, my mom stared at me with a sudden knowing and exclaimed, "Amber, I think you're having contractions!"

This thought had not even crossed my mind. With my first son born so early via c-section, I had never experienced a contraction. Besides, it was way too early for contractions, wasn't it? I quickly called my doctor, doubtful but wanting to verify that what I was experiencing was not related to my baby.

Within a couple of minutes chatting with my OB-GYN and explaining what I felt, she told me that I needed to go to the hospital. I was, in fact, having contractions.

Shocked and in disbelief, I agreed to go, explaining that after I took care of a few things that I needed to do and then once I gathered my belongings from home, I would head that way. She kindly, yet firmly replied, "There's no time for all of that. You need to go now. Your contractions are very close."

Oh! Familiar anxious thoughts began to creep in as I recognized the urgency of my situation. I ended the call with my doctor and immediately dialed Rob at work. He assured me he would meet me at the hospital as soon as he could.

I stowed my 20-month-old toddler in his car seat in the back of my mom's car and slid carefully into the front passenger seat, more aware than ever of the pains persisting in my abdomen. Silently, I prayed for God to protect my unborn child and for His peace to flood my heart and my mind.

I stared out the window at the wintry scenery as my favorite verse in Philippians scrolled through my mind once again *(Do not be anxious about anything*[4]*...).* I took my thoughts captive,[5] praising the Lord for a healthy baby and for His provision over the day ahead.

We approached the hospital's maternity unit and explained my situation to the friendly attendant, who quickly completed my check-in. They promptly assigned me a room in the delivery department and set up an IV for me and heart monitors for the baby.

Rob arrived shortly after us, and a sense of peace and protection filled my hospital room. Grateful for his loving presence and support, I attempted to fill him in on the morning's happenings in between surges of breathtaking pain.

"Contractions," I informed him, "are no joke!" I attempted to make light of my suffering; however, I failed miserably when he tried to carry on a conversation with me during one of the increasingly intense stabs of pain. I snapped at him through gritted teeth. "Don't talk to me while I'm having a contraction!" Thankfully, for my sake and my marriage's, I received an epidural shortly after that.

Suddenly remembering that I had been on my way to work when my impromptu labor transpired, I called my boss to inform him of the circumstances. Laying on my side, facing the opposite direction of the nurse and Rob, I was finishing up my phone call when Rob's frantic voice interjected, "Amber, get off the phone! Something is wrong!"

---

4   Philippians 4:6-7
5   2 Corinthians 10:5

I turned to see the nurse frenziedly checking monitors and hurriedly moving around my bed. She announced in an urgent, yet controlled voice, "We have to take you back to surgery right now. The baby is in distress—his heart rate is dangerously low."

Within seconds, I was rushed through doorways and carted into the operating room, a blur of other patients, medical equipment, and hospital personnel whizzing by in my peripheral view. My head churned with anxious thoughts of the unknown. I resisted the urge to panic, unavoidable tears streaming down my face and silent prayers swirling in my mind while the medical staff kindly and swiftly walked me through what was happening and prepared me for surgery.

The house surgeon introduced himself and informed me in a compassionate, yet no-nonsense tone, "Your doctor is on her way, but there is no time to wait. I have to begin the c-section right away."

Just minutes after the surgery began, my OB-GYN emerged into the room and assisted with the remainder of the operation. I later learned that my doctor had been standing outside the operating room not long after the surgery began, banging on the door, demanding (with a certain expletive) that someone open it. A detail that now adds a bit of humor to a somewhat traumatic and tense experience.

My mom and Rob followed my doctor through the door of the operating room and settled in just in time to see our second-born brought into the world.

My second sweet son was born that wintry whirlwind of a day, three weeks early, weighing five pounds and sixteen ounces. I stared anxiously as the medical team examined him across the room. The pent-up breath that I unknowingly held in my lungs released in a rush when they handed our baby to Rob and informed us that he was perfectly healthy.

Flooded with overwhelming relief, tears of joy flowed from my eyes as I gazed at my precious baby boy. I held him close and fell in love all over again, my heart swelling with gratitude.

I endured four surgeries in under two years, the first three of which took place in a seven-month time crunch. Each surgery involved weeks of recovery, not to mention the adjustment and strain of caring for new babies. Despite the toll this had taken on my body, I was optimistically on the road to recovery.

However, I became increasingly sensitive about every aspect of my health. Every tinge of pain spun into suspicion as I imagined and researched all the possible conditions from which I could be suffering. Every symptom or sickness left me searching tirelessly for underlying diseases or conditions that needed to be cured.

I entered into a season of being consumed by my health and medical mysteries—of which there seemed to be a plethora to address—and made it my mission to solve and resolve every last one.

14
AWAKENED AMBER

In early 2013, now with two children under the age of two and around the same time that I first began to cut back on my alcohol consumption, I received a medical diagnosis that prompted me to further evaluate my lifestyle.

For months, I had been in pursuit of the truth regarding my latest and most prominent ailment. Rundown from years of battling chronic headaches, constant pain throughout my body, extreme fatigue, brain fog, restless nights, and many more undesirable symptoms, I was desperate for answers. My condition seemed to be getting worse, and I wanted to know what was wrong with me.

I spent so many years fighting what felt like an invisible opponent—struck over and over with aches and ailments without any idea where they were coming from. My arms flailed aimlessly at the air around me in a futile attempt to fight back. I stole naps on my lunch breaks at work to fight the fatigue, downed sugary soft drinks and over-the-counter medication for energy and pain relief.

I mustered up as much willpower as I possibly could to endure each day's responsibilities, all the while wondering what was wrong with me and why everyone else wasn't as drained and depleted as me. Not only did I want to know what adversary was responsible for my misery, but more importantly, I also wanted to know how to defeat it.

After what seemed like a never-ending slew of doctors' appointments and medical tests to rule out all the possibilities, I found that my suffering was caused by a condition called fibromyalgia.

I quickly learned from a deep dive into researching my doctor's diagnosis and the related symptoms that this condition fit me like a new tailor-made wool suit—just my size, but itchy and uncomfortable. Relieved to have clarity, to finally have answers and an opponent to fight, I gladly donned my new outfit and wore my diagnosis willingly.

Determined to make medication a last resort, I delved into all the possible ways to alleviate my symptoms. Aside from hearing the term before, I knew very little about fibromyalgia. I dove into researching and reading to gain a better understanding of what I was up against, a skill I had fine-tuned over the years as a self-made diagnosis detective. I quickly learned that most symptoms of fibromyalgia could be drastically reduced, even eliminated, by making healthy lifestyle choices. This gave me hope, a sense of control.

In impeccable timing (another God-incidence), a friend reached out to me about a health and wellness company she recently joined, and I knew it was the solution I was looking for. I dove headfirst into the endeavor, eager to not only become healthier and potentially alleviate my physical suffering, but to also help others who wanted to do the same.

For the first time in my 30-plus years of life, I began to learn how to use food to properly fuel my body. I learned about clean eating—a concept that was completely foreign to me—to eliminate the foods that were harming rather than hurting me, like sugars, simple carbohydrates, dairy, and processed foods to name a few.

As a self-proclaimed carb-and-cheese-aholic, not to mention a recovering Taco Bell® addict, this was certainly new territory for me. It was an equally challenging change for Rob, as he joked that in his bachelor days, he prided himself on eating well because he selected the "healthier" options from the menu for his nightly fast-food dinners. We both wanted to be healthy and feel well, but that would require major changes to our diet.

Rob and I eagerly dove into a new, healthy lifestyle and consequently had positive physical results. Rob lost thirty pounds and began a workout routine to build muscle and stay in shape. I trimmed down as well, losing a pant size, which was certainly a perk. However, I was admittedly not as concerned about losing weight as I was about feeling better.

Changing my eating habits, adding vitamin supplements to help fill in the gaps, and consistently exercising made a massive difference in how I felt. I began to have more energy, my mind was clearer, and I felt more hopeful about my health than I had in a long time. I felt empowered because this was something I could fix.

Nevertheless, there seemed to always be something causing me strife. No matter how many ailments I conquered, another one appeared. Stuck in a real-life game of Whac-A-Mole®, I hastily pounded each medical incident, each diagnosis, only to have several more pop up in other places. The menacing moles outmaneuvered and outnumbered me every time.

For much of my adult life, I chased a solution to one health condition or sought healing from one medical crisis after another. A broken hand, a torn ACL, a broken scapula, allergies, headaches, gallbladder, appendix, kidneys, high-risk pregnancies, fibromyalgia, carpel tunnel, and the list goes on. Thousands of dollars and countless hours spent on surgeries, physical therapy, supplements, and health plans galore.

Figuring out what was wrong with me and managing my rollercoaster ride of health crises became an obsession.

My years of medical mayhem and my preoccupation with fixing myself all came to a head when I received one of the scariest and most serious diagnoses yet.

Miserable Mystery

As I lay on the living room floor of my friend Dawn's house praying for the impromptu pain in my abdomen to subside, I contemplated which was worse: the embarrassment of being involuntarily laid out on the carpet or the ever-increasing, breathtaking waves of pain that left me feeling miserable and helpless.

Friendly, worried faces peeked in the doorway from time to time to see if I felt better or needed anything. Nearly an hour passed as

I lay there, immobile, trying to stifle my groans of anguish while politely thanking people for checking on me.

Unable to bear the pain any longer and beginning to worry about what could be causing this unexpected ailment, I finally agreed to two things: First, to take a dose of the pain medication I had on hand from my recent carpel tunnel surgery (I was only a few days post op with stitches and bandages intact) and second, to go to the emergency room.

I waited as patiently as possible for the latest agonizing pangs to pause, and then Dawn and her husband helped pull my weary, weak body from the floor and escort me to my friend Andrea's car. I cautiously slumped into the passenger seat, exhausted but grateful to be on my way to get help.

I reached out to Rob to let him know what was going on. "I'll be there as soon as I can," he promised, concern in his voice.

Andrea graciously sat by my side in the waiting room while I impatiently anticipated my turn to be seen. Fortunately, the staff called my name after only a short wait. I thanked Andrea and reassured her that Rob would be there soon as she reluctantly said goodbye. "Let me know what you find out. We will be praying for you!"

Before I had much time to reflect on how grateful I was for such kind and compassionate friends, the ER staff shuffled me to an exam room and then off for testing. As soon as my blood work came back, I was promptly admitted to the hospital and informed that, while they didn't yet have conclusive results about what was causing my pain, they would need to monitor me due to my extremely high liver enzymes.

Rob arrived shortly after I settled into my hospital room, and I held back tears of frustration and helplessness as he hugged and comforted me. "Here we go again," I said with a half-hearted smile, trying to make light of the situation. Thankful for his always strong and stable presence, we talked through the day's events and waited anxiously for an update.

Another blood test and several hours later, the nurse came to my room with unpleasant news, "Your liver enzymes are still too high. We will have to monitor you until they come back to a normal range, which means you will be here overnight."

I felt a deluge of disappointment. With Christmas just a few days away, my post-surgery wrist already aching and incapacitated, and my nearly two-year-old and three-and-a-half-year-old toddlers at home with their grandma, that was not the news I hoped to hear.

"Does the doctor have any idea what was causing my pain?" I asked hopefully.

"No, not yet," she replied straightforwardly. "We have ruled out any critical issues, so that's good. We just have to keep an eye on your enzyme levels for now."

More frustration. More confusion.

At least my pain was gone. Whether it was the medication they gave me or that it had simply just passed, I was thankful nonetheless. Still, I couldn't help but wonder why it happened in the first place.

Rob stayed with me all evening, and we did our best not to allow our bewilderment and the inconvenience to dampen our spirits. He kissed me goodbye before he left for home to put our boys to bed, and I promised to pass along updates as soon as I received them.

My night was restless—machines beeping, medical staff poking and prodding, and thoughts swirling.

Lord, please give me peace. Give the doctors wisdom, give us answers about what is going on, and heal my body. Please get me home safely to my family.

First thing in the morning, they ran a new blood test. I soon found out that my enzymes were back to normal, and I was released to go home. *Thank you, Lord!*

While I was thrilled to go home, my relief was diminished by the lack of answers. The doctors could not determine any underlying issues nor come up with any conclusions. The medical staff threw around guesses like gal sludge or kidney stones as possibilities but no definitive answers.

As if one medical mystery wasn't enough, the doctor also informed me that they discovered an unusual spot on my kidney. I received orders to get an MRI and follow up with a urologist.

A couple weeks later, an MRI confirmed that I had a small lesion on my left kidney that needed to be closely monitored. I attempted to interpret each line of the medical gibberish of my test results, leading me down a rabbit trail of grim and worrying possibilities. Questioning thoughts set in, and internet searches commenced. My doctor provided reassuring guidance, admitting that this type of lesion was troublesome but pointing out optimistically that it was very small. The goal, he informed me, was to ensure that it was not growing.

Six months passed, and I underwent another test. The lesion seemed to be growing, ever so slowly, as were my concerns. With even more trepidation, I sought the counsel of my doctor. This time, he introduced the possibility of a future surgery and reassured me, once again, that we would do all we could to monitor my condition in the meantime.

Still an eternal optimist and refusing to believe the worst in any situation, I leaned on God, and my endlessly supportive, constantly level-headed husband, for peace and strength as I faced whatever was ahead.

In November 2015, almost a year after the ER stay, I set out for another follow-up MRI. The months in between my checkups, I felt peace and trusted the Lord with the outcome. Yet, as each appointment came near, I felt the intensity of my emotions increase. I had to repetitively capture the anxious thoughts or what-ifs and replace them with the truth of God's word.

I had to repetitively capture the anxious thoughts or what-ifs and replace them with the truth of God's word.

Anxiety in a man's heart weighs it down, but a good word makes it glad. (Proverbs 12:25 ESV)

A ball of nerves and my head filled with a plethora of outcomes found from months of internet searches, I methodically replaced my clothes with an awkward, oversized medical gown and followed the attendant to my assigned room.

The friendly technician conversed with me briefly as he administered an IV.

I chatted nervously about the lesion and explained this moment-of-truth scan to evaluate what my doctors had monitored for the past year. "I'm sure it's nothing," I added, only half-believing myself.

I had plenty of time the past ten months to research, to mull over, and to pray over this unfortunate finding. My faith was strong, my confidence rooted in Christ; therefore, I felt a sense of peace knowing that I could handle whatever was next.

However, I still battled underlying uneasiness that accompanied the unknowns. Will this be something serious that I will have to walk through? Is my next season one in which I demonstrate what it looks like to battle a significant illness or diagnosis with a steadfast faith, trusting the Lord no matter what?

Regardless of what was ahead, I had resigned to the fact that God would sustain me and that I could give Him the glory every step of the way. I prepared for the worst and hoped for the best.

For the next thirty minutes, lying flat and tucked inside the man-made medical cave, I attempted to keep my body and my mind still, finding an unusual comfort in the loud hum of the monstrous machine as it muffled my thoughts.

The test concluded. The noise quieted. The nerves must have shown on my face because as the technician helped me up from the table, he said in a reassuring tone, "I'm not allowed to diagnose anything but from what I have seen today, I wouldn't worry." I left the hospital and headed home feeling hopeful.

Within a few days, the results of my MRI appeared on my online medical chart. I quickly opened the document, prepared to trudge my way through the confusing medical lingo and look up a plethora of words and phrases to surmise my own summary of the findings, not willing to wait another few days to hear directly from my doctor.

Within just a few seconds, my eyes locked on a sentence in the very first paragraph, and my blood ran cold. The words were written, not in unintelligible medical gibberish but in clear, understandable layman's terms just two lines into the document: "It is most suggestive of renal cell cancer until proven otherwise."

My heart sank. *This can't be true!* A thousand what-ifs dashed through my mind in mere seconds. Then I forced myself to take deep breaths, and I began to pray.

Lord, I trust You. I know that You will take care of me. Whatever I face, I pray for Your hedge of protection around my family and me. I pray for Your peace that passes all understanding[1] in all circumstances and for Your light to shine through me. In Jesus' name. Amen.

When Rob got home from work, I shared the results with him. He hugged me and encouraged me that we would get through whatever was ahead. Together, we decided to choose optimism and to trust God.

Within a few minutes of meeting with my urologist, he made a clear recommendation to have surgery to remove what was presumably a cancerous lesion on my left kidney. I tried to retain the information he gave me, grasp the reasoning for the drastic measures, and ask as many questions as possible.

"Does it have to be now?" I asked, still trying to wrap my mind around this news, not quite ready to commit to a solution that seemed so severe so soon.

"With this type of lesion, surgery is inevitable," he persisted. "Whether you do it now as I recommend or later, it will eventually need to be removed."

He also pointed out that we only had a few weeks until the end of the year, so it was a good time to schedule a surgery if my insurance deductible had already been met, which it had.

I left the doctor's office feeling burdened by indecision and disbelief. *Was I really going to have another surgery?!* It seemed surreal. The phrase "surgery is inevitable" tumbled in my thoughts for the hours and days following—like an annoying commercial jingle on replay.

---

1 Philippians 4:7

A little shocked, but refusing to be shaken,[2] I focused on finding a solution to this problem. Rob and I spent time discussing the seriousness of my most recent medical crisis, reviewing our concerns, and considering our options. More than ever, I felt consumed with gratitude for my husband, for his stability, his strength, his compassion. I felt safe with Rob and knew that with him by my side and with our faith in God, we could face anything. We continued to pray for the Lord's provision and His guidance as we contemplated the best path forward.

Unwilling to move forward with such a serious decision without getting another opinion and feeling unsettled in my spirit about the prospect of surgery, I scheduled an appointment with a second urologist. His verdict was the same: Surgery was the next step.

My uncle and trusted father-figure, Randy, immediately showed his care and concern. He connected me with his friend who was a urologist and agreed to review my results as a favor. Once again, this urologist gave the same conclusion.

Still not satisfied with the answers I was getting, I consulted yet another doctor. His feedback was the same.

After consulting four separate urologists, I started to feel backed into a corner. Surgery seemed like the only logical next step, and the year-end approached quickly. I reluctantly accepted that surgery was in my near future and researched for the best surgeon.

For several days, I sought referrals and recommendations. My uncle's urologist friend had a colleague, Dr. Z, whom he highly recommended. After doing some digging, I discovered impressive credentials and rave reviews and felt confident Dr. Z was the best choice. Aware of the time crunch, I quickly called his office and scheduled my surgery for December 30, 2015.

For the first time, my medical crisis felt real. Up until this point, I had shared what I was going through with only a handful of close relatives and friends. I hadn't spoken openly about it because I had hoped and prayed that it would simply go away. I arranged for time off work and notified family members and friends. I filled them in on what I had been dealing with for the past year, asked them

---

2 Psalm 16:8, Acts 2:25

for prayer, and reassured them that it would all work out, and I wholeheartedly believed that.

The following week, just a few days before my surgery, I saw Dr. Z for a standard pre-surgery touch point. Leading up to this appointment, I felt internally unsettled. Something was off. No matter how many professionals told me that surgery was necessary, I did not have peace.

During my appointment, I asked questions and shared some of my concerns. Dr. Z patiently listened. When he responded, his words were weighty and prompted even more consideration. "Keep in mind, this is a major surgery," he advised. He candidly discussed the seriousness of the procedure and the lengthy recovery process.

I hadn't thought about that. Up until that point, it was just another surgery.

"There's even a chance that I won't be able to get to the lesion—which would require me to perform an even more involved surgery," he solemnly said.

Dr. Z clarified that the lesion was very small and in a precarious place, and he might not be able to get to it. If that happened, he would have to remove the entire kidney.

Dr. Z encouraged me to consider my next steps thoroughly and emphasized that it was not a decision to take lightly.

For the first time since consulting doctors about this surgery, I felt heard by a medical professional, and I was not alone in my reservations. I left that appointment feeling even more aware of the gravity of the surgery and more hesitant to proceed with this plan.

Let Go and Let God

I continually prayed for God to guide me. I sought His wisdom for next steps and talked through everything with Rob, determined to make the best possible decision for my health and for my family. Settling on surgery and having a distinct plan to rectify the problem, I presumed, would make me feel better. But that was not the case.

So many thoughts had been racing through my mind during the months since receiving my first unfavorable MRI result. Monitoring my lesion felt like walking near a rocky cliff prone to landslides. I carried on with my days as usual, walking the path of my everyday life; however, I was constantly aware of a bank of boulders overhead threatening to tumble down at any moment. I recognized the possibility of my whole life getting knocked off course based on this one diagnosis.

Despite the threat, despite the potential danger ahead, I wasn't scared. Sure, I had little pebbles of dread or uncertainty that trickled into my mind, but I wholeheartedly trusted the Lord to see me through this medical ordeal, no matter what.

When it came to this surgery, it wasn't fear that held me back. I had plenty of surgeries in my life, after all. In fact, surgery had been the go-to solution for fixing many medical matters throughout my adult life.

I began to contemplate that truth. Did I, unknowingly or unnecessarily, default to surgery or medical intervention to fix my problems?

Just two years prior, I had carpel tunnel surgery on both of my wrists to try to rectify yet another one of my health conditions—a surgery I had regretted after the fact because of the slow recovery process and unsatisfactory results.

I thought back to all the medical issues I had over the years and the countless appointments and tests and hours spent researching, analyzing, and attempting to fix each problem.

A conversation I recently had with my gastroenterologist replayed in my mind. As I sat in her office, going over the results from an upper GI endoscopy—on a quest to solve one of my numerous mysterious ailments—she said something so simple yet so profound: "Sometimes, we may not find an underlying issue to every discomfort, pain, or ailment. We don't always know what is going on in our bodies. And that's okay. We have to be able to let some things go without getting an answer."

The results of my test showed no noticeable issues, and while I was relieved that it was nothing serious, I felt a pang of disappointment because I knew that meant I had reached a dead end. It meant there was no solution, no next step to fix my symptoms.

Yet, my doctor's simple statement of truth unlocked something inside of me. I felt different. Her straightforward, yet insightful, remark somehow gave me permission to release my grip on the luggage full of medical burdens that I hauled with me everywhere I went. My invisible baggage no longer had the power to weigh down my thoughts or consume my time.

Not long after that conversation, I heard a message from a ministry leader about how the enemy is relentless. She pointed out that the enemy will do whatever it takes to keep us from what God has for us. If he can't keep us stuck and bound up in sin, then he will simply distract us.

As I pondered my upcoming surgery, a light suddenly switched on, illuminating the devious diversions that lurked in the hidden rooms of my mind. I could see clearly how consumed I had been for so many years.

> ...the enemy will do whatever it takes to keep us from what God has for us. If he can't keep us stuck and bound up in sin, then he will simply distract us.

The countless hours researching ailments and sitting in doctors' offices. Thousands of dollars poured into medical tests and surgeries. My time, my thoughts, my resources inundated with medical obligations.

I had walked away from significant areas of bondage in my life, and the enemy knew he couldn't trap me in those places anymore, so he successfully schemed to steal, kill, and destroy[3] God's plan and purpose for me through a new obsession.

And even though I was no longer walking in blatant rebellion and sin, could the open wounds in my soul have affected my body?

> I no longer spoke words of sickness or disease or calamity over my health.

I didn't deny that I had real-life medical issues, but what I did recognize was the persistent cycle of dysfunction in my health and my tendency to be distracted by it.

Reminded of my authority in Christ, I began to pray fervently. I commanded the attacks against my body to leave in Jesus' name. I began to take every thought captive and make it obedient to

---

3 John 10:10

Christ. I no longer spoke words of sickness or disease or calamity over my health. I removed the cloaks of toxic conditions that I had so willingly worn. I no longer allowed diagnoses to be my identity.

I resolved to speak life and speak the truth of God's word. Jesus instructed us to pray for His Kingdom to come and His will to be done on earth as it is in heaven[4]—and there is no disease or sickness in heaven!

I had a newfound clarity and an awakening to the truth revealed in God's word. I was determined not to allow the enemy to kill, steal, or destroy any part of my life.

With eyes wide open, an awakened spirit, and a heart surrendered, I prayed and sought the Lord's wisdom for what to do about my impending surgery. Clarity set in. As if tiny windshield wipers in my brain swished away the muck and confusion, I knew that I was not supposed to move forward with this surgery. I shared my revelation with Rob, and he wholeheartedly supported me. The day before my scheduled operation, I canceled.

Peace like a river flooded my entire body, and I knew I had made the right choice. Dr. Z, who, not surprisingly, supported my decision simply asked that I agree to get follow-up tests every six months to monitor the lesion. I happily agreed.

I began praying for the lesion to disappear. I began claiming healing over my kidney and believing for complete healing in my body. My friends laid hands on me, prayed for me, and agreed with me for healing. Before each test I prayed, with the authority of Christ, that anything that meant me harm had to leave my body in Jesus' name.

Several ultrasounds into my six-month follow-up rhythm, I felt validated and hopeful when the results showed that the lesion was shrinking. A few more visits later, I giggled to myself when the technician had difficulty finding the lesion at all. "I'm not surprised," I said with a triumphant grin. "I've been praying for God to heal me."

After over a dozen CT scans, continually favorable test results, and nearly four-and-a-half years after my abandoned surgery, my

---

4   Matthew 6:10

doctor ordered an MRI to get a better look. He wanted to be certain that we weren't getting inaccurate results.

Several days after my MRI, I opened my online medical chart and read the results with sheer delight: "Lesion has been stable in size…and is almost certainly benign." On a quick phone call, Dr. Z congratulated me and released me from further medical testing, pending any future issues.

As far as I was concerned, God had healed me and would continue to heal me, so I had no plans of returning. *Thanks, and adios, Dr. Z! No offense, but I hope I don't see you again!*

I praise God for the healing that took place, not only in my body but also in my mind. I am no longer a slave to medical mayhem.

> *It is for freedom that Christ has set us free. Stand firm, then, and do not let yourselves be burdened again to a yoke of slavery. (Galatians 5:1 NIV)*

In fact, following that incident, I had so few medical issues or concerns that when I called my primary care physician to schedule routine blood work one day, the receptionist informed me that I was no longer a patient. Apparently, since I allowed an extended period of time to pass since a visit, they dropped me from my doctor's care. Time flies when you're not distracted by an onslaught of health issues!

I am truly amazed at the improvement in my physical health after the shift in my mindset and my choice to speak life, not death over myself.

I had also been on a journey of experiencing extensive emotional healing and finding freedom from past trauma, beginning years earlier when I addressed my abortion wound for the first time.

As my emotional wounds healed coincidentally, or rather God-incidentally, so did my body.

As my emotional wounds healed coincidentally, or rather God-incidentally, so did my body. The positive progress and the alignment in my physical, emotional, and spiritual well-being was unmistakable.

It doesn't mean that I never get sick or that my family never has health concerns, but I no longer allow such things to consume me or create any distraction in my life.

I came out of agreement with every diagnosis and every false identity. I pay close attention to the words that come out of my mouth and the thoughts that I entertain about my health and the health of my loved ones. And, regardless of what I see in front of me, I know that God is faithful to fulfill His promises.

But the Lord is faithful. He will establish you and guard you against the evil one. (2 Thessalonians 3:3 ESV)

FINDING
FREEDOM

Now the Lord is the Spirit, and where the Spirit of the Lord is,
there is freedom.
(2 Corinthians 3:17 ESV)

15
GRATEFUL AMBER

During the months that I faced my medical dilemma with my kidney, I simultaneously struggled with feeling discontent at work. From the time I was young, I desired a career. I remember daydreaming about my future as a businesswoman—successful, independent, career-oriented, and looking the part in a stylish two-piece pantsuit.

Shortly after graduating college, I was well on my way to achieving those goals. I wet my feet in corporate America with the most corporate-y job out there—I accepted a position as a marketing specialist at a large bank in the affiliate corporate office.

Fleeting Fulfillment

I sky-rocketed to businesswoman status—cubicle in a high-rise building (well, as high as they get in small-town Ohio), lunch breaks and happy hours at the local downtown establishments, fancy conference room meetings and, of course, the eagerly anticipated mandatory professional attire.

For close to eight years, I broadened my knowledge and skills, held various roles within the department, gradually worked my way up the pay scale, and even completed my MBA at a local university. My life looked like the picture I had painted in my youth.

Yet, something was missing.

Not all that surprising, I found the banking world to be quite boring. Granted, of all the jobs to have at a bank, I believed mine was the best. In my marketing role, I planned company events and fundraisers, I traveled locally to assist various banking sites with marketing initiatives, and I helped manage the company's sponsorship with the local minor league baseball team, which involved lots of entertaining activities and social interactions.

The company even sent me to a couple corporate trainings in Florida where I got to bask in sunshine at a luxurious hotel pool in between riveting sessions teaching the most effective way to procure customer data for direct mailings. Not to mention, as a young and single 20-something,

I truly felt like I was living the life I had dreamt of, but somehow it didn't measure up.

I had plenty of opportunities to hang out with my coworkers after work for drinks or go out on the weekends, consequently developing some great friendships and, inevitably, a few flirtatious flings. I truly felt like I was living the life I had dreamt of, but somehow it didn't measure up.

Assuming it was the lackluster banking industry that was the problem, I began looking for other options. I ultimately settled on a sales position with a company that developed software for public transportation like airports and trains. Surely the transportation industry would prove to be much more interesting than banking, right? Spoiler alert: It most definitely did not.

However, the allure of a career change, especially one that involved jetting off on sales calls across the country and working closely with counterparts all over the world, drew me in. The cherry on top was a significant salary increase plus quarterly bonuses. If my downtown corporate banking job was an entrée at a fancy restaurant, this new position felt like a five-course meal in the lavish VIP lounge. Achieving this new level of corporate success meant that I had reached new heights in my career goals.

But where, exactly, was I headed?

My flight landed at my home airport late on Thursday night. Exhausted from another week of travel and ready to sleep in my own bed, I grabbed my luggage from the overhead compartment and waited for my turn to exit the plane. My drive home was a daze of hazy headlights, glowing road signs, and brooding thoughts.

Traveling half the month was not as exciting or enjoyable as I anticipated it would be. Turns out the new product I was assigned to sell wasn't flying off the shelves either. Lastly, glaring me in the face just like the oncoming traffic during my late-night drive was the fact that I found transportation software to be utterly uninteresting. I had pushed myself to flourish in my role, I was determined to find purpose in my position, all to no avail. No matter how hard I tried to force it, I could not find a passion for my job.

Thankfully, I soon transitioned out of the sales position and into a support role for the sales and marketing department. My spirits rose and my job satisfaction grew as I now had the opportunity to do things that I loved—like more behind-the-scenes projects, planning company events, and facilitating fundraisers. I also highly respected the company's leadership, had great coworkers, and thoroughly enjoyed my work environment—a huge plus.

Nonetheless, the sentiment didn't last. I spent close to eight years in that role feeling like I didn't fit. The industry wasn't appealing to me. The days were long and boring.

During my time at that software development company, I met and married Rob, and shortly thereafter we started having children. Once our boys were born, my discontent at work became almost unbearable. I longed for the opportunity to be at home, to be a part of each day with my kids. I recognized how quickly they grew and how fleeting the time was.

Shifting restlessly in our weekly sales meeting, my mind wandered as the conversation droned on about our strategy to win the latest airport system bid. Software jargon, hardware specifications, and technical terms sailed over my head while I held back tears and silently pleaded in frustration. *Lord, is this really what I'm supposed to be doing with my life?*

My heart was not in my job and the desire for donning uncomfortable professional clothing had long since lost its appeal. While I worked for a great company and had wonderful coworkers, I wasn't able to muster up much enthusiasm for or interest in my day-to-day responsibilities at work, no matter how hard I tried to force it. Even the perks and income had lost their appeal.

Instead, I felt jaded and disappointed because my high hopes of a lucrative career bringing fulfillment and happiness had fallen flat. For a long time, most of my adult life in fact, I assumed that I just had to deal with it. I reasoned that nobody really loved their job, and it was just a part of life—that if you made good money and became successful, then it was worth the unhappiness.

But as much as I tried to reason with myself, to force myself to push through, an unsettled, uncomfortable feeling persistently pricked in my heart—like an itchy sweater you endure because it looks nice but makes you miserable the whole time you're wearing it. Was the discontentment, the dissatisfaction, the sacrifice really worth it?

A Leap of Faith

I began to dream about quitting my job and being a stay-at-home mom—something that I had never before dreamed of doing. I began to envision spending my days immersed in things I was most passionate about—ministry work, health and wellness, and my family. I had a deep desire to wholeheartedly serve God with my time, talents, and treasures,[1] whatever that looked like. I felt pulled in a direction that seemed out of the ordinary and contrary to what I had always perceived as normal.

The more I pressed in and prayed, the more I realized that the change I contemplated was not a selfish desire but rather one that the Lord was gently nudging me to consider.

I walked in the door after a later-than-usual evening at work to a bustling home—bouncing boys playing in the living room, toys and snack dishes strewn about, and my amazing husband faithfully preparing dinner. I quickly laid my coat and bag on a chair, grabbed kisses and hugs from everyone, and began helping Rob.

---

1   Matthew 6:19-21; 25:14-30

"Wouldn't it be great if I could be here with the kids and didn't get home so much later than you from work?" I prompted, as Rob and I cleaned the slew of dirty dishes after dinner.

He shrugged, less interested in my inquiry and more focused on clean-up.

I continued, prodding a bit more. "I just don't know how much longer I can do this. It's so hard being at work when what is most important to me is at home. The boys are getting so big so fast!"

This wasn't the first time I had mentioned my inclination to quit my job and come home. I had been praying for months and brought it up to Rob every so often to gauge his feelings. Aware that my desire to come home would affect our lives immensely, I knew I could not take such a big step without him being on board.

Rob scoffed and blew it off as illogical. "Yeah, seems like a nice idea, but I don't see how that could work." He reasoned, rightfully so, that it didn't make sense financially and would put our family in a tough position. "You never mentioned wanting to be a stay-at-home mom—that wasn't the arrangement we had discussed before we got married," he added in a familiar half-joking tone that told me his remark had underlying true sentiments.

Rob never said it outright, but it was clear he did not have the same view as me about my proposed plan. Feeling dejected and discouraged, I put my desires on the back burner, praying and hoping that the Lord would work on Rob's heart.

I knew that quitting my corporate job and cutting our household income in half seemed irresponsible and unreasonable on the surface. I knew that what I proposed made no sense in the logical world. Even when I factored in earning supplemental income from my small health and wellness side business, the numbers just didn't add up. My practical mind sought out a solution to the deficit in our budget, but no matter how many times I rearranged the numbers or recalculated our income and expenses, I couldn't get it to line up in our favor.

Yet, I couldn't shake the feeling that the Lord was leading me in this direction. Journal entry after journal entry, I poured out my prayers: my desire to be all-in for God and to live out my life for the purpose He called me to.

While I couldn't see exactly what that future looked like, I knew that I wouldn't get there as long as I clung to the norms and comforts of my life. My sense of security, coincidentally, seemed to be holding onto me as much as I was holding onto it.

In desperation, I sought God's guidance, month after month, and surrendered the outcome to Him. By December 2015, the same month I was scheduled to have kidney surgery, this topic moved from simmering on the back burner to a full-blown boil on the front flame.

To my surprise, when I revisited the issue with Rob, his position had shifted from unwilling and unsympathetic to supportive and understanding. By God's grace, his heart had changed. I praised God because I knew that my husband's support was the green light I had been waiting for. Pent up excitement and joyful anticipation of what the Lord wanted to do began to bubble to the surface.

While considering my next steps and how to implement this new life plan, I received a call from the executive director of the pregnancy center where I volunteered for the past five years. Sarah, who was a mentor and quickly becoming a dear friend, informed me of a job opportunity at the pregnancy center and encouraged me to apply. I eagerly accepted her invitation. Not long after my interview, I received the job offer.

My heart leapt with eagerness at the idea of working daily on this mission where my passion would be ignited, doing something that was so meaningful to me and so impactful for families. Could this be the answer to my prayers?

My heart pulled toward the pregnancy center, yet I felt a hesitation in my spirit. I was conflicted because I desperately wanted to have a career full of meaning and purpose, but my heart yearned to be home during these precious years with my young boys.

Additionally, I felt guilty for creating such a deficit in our finances. While I had my husband's approval, I still felt self-imposed pressure to pull my weight financially. Bogged down by the worry that Rob would one day resent me, I considered solutions to soften the blow of a drastic income cut. The pregnancy resource center would only provide a meager ministry salary and a fraction of what

I had been making, but I reasoned that it would still be *something* steady that I could contribute to our household income.

Riddled with confusion and uncertainty about how to move forward, feeling pulled in different directions, I prayed for God to provide perfect clarity. If we were going to make such a drastic change in our lives, I wanted to be sure I was doing what God wanted me to do. I knew He would show me if I asked and had the patience to wait for His answer. I clung to His promises in scripture to guide me and show me my next steps.

I will instruct you and teach you in the way you should go;
I will counsel you with my loving eye on you. (Psalm 32:8 NIV)

Sitting in bed late one night, Rob and I hashed out the plan we had been discussing. With the job at the pregnancy center now seeming like the obvious next step, my thoughts spilled out as I contemplated the pros and cons aloud.

Rob gently challenged me with a simple question: "I thought the whole point of you quitting your job was to be home with the kids. Then, why would you leave one full-time job for another?" he asked.

Shocked that he was not pushing for me to take the path that involved a guaranteed income, I began to confess the burden I felt to help contribute to our family financially. He lovingly reminded me that he supported my decision to quit my job because he knew how important it was to me to be home and how valuable that time would be not only for our kids but also for our entire family. He reassured me that he was fully on board—no resentment, no expectations.

Despite how crazy this decision seemed to the outside world, I completely trusted God with the outcome. I knew that if He led us to this, He would get us through it.

Instantly, a flood of peace washed over me. God made it perfectly clear. Despite the uncertainty of our finances, despite the fear of the unknown, despite how crazy this decision seemed to the outside world, I completely trusted God with the outcome. I knew that if He led us to this, He would get us through it.

Trust in the Lord with all your heart and lean not on your own understanding; in all your ways submit to him, and he will make your paths straight. (Proverbs 3:5-6 NIV)

On January 27, 2016, I worked my last day in corporate America. I came home from work that day, overflowing with emotions, to a deluge of heart-felt hugs and kisses from my two sweet boys and Rob. A new chapter had officially begun in my life. I had no idea how abundantly the Lord was going to bless me—not in the ways that I expected, yet far beyond all I could ask or imagine[2]—as I stepped out in obedience in this new season.

Heart of Gratitude

Each day after quitting my job felt like a gift that I got to wake up and unwrap. I couldn't help but find joy in every single thing, big and small.

All the remedial responsibilities that had once been packed into tiny pockets of time throughout my tiring work weeks now gave me a sense of enjoyment because they were sprinkled into days I designed: Running errands with my little sidekick, as he became known, while big brother was away at kindergarten. Grocery trips on Tuesday mornings to avoid the weekend rush. Cleaning my bathroom floors on a random Thursday instead of my typical Saturday because, why not? Taking extra time and care to prepare healthy meals for my family.

Some of the biggest blessings, though, were those moments of peace in solitude and the precious memories with my children. Quiet time doing my Bible study outside in the sun. Picnic lunches at the park, games, crafts, and countless adventures with my sweet boys. My heart overflowed with gratitude for this gift of time.

---

2   Ephesians 3:20

I continually thanked God for this new life that I could hardly believe was mine.

Even when, or perhaps especially when, hard times and tragedy struck, I felt the Lord's peace and purpose in my new, flexible schedule.

Just a couple of days after quitting my job, Rob's mom underwent knee surgery to repair extensive injuries she suffered from a recent fall. We arranged for her to stay with us during her recovery. Having the opportunity to care for her and enjoy extra time with her while she healed was one of the first of many blessings that came from my new-found freedom. I truly felt that the Lord allowed our family that season to connect with her more deeply, to strengthen our relationship, and to demonstrate Christ's love for her in a tangible way.

Within only a couple months of becoming a stay-at-home mom, my stepdad's health drastically declined. After years of battling dementia (later diagnosed as Chronic Traumatic Encephalopathy or CTE,[3] which is caused by repeated traumatic brain injuries, in his case, related to his high school and college football careers), Frank's symptoms became so severe that my mom made the difficult decision to move him into an assisted living home with an Alzheimer's unit. He needed care around the clock, and she could no longer do it on her own.

My stepbrother and stepsister lived out of state with their families. Both had strong relationships with their dad and would have spent every possible minute with him in his time of need if they lived nearby—of that, I'm sure. Although, I often think it may have been a blessing that they didn't have to experience the anguish first-hand or endure the unbearable heartache over and over of his declining health.

I resolved to help as much as I could. I knew that my new freedom was a gift from God and an unexpected blessing in this tragic, heartbreaking, demanding season.

---

3 "Chronic Traumatic Encephalopathy," Mayo Clinic, November 18, 2023, mayoclinic.org/diseases-conditions/chronic-traumatic-encephalopathy/symptoms-causes/syc-20370921.

I parked in the front lot of the increasingly familiar assisted living home, a sprawling tan apartment-type building with large white columns and neatly trimmed bushes. The facility's tidy lawn, perfectly arranged furniture, and elegant decor almost succeeded in distracting me from the tragedy of the hundreds of diseased and declining residents housed within. Almost.

Breathing deeply and praying silently, I prepared myself for another day with Frank. The weeks since he had moved into the memory care unit had been some of the most emotionally draining, physically exhausting, spiritually challenging times of my life.

I entered the large sliding glass doors and made my way through the lobby and up the stairs to the locked entrance of my stepdad's Alzheimer's unit. Once admitted, I walked the short trek to his room, reciprocating cheerful greetings from the saintly staff. We often noted what a blessing it was to have such kind and compassionate people taking care of our loved one.

I tentatively peeked through the doorway of Frank's one-room living quarters to find him awkwardly slouched in a wheelchair, staring blankly at the wall while my mom tenderly smoothed his hair with her hands. No matter what time of the day or night I visited, she was almost always there. I could see the sadness and exhaustion in her eyes as she greeted me wearily.

I crouched down to give my stepdad a hug and tried to meet his downcast eyes. "Good morning, Frank!" I said joyfully. "Looking good!" A slight twitch in his eyes and whispered mumble signified his acknowledgment of my greeting.

I held back tears and turned to my mom. "I'll wheel him around for a bit. Why don't you take a break?"

Frank and I cruised the hallways, stopping every now and then to look out a window or adjust his position. When we turned the corner, I spotted a tiny, tucked away room that served as the floor's chapel. I pushed him through the open doorway, positioned his wheelchair in front of the hanging cross, kneeled next to him, and began to pray.

Lord, thank You that You love Frank more than I could ever know. Thank You for the blessing he is to so many people. Father, you know what he needs. You know what is best for him. Please comfort him and help him. Have mercy on him in his pain and frustration. Give the nurses and caregivers everything they need to care for him and supply my mom the strength and energy to love him well. Protect all of our sad and weary hearts through this difficult time. We love You, we trust You, and we know that You are always good. Amen

After concluding my prayer, I felt an overwhelming desire to intercede for Frank. I had a sudden awareness that I didn't know where he stood with God or if he had ever officially accepted Jesus as His Lord and Savior. Yes, he had gone to church as a kid and sporadically as an adult, and I knew he believed in God, but I was unsure of his relationship with Jesus. Not willing to leave his eternity to chance, tears trickled down my cheeks as I prayed a heartfelt prayer aloud:

Lord, I thank You that You know Frank's heart and that Your desire is for all to know You and come to You. I pray, Lord, that if he has not yet made a decision for Christ, that You would create an opportunity for his heart to turn to You. I recognize that he is not in a frame of mind to understand or respond to my words, so I trust You, Lord, that You will make a way. I know that You are beyond time, beyond sickness, beyond any barrier that would try to stand in the way of Frank giving his life to You. I submit him to You, Lord, and I pray for his salvation, for his eternity to be secure in You, in Jesus' name. Your kingdom come, Your will be done, on earth as it is in heaven. Amen.

After sitting with Frank in silence a little longer, I took him back to his room. I did my best to help him eat, supporting his hand while he clumsily aimed for his mouth. I talked to him about my day, shared updates about his kids and grandkids, and told him how much we all loved him.

Each moment I spent with my stepdad in this environment, under these conditions, my little-girl heart shattered all over again as I wrestled with the distress of yet another father ripped prematurely from my life, from my mom's life, from his kids' and grandkids' lives, and from the many lives of those who adored him.

Being with Frank day-in and day-out and watching him slip away was unbearable. My heart felt like it was being torn to pieces with each vacant stare from his eyes and every labored breath he took. I longed to be there for him, to be sure he felt loved and cared for, even though he barely seemed aware of his surroundings or who the people near him were most of the time.

My little-girl heart shattered all over again as I wrestled with the distress of yet another father ripped prematurely from my life

When it was time for me to go, I hugged him again. "See you tomorrow! Love you!"

I felt my heart weighing heavy inside my chest as it did every day after leaving him. I drove home to my family, weariness and sadness bombarding me. Every day I pleaded with God for help. I begged him for mercy for my stepdad, for guidance for the medical team, and for strength, comfort, and peace for those of us who loved him and were caring for him.

Witnessing our loved one become a shell of the man we once knew—strong, vibrant, and otherwise healthy in his mid-60s—was traumatic for our entire family.

After nearly two months in the assisted living home, Frank's struggle came to an end. Late on a Saturday night in April of 2016, we gathered in his room—my mom, stepbrother, stepsister, and me by his side, along with other friends and family nearby—and prayed over him as he took his last breath. Knowing he was no longer suffering comforted our tired and grieving hearts. Imagining him in a new body in heaven, young and vibrant as in his youth with his joyful smile and jolly laugh, provided peace in the midst of our sorrow.

As strenuous and distressful as those weeks of caring for my stepdad were, I am so grateful that I had the opportunity to be by his side during such a critical time. I thank God for the sweet moments of praying with him, sitting with him, feeding him,

I can see, more clearly than ever, how God's blessings come to us in ways we least expect.

and comforting him. I thank God for the help I was able to provide my mom and the peace of mind it gave my stepsiblings to know I was there helping to care for him.

I even thank God for the heartache and the pain because I can see how faithful He was to carry me through and sustain me even during the hardest of times. I can see, more clearly than ever, how God's blessings come to us in ways we least expect.

Had I ignored the promptings to quit my job, I wouldn't have had the additional time, energy, or freedom to clear my schedule to support my mom and care for Frank. I will forever cherish that time and count it as one of the biggest blessings that came from my season of obediently following the Lord's guidance to step away from the norm and step out in faith.

16

CODEPENDENT AMBER

As I continued down the path of obediently following God's lead and seeking His guidance more diligently than before, doors continued to open. A series of heart-felt prayers, chance meetings, and God-incidences led me to one of the most transformative seasons of my life.

After engaging in a rare one-on-one conversation with our pastor, Charlie, after church service one Sunday morning, I felt charged with purpose and direction. I had previously shared my abortion testimony with him, my mission in pro-life ministry, and the work I was doing at the pregnancy center. His shared passion for this cause and his enthusiasm for what the Lord wanted to do through me radiated in his excited eyes and inspiring words as he charged me to walk even more boldly in my assignment—suggesting that I share my testimony to the congregation and prompting me to start and lead a pro-life group at our church.

Charlie's encouragement, his belief in me, and his sound wisdom for next steps were like a catapult launching me off into the mission field. I went home that morning with resolve in my spirit, confidence in my purpose, and a determination to forge ahead in what I knew to be God's calling on my life.

Although I was excited about the future and knew I was on the right path, I still had no idea what that looked like or what exactly to do. I continued to pray for God's guidance and for clarity for next steps. I also began praying for the Lord to put people in my life who could help me—specifically, I asked God to bring me a mentor. I desperately wanted to grow in my relationship with the Lord, and I knew that partly comes from the guidance of someone who is wise and willing to share their experiences. I needed direction; I needed to be discipled.

A wise man will hear and increase in learning, and a person of understanding will acquire wise counsel. (Proverbs 1:5 NASB)

Right Place at the Right Time

Shortly after my Sunday morning chat with Charlie, I attended a large leadership event that my church hosted. During the lunch break, I sat down across from a couple, Richard and Rena, whom I had admired from a distance for their well-known ministry that helps support those battling cancer.

As I got to know them and learned more about their ministry, I also shared some of what was on my heart and the prompting I felt to do something more with pro-life ministry. During our short time together, I felt an immediate connection and anticipation for what the Lord might do through this new-found friendship.

Richard and Rena graciously agreed to meet with me again and to follow up with the help I needed to move forward with my ministry plans. I was overjoyed at the prospect of staying connected with people from whom I could learn so much.

Within a couple weeks of our happenstance encounter, I received a text from Rena inviting me to join her small discipleship group starting in the fall. Grateful tears spilled from my eyes as I praised God for answered prayers.

In November 2016, I began a two-year journey committed to diving deeper with the Lord than I ever had and learning what it looked like to truly live a life surrendered to Christ. My heart leapt with excitement about learning from someone I admired for her dedication to knowing God and His word.

My heart overflowed with gratitude and awe as I recognized God's perfect timing in all these circumstances. My small group was set to meet on Friday mornings, a time that would not have been feasible had I not quit my job earlier that year. Once again, the Lord reminded me of the blessings that freely flowed from that one decision to follow His lead when it seemed irrational.

Like many of my endeavors, I entered with high hopes and a preconceived notion of how it would go—what I thought I would and should gain from it. I loved to learn, and I loved the Lord, and I fully anticipated a lighthearted experience of studying scripture, growing in my faith, and developing a closer relationship with Jesus.

> *Once again, the Lord reminded me of the blessings that freely flowed from that one decision to follow His lead when it seemed irrational.*

Little did I know that this would be one of my most intense seasons of self-reflection and that growing in my walk with the Lord would require uprooting some of my deep-seated habits and thoughts still stealthily wreaking havoc in my life.

Week after week, the Lord pulled back the layers of trauma and false beliefs and brought to the surface areas I didn't know needed healing, or lies I believed about myself or others that needed to be reformed.

The Insanity Cycle

My insides felt like I had swallowed a cupful of thistles, and my mind raced with troubled, self-conscious thoughts. Unwilling to wait a minute longer in the captivity of my stewing frustrations and angst, I dialed Rena's number as I rode home from a family outing. I stared distractedly at the scenery passing by my window as I waited anxiously for Rena to answer.

Thankfully, her kind voice soon responded on the other end of the line. After a quick greeting, I briefly rehashed the most recent drama with my friends Gloria and Brook. Brook made false accusations about me and my intentions, invoking division and hurt feelings with Gloria.

What had I done to make Brook dislike me so much? She was once a close friend and confidant but had recently resorted to hateful and vindictive behavior, most often with an intent of turning Gloria and others against me.

Mutual friends had started sharing how she talked about me behind my back, the lies she spewed about my character, and her incessant indignance toward me. I was devastated. Brook had been a good friend, a mentor, and someone I once trusted wholeheartedly.

When I first got to know Brook, she was encouraging and supportive and went out of her way to make me feel like a valued friend. But lately, she had distanced herself from me, ignored me in group settings, and was seemingly openly against me. I felt betrayed, violated, and distraught to learn that, not only did she no longer support or care about me, but she was also actively trying to sabotage me.

Like I had many times before, I shared with Rena the anguish I felt over being betrayed and defamed. "I can't believe Brook is saying these things about me! How can Gloria possibly believe her? Can't she see the manipulation and lies?"

Brook's hurtful and deceitful words were a never-ending merry go round in my mind, circling, replaying, and nauseatingly persistent. Not only was I nursing wounds from her ongoing malicious attacks against me, but I was outraged by her blatant disregard for the truth and her ability to manipulate others to believe her.

"I need to confront Brook and make her see what she is doing and saying is wrong. And, somehow, I have to repair the damage with Gloria. I can't stand that she is hurt and upset with me!" I was exasperated.

Rena sat on the other end of the phone in silence as I rambled through all my offenses and talked myself into calling each of them to set the record straight. I was determined to make this right, to make the truth known, and to find a solution that would result in a happy ending, where everyone believed me and liked me. I just needed Rena to help me figure out the best approach to achieve my goal.

As usual, Rena didn't give me the answer I was looking for nor did she validate my quest for justice. Oh, how many times I wished she would just tell me what to do! Instead, she compassionately acknowledged my feelings of distress and began digging deeper with a series of familiar questions: "What is your motive for calling Brook? Or trying to fix things with Gloria?"

"Well, what Brook is doing is wrong, and she needs to know that!" I retorted. "And I feel terrible that I hurt Gloria."

Rena reminded me that this turmoil with Brook had been going on for months and lovingly asked, "Has she ever changed her behavior because of something you confronted her about?"

"No," I mumbled, "she doesn't even see that she's being manipulative with Gloria, and she thinks she's right about me, so anything I say is completely lost on her."

"Then, what is your real motive for wanting to confront Brook?" Rena repeated.

I pondered that question for a moment, asking the Lord to reveal any brokenness in me, any impure motives. Suddenly I knew. "I want justice. I want her to understand what she is doing is wrong. I want to clear my name. I want her to change her mind about how she feels about me."

Revelation set in as I recognized that my desire to manage my image, to please others, and to be liked was the driving force for addressing things with Brook. I had learned from experience that Brook was not receptive to what I had to say. Trying to defend myself with her had only led to more distress and more frustration on my end. Rena knew that, as she had been around this mountain with me several times before.

I was reminded of three lessons I had recently learned:

❖ Insanity is doing the same thing and expecting a different result.[1]
❖ You can't reason with the unreasonable.
❖ My identity does not come from what others think of me.

---

1   Misattributed to Einstein according to Albert Einstein, *The Ultimate Quotable Einstein*, ed. Alice Calaprice (Princeton, NJ: Princeton University Press, 2013). The quote was by an Al-Anon meeting attendee as quoted in Betsy Pickle, "Al-Anon Helps Family, Friends to Orderly Lives," *The Knoxville News-Sentinel*, October 11, 1981.

Many times before, I had tried to defend myself to Brook to no avail. Her behavior didn't improve and her demeanor toward me did not change. As much as I desired to make a difference in this circumstance, I could not control what Brook thought or did. So, why should I expect this time around to be any different?

Rena continued to dig, "As for Gloria, I heard you say that you feel terrible that you hurt her. Did you *actually* hurt her? Or are her feelings hurt about something she thinks that you did or said?"

"Her feelings are hurt because of me. Isn't that the same thing?"

"No, it's not the same thing," Rena pointed out matter-of-factly. "If you have done something wrong and it causes harm to another person, physically or emotionally, then you should take ownership of what you have done. But just because someone has hurt feelings doesn't mean you have done something wrong. It certainly does not mean that *you* hurt them. Other peoples' offenses or hurt feelings are not ours to own, whether they hold us accountable or not."

My mind reeled as I tried to catch the truth Rena was pitching. Like the rising sun dissolving a lingering morning haze, my understanding of my co-dependent nature became clear.

My whole life I had been driven by the need to be liked and for all my relationships to be in good standing. If, for some reason, things were not in perfect harmony or I thought (or knew) someone had an issue with me, I would obsess over that situation or person, worrying, fretting, and doing whatever I could to make things right. I could not rest or feel okay unless everything in my life was in order and all the people I knew were happy with me.

> *My whole life I had been driven by the need to be liked and for all my relationships to be in good standing.*

Rena, with wisdom and determination, persisted with one last series of questions to drive this much-needed lesson home. "Where are you not trusting God in this situation?"

I reflected on my thoughts and feelings about Brook and Gloria and many similar tumultuous instances, and the ongoing feelings of anger, frustration, anxiety, and restlessness that persisted. I had tried so many times to make things right in order to feel at ease.

"I'm trying to control things—other people's actions and thoughts. And I'm not trusting God with the outcome," I finally said.

I was beginning to realize that I had a preconceived notion of what I thought needed to happen for me to have peace. I needed (or wanted) reconciliation. I needed (or wanted) justice. I needed (or wanted) harmony and truth and for my reputation to be repaired.

> *Where does my value, worth, and peace come from—from people and circumstances, or from God?*

But much of that depended on outside circumstances that were beyond my control. Lessons I had learned about codependence and questions that Rena had asked me numerous times before surfaced in my spirit: *Can I be okay, even when the situations or relationships in my life are not okay? Why do I feel the need to defend myself? Where does my value, worth, and peace come from—from people and circumstances or from God?*

Who Does God Say I Am?

I took time to pray and seek God's wisdom and truth. I began recounting aloud with Rena all I had learned and all the progress I had made in having genuine confidence and authentic peace. I believed with certainty that my identity comes from God because He calls me His daughter,[2] and that my peace is not dependent on my circumstances but rather comes from the Prince of Peace.[3]

I knew wholeheartedly that my value and worth did not come from what others think about me or who does or does not like me at any given moment. My identity and my worth come from God, and His opinion is the only one that matters.

I knew that because of who I am in Christ, I had nothing to prove, and I could trust God with the outcome.[4] And I knew in my heart that I could and would be fine, even if relationships in my life were not as I wanted them to be.

---

2   John 1:12
3   Isaiah 9:6
4   1 Peter 2:23

I have told you these things, so that in me you may have peace. In this world you will have trouble. But take heart! I have overcome the world! (John 16:33 NIV)

My peace comes from a deeper place of contentedness in all circumstances, not just when my life is harmonious and everyone likes me.

That day, in the middle of a car ride home with my family, I released Brook and Gloria and the whole tumultuous situation. I resolved that I would no longer let this drama steal my joy or my peace.

I decided I would no longer get caught in the snare of needing their approval or trying to control their thoughts and feelings about me. I let go of anything I thought they owed me. I forgave them of the hurts and the offenses I had endured over the past months. I turned from my anxious thoughts and the need to be in control. Once and for all, I surrendered my circumstances, these relationships, and the outcome to the Lord.

As if dozens of tiny weights attached all over my body were suddenly cut loose, I instantly felt lighter and freer, no longer bogged down by the burdens of my unhealthy thoughts and habits or tethered by the constraints of toxic friendships.

I had no idea how this situation represented so many areas of my life where I was bound by codependency, people pleasing, and image management.

The relentless need to be liked.

The never-ending search for validation and approval.

The desperation for love and acceptance and harmony no matter what.

The consuming angst in my life when situations or relationships felt unsettled.

The constant stress of wondering whether or not someone was mad at me or worrying that when people didn't reach out or respond to me somehow meant that I did or said something wrong.

I began to realize how much of my identity, my value, and my peace came from others and my circumstances. I began unraveling

Determined to be set free of all that held me in bondage, I gratefully tackled each new challenge, trusting that what the Lord revealed, He intended to heal.

my giant ball of codependent behaviors acquired and entangled in since childhood.

Over the course of coming months, the Lord lovingly revealed other areas of my life and various relationships that were subject to the same destructive snares. Determined to be set free of all that held me in bondage, I gratefully tackled each new challenge, trusting that what the Lord revealed, He intended to heal.

I praised Him for uncovering this stronghold in my life and for showing me how to break free from these shackles.

17
UNSHACKLED AMBER

In December 2016, I received an invitation from my friend Dawn to join women who were gathering in a private online group to connect, study the women of the Bible, and pray in preparation for a large conference taking place the following December. Intrigued by the opportunity to connect with women I knew were godly and faith filled, I eagerly accepted the invitation.

As soon as I tuned into the online gatherings, I heard men and women on fire for the Lord in ways I had never experienced before. I was blown away by their passion and authentic love for Jesus and for God's word. A stirring arose in my spirit as I recognized that these new friends had something I didn't have.

They were not your run-of-the-mill Christians but full of life, full of passion, raw and real. They had an undeniable joy. A peace that passed all understanding. A confidence and authority in their identity in Christ. I didn't fully understand it, but I knew I wanted it.

As the date of the conference quickly approached, anticipation bubbled up in my belly. I had been praying, journaling, and asking God for what I hoped to receive.

Intentionally putting aside all the obligations or distractions at home that could pull me away from this long-awaited adventure—I boarded a plane.

In early December of 2017, I attended the first national Her Voice Conference in Portland, Oregon. Bob and Jenny Donnelly, founders of Tetelestai Ministries and Her Voice Movement, lead the Her Voice events and host various nationwide gatherings, along with other incredible pastors and leaders.

Within just the first few minutes of entering the atmosphere, I knew something was different.

This wasn't a group who just gathered on Sundays for an hour to be entertained by a worship band and spoon-fed a message and then just carried on with their week. These were people who hungered for God's truth and were wholeheartedly devoted to their Lord and Savior Jesus Christ. The environment emanated an authentic love for and pursuit of God.

I prayed fervently for the Lord to reveal Himself to me. I wanted a deeper connection with Him. I wanted to be head-over-heels in love with Him the way they were. I longed for that same boldness and confidence. I had made up my mind: I would not go back home to Ohio without it.

Unexpected Healing

My thoughts were inexplicably and repetitively sprinkled with memories and emotions surrounding my dad's death. I kept feeling a nudge from the Lord to address that time of my childhood, but I couldn't make sense of why. I had such an anticipation for what the Lord wanted to do in me at this conference, and I was sure that losing my dad when I was 13 years old had nothing to do with it. I was even a little annoyed that God would bring this up. Over two decades had passed since my dad died, and I had dealt with and healed from it long ago. I was over it.

On day two of the conference, I gleaned from incredible messages about our authority in Christ and abiding in Him, with an emphasis on one of my favorite verses: Be still and know that I am God.[1]

---

1   Psalm 46:10

I was reminded that the translation of "be still" in Hebrew is "let go." Prayers flooded my journal as I asked the Lord to show me anything that I needed to let go of, anything that was standing in the way of fully abiding in Him, knowing Him, and walking in my authority in Christ.

The next sentences that I scribbled in my journal were:

Lord, please let me understand why I am so overwhelmed by the memories of my dad right now and why these memories have been so prominent the entire weekend. Help me see why. Lord, what are You saying to me?

Not long after I penned that prayer, as if being pulled by a giant magnet, I stood up and methodically made my way through the rows of chairs to the back of the grand meeting hall. I tentatively pressed through the door of the prayer room, not even sure why I was there. I stood, hovering near the doorway and waited. I had never been to a prayer room before and had no idea what to expect or what to do. Nervous and insecure, I prayed for God to lead me and show me why I was there.

Overcome with emotion, I suddenly lost all concern for what I looked like, who was watching, or what people would think, and I melted onto the floor in tears and silent prayers. Loving and patient ministry team members tended to me, prayed for me, and asked prompting questions.

As I gradually articulated the events of my dad's death and the memories that taunted me, these prayer warrior women interceded for me. Soon, a wave of emotion flooded my entire body, and I was delivered from spirits of abandonment, rejection, trauma, and anger.

As if chains were breaking off my body, a lightness and freedom I had never felt began to sweep through me from my head to my toes. In those moments of complete surrender, the Lord met me and healed deep wounds I didn't know I had. Without fully understanding how or why, I knew that I was different.

I returned to my seat and immediately captured these thoughts in my journal:

I am set FREE! Thank You, Jesus! I am lighter. I feel different. The ties have been broken. The bondage is gone.

Thank You for letting me see what I was holding onto.

Thank You for the release of stored up tears—stored up grief of losing my dad—unexpected loss and insecurity. I had no idea that is where so much bondage was rooted.

Thank You for breaking those ties.

Thank You for being my Daddy and letting me see You as a little girl—as my 13-year-old self, taking my hand and holding me in Your arms.

Lord, I know You will NEVER leave me. You were there when I needed You. I ran away, but You never stopped running after me. I love You with my whole heart. Ahhhh! Jesus, You are so good! I feel like a new person—the joy coming from my insides is overwhelming. I AM NEW! I am stronger! I am lighter! Thank You, God, that You are the same yesterday, today, and forever.

Reading those words even now brings tears of joy and gratitude. I'm so grateful that I followed wise advice years ago to journal my thoughts and prayers and important events so I can look back to see what God has done in my life! What a wonderful reminder of His faithfulness and His goodness.

> *Once I got a taste of this kind of freedom, there was no turning back.*

Once I got a taste of this kind of freedom, there was no turning back. This was just the beginning of so much healing, countless prayers answered, and a deeper intimacy with the Lord.

Baptized with Fire

The final night at the end of the last session, the attendees were invited to come to the front and receive prayer for the things we were seeking from God. Like one of those toy race cars that you pull back to create resistance and then let it go to speed ahead, my feet zoomed to the front as fast as they would take me.

Desperate for the Lord to consume me and have His way in me, I stood near the front with dozens of other women, praying silently to myself and allowing others to pray over me.

Then BOOM! A feeling like nothing I had ever experienced before enveloped me. My entire body felt as if it was engulfed in flames, and I dropped to the floor overcome with joy, sweat seeping from my pores, and tears streaming down my face.

The Holy Spirit began to flood me like a wave of heat and exhilaration from my head to my toes, and my prayer language poured from my lips for the very first time. I praised God for allowing me to experience Him in new ways, for opening my eyes to His power in me, and even for the struggles that led me to this very moment of complete surrender and baptism of the Holy Spirit.

I baptize you with water for repentance. But after me will come one who is more powerful than I, whose sandals I am not fit to carry. He will baptize you with the Holy Spirit and with fire. (Matthew 3:11 NIV)

From that point on, I began chasing after the Lord with fervency like never before. My eyes were wide open to the marvels of God's truth and the power of the Holy Spirit in me.

I arrived back to Ohio feeling nine feet tall. I swept through every inch of my home and prayed over my family and my household with a newfound authority and boldness. I claimed every promise in scripture I had read, every word spoken over me, every truth that God revealed to me, and recited them with conviction over myself, my marriage, and my children. Something in me had shifted, and I would never be the same—in the best possible way.

It's safe to say I had totally gotten it wrong as a teenager when I presumed that being a Christian was boring and lame.

It's safe to say I had totally gotten it wrong as a teenager when I presumed that being a Christian was boring and lame. What a marvelous, exciting, breathtaking ride it is to be a follower of Christ! And that was just the beginning.

Deeper Still

Shortly after attending my first Her Voice event, I crossed paths with a friend I had met on a previous trip for my health and wellness business. Walking through the corridor of an arena filled with thousands of team members at a business training, Kelly and I coincidentally (God-incidentally) walked right by each other and eagerly embraced. We quickly started catching up, and she shared what she had been doing since I last saw her almost a year prior.

Immediately, I noticed something different about her. She exuded a joy, light, and excitement for the Lord that she did not have the first time I met her. She was completely different!

My sweet friend shared her story of transformation. She shared how she encountered God on a mission trip to Ghana and had been radically changed. Her vigor and enthusiasm for the Lord were evident, and I felt an instant kindred connection with her.

After another chance meeting (God-incidence) at a business event a few months later, with another joyful reunion and a jubilant conversation about all the things the Lord had been doing in each our lives, we instinctively knew that our friendship was meant to be more than randomly running into each other every few months. We parted ways after the event—Kelly to Kentucky and I to Ohio—but this time we made plans to stay connected. Determined to stay in touch, we set up a weekly phone call so we could check in, share what the Lord was teaching us, and encourage one another.

Kelly was on what seemed like a rocket-ship ride of faith and growth in the Lord. I had never met someone who so radically transformed in such a short amount of time. She was studying God's word intently and growing in her God-given gifts rapidly. Her passion and fire were contagious, and I felt excited and grateful to invest in such a meaningful relationship with a sister in Christ.

Our weekly phone calls continued for over a year, and our friendship blossomed as we intentionally intersected our lives through various get togethers, trainings, ministry events, and spiritual retreats. I loved being on this journey with such a dear friend as we grew in our spiritual walk with the Lord. We often prayed together and dreamt about what God had in store for each of us in our individual ministries as well as together.

One afternoon, more than a year after our sisterly bond began, I received an ambiguous text from Kelly asking me what I was doing during an upcoming weekend. "I'm available, why?" I asked curiously.

"Would you like to join me for our first freedom retreat?" she responded. I felt a leap in my spirit and called her immediately.

Kelly had recently followed the Lord's prompting to launch a mentorship program, essentially teaching others what she had been learning, guiding them into a more intimate relationship with Christ, and helping equip them to step into their kingdom assignment. The first session of mentorship was wrapping up soon, and the final step of the program would be a three-day deep-dive spiritual retreat for the mentees.

"Count me in!"

I could not pass up a weekend like this. Not only would I spend time with my close friend and other amazing women, but I knew that leaving all the cares of the world behind and focusing all my attention and adoration on the Lord would be life-giving and transformative.

Moreover, this retreat had a higher purpose to walk attendees through in-depth healing and deliverance—in which I was more than eager to partake.

Ever since my first profound encounter with God's healing hand at Her Voice in 2017, I had been on a deliberate journey of seeking the Lord for healing and freedom in multiple areas of my life. Over the past two years, I had read books, studied the Bible, gleaned from others' experiences, and knew that I was ready to take a step further into the liberated life God had for me.

Almost a year had passed since that impactful incident in Portland, and I pondered the many powerful experiences that had led me to this current opportunity. Over the past year, with each retreat, each encounter, and through seeking the Lord with all my heart, the barriers and bondage in my life were breaking down and dissipating. I eagerly prayed, journaled, and prepared for the upcoming getaway.

Leading up to that weekend, I anticipated the struggle: The physical strain of my first three-day fast from food (a recommendation for all attendees based on Mark 9:29), coupled with long days of intense introspection away from the comforts of home. The mental fight of staying focused on God's truth; not allowing shame or condemnation to rule my thoughts as I confessed my sins and struggles. The emotional stress of revisiting painful places in my past or present. The spiritual battle of denouncing any oppressive influences in my life, and releasing any strongholds that I still, knowingly or unknowingly, clung to for comfort.

Despite the struggle, I knew that every bit of the physical, emotional, and spiritual work I was committing to would be worth it.

After a three-hour drive to a small town in Indiana, I arrived at the modest women's community center that would serve as my heavenly haven for the next three days. I entered the building, squealed a few enthusiastic greetings to friends I hadn't seen in person for some time, and then plopped my belongings on my bunk bed of choice. Just like that, my long-awaited weekend wheeled into motion.

Worship music filled the atmosphere as two-dozen women cozied around the rec-room-turned-sanctuary on exercise mats, blankets, and pillows with Bibles and journals in-hand. Heart yielded, mind opened, and body relaxed, I submerged into a state of deep surrender, peace, and attentiveness to the Lord.

Kelly brought the gathering to an official start with prayer and then turned to Ella, one of the other ministry leaders, to share what was on her heart. Ella's message lured me into a deeper revelation of intimacy with the Lord and invigorated me for what was ahead: "With intimacy comes identity, with identity comes authority, with authority comes victory." Throughout the weekend, my heart softened, and the Lord lovingly revealed work that needed to be done:

The hard deposits that He wanted to chisel away.

The crooked places He wanted to straighten.

The dark corners He wanted to expose.

The shackles He wanted to break.

God drew me closer and uncovered new layers of His love. Each of us women had an opportunity for focused prayer and intercession with the ministry leaders. As my turn arrived, I eagerly surrendered to the process and let go of pride and control. Loving prayer warrior women surrounded me, prayed over me, commanded demonic oppression to leave me, and guided me toward God's healing touch.

As I boldly faced my strongholds—denouncing the lies and severing ungodly ties—I was encapsulated in God's cocoon of unconditional, unchanging, unwavering love. I basked in the truth that the battle was already won![2] I simply had to surrender and let the blood of Jesus Christ cleanse me from all the remnants of unrighteousness and sin that still lingered in the dark and hidden places of my soul, to command the enemy who no longer had authority or permission to torment me to leave in the name of Jesus Christ.

> *As I boldly faced my strongholds—denouncing the lies and severing ungodly ties—I was encapsulated in God's cocoon of unconditional, unchanging, unwavering love.*

> *Submit yourselves then, to God. Resist the devil, and he will flee from you. (James 4:7 NIV)*

A familiar invigorating feeling surged through my body—old, tattered rags of emotions, trauma, and bondage fell away as new, clean garments of righteousness and purity covered me. I lay still on my mat, eyes closed, content to linger in my liberation while waves of peace and praise washed over me.

> *"There is no pit so deep, that God's love is not deeper still."*
> *— Corrie Ten Boom*[3]

Revitalized by a new sense of freedom and deep gratitude, my heart overflowed as I wrapped up this unforgettable experience.

---

2   1 Corinthians 15:57
3   Corrie ten Boom, John Sherrill, and Elizabeth Sherrill, *The Hiding Place* (Bantam Books, 1974), 217.

Just as it began, our weekend concluded with heartfelt worship and praise for our Rescuer, our Redeemer. Praise spilled onto the pages of my journal as I thanked God for all He had done:

I praise You, Lord, for freedom! For releasing me of the things that have been holding me captive. During this weekend, there was SO MUCH release! I praise You, Father! You are so good and so loving...Thank You for pursuing me. Thank You for loving me so much! I can barely comprehend the depths of who You are, but I want to know You more. I invite You into every part of me—every piece of my heart is Yours, Lord! I praise You and give You all the glory! In Jesus name—Amen!

Shortly after that powerful weekend, I felt a nudge from God to partner with Kelly and join her ministry team. When I told her, she joyfully confirmed and welcomed me with open arms. I enthusiastically hopped onto the high-speed shuttle of faith and growth with my dear friend, eager to seek the Lord and His will through this new adventure.

With a group of amazing ministry leaders, we taught mentorship classes, hosted freedom retreats, and served alongside one another as we sought the Lord with all our hearts.

What a privilege to walk others through the same process I went through! All the while, God strengthened my gifts, enhanced my courage, and deepened my connection with the Holy Spirit.

18
UNTANGLED AMBER

In December of 2019, I found myself, once again, preparing for a trip across the country to Portland for the second Her Voice Movement conference. The past couple years had been filled with soaring spiritual growth—a deeper connection with the Lord, stepping into and recognizing spiritual gifts, witnessing God's signs, miracles, and wonders not only in my own life but in the lives of those around me.

With each passing day, month, year, I shed the layers of lies I had believed for most of my life—that my value and worth came from what I achieved, how full my social calendar was, or from pleasing others—and my hunger for the Lord intensified. He became my obsession.

The more I knew Him, the more I wanted to know Him. The closer I got to Him, the more I recognized a deeper closeness with Him that was available to me. The more I experienced His goodness, peace, and grace, the more I wanted to bask in His presence and surrender to His will.

As I prepared for the trip, my eager expectation fizzed like a shaken up two-liter bottle of soda. I was ready to burst with excitement. I prayed and fasted for 21 days leading up to the event, believing wholeheartedly that God had something special in store for me and wanting desperately to draw closer to Him.

As I entered the double doors to the venue's large meeting hall, my breath was taken away by the beauty of a run-of-the-mill hotel meeting space transformed into a mesmerizing sea of tranquility. Like a blanket of freshly fallen snow, a thousand white fuzzy chairs and matching rugs formed neat rows stemming out on all four sides of the square platform in the center of the room, covering the vast space. True to the theme of this year's event, "Lavish," the room permeated lavishness and beauty.

I settled into my cozy chair next to my friends, excited to glean all that the Lord had for me these next few days. Once again, I arrived at the event eager to level up in my spiritual growth, determined to gain a deeper knowledge and understanding of my power and authority in Christ. I enthusiastically set my hopes on a deeper connection with the Lord and a greater understanding of His plan and purpose for my life.

As the worship and teaching ensued and I pressed into the presence of the Lord, I felt something unsettled in my spirit. Shackles that had not yet been unlocked. Wounds that had not yet healed. I discovered a deep, hidden root of unforgiveness and bitterness.

Bitter Roots

As with my first Her Voice Movement conference two years prior, my mind was involuntarily flooded with memories of my childhood, memories I had not intended to revisit. Memories of growing up and the years following my dad's death scrolled through my thoughts as if I were watching old home movies on a tiny projector. Fiery darts penetrated my heart. I felt the sting of rejection from my brother and a sense of neglect from my mom.

Where was this coming from? Those memories were long ago, and I currently had a great relationship with both family members. Yet, I trusted the Lord and where He was leading me.

Lord, help me to understand what I'm feeling and reveal anything that needs to be healed. What do you want me to know about this?

Deep-seated anger and defenselessness burned like lava rising to the surface of a dormant volcano as I recalled years of torment at my brother's hand. The times he pinned me to the floor until I begged for mercy. The countless instances when he picked, punched, or poked until I pleaded sufficiently enough for him to stop or until someone else intervened. The hurtful, belittling, malicious words slung at me to manipulate or irritate or simply create angst. The endless tears, bouts of frustration, and surges of anger.

Darts of rejection penetrated and pricked my wounded heart as I relived the deep hurt I felt in each moment. I relived the sadness of every physical or emotional wound inflicted by him, someone for whom I cared greatly but didn't seem to care for me.

I remembered the twisted feelings of anger and sadness, as I fought the innate need for his approval mangled with a hate for his ongoing harassment. I felt all over again the dejection and disappointment of realizing that, growing up, he was not the protector and supporter I so deeply desired my big brother to be.

My thoughts shifted to my mom, and I felt tinges of woundedness and frustration as I recalled the times that she seemed absent or emotionally unavailable after my dad died. Searing feelings of lonesomeness seeped to the surface. I saw flashes of an absent mother, an empty home, numerous endeavors and incidents without supervision or discipline, and a sense of helplessness as I tried to console a fragile, heartbroken, widowed mother.

I remembered feeling the desire and duty to comfort my mom yet not feeling comforted myself. I recollected the years in my youth with seemingly no rules or oversight as I succumbed to sexual immorality and self-indulgence under her supervision, or lack thereof. I gazed upon the vivid scene in the living room of my childhood home where my mom, without protest, conceded to my decision to abort my child, her grandchild.

Unbeknownst to me, these deep-seated feelings of resentment toward my mom and brother had been entrenched and burning in my heart like a hidden, deadly poison. Disappointment and anger had been percolating in my bloodstream for years, unchecked and unresolved, allowing a spirit of bitterness to take root.[1]

Overcome and overwhelmed by the revelation of the effect these feelings had in my life and how they robbed my peace, I surrendered them to God and asked Him to set me free.

I heard one word: *Forgive.*

But, Lord, that was years ago? I protested. Surely, I don't hold anything against them... Do I?

Given the slew of memories I had just revisited and the unmistakable heartache they still invoked, it took only seconds for me to recognize the answer to that question. So, I relented.

Once again, I knew that if the Lord revealed it, He wanted to heal it—regardless of how insignificant it seemed or how long ago it occurred. I had learned that the journey to and through these hard places, despite the pain, was worth the reward of freedom.

> *Disappointment and anger had been percolating in my bloodstream for years, unchecked and unresolved, allowing a spirit of bitterness to take root.*

On the ground, my face flat on the fuzzy white rug, I began verbalizing feelings that had been deeply buried for so long. One by one, I forgave each offense that came to mind. Like a clogged pipe that could no longer withstand the built-up pressure, emotions burst from me in cries, coughs, and convulsions.

I felt comforting hands on my back and knew friends were covering me in prayer as the Lord lovingly liberated me from years of bondage. By the power of the Holy Spirit, I took authority over my mind and my body and commanded unforgiveness and bitterness to leave me in Jesus' name.

As quickly as the gush of emotion had engulfed me, the peace of God flooded and calmed me. My entire body melted into the tear-drenched rug beneath me as I felt the angst release, the shackles

---

1   Hebrews 12:15b

unlock, the wounds heal. I felt the Lord console me as I lay drained and depleted, yet peaceful and content.

Then I saw an image of a beautiful fruit tree on a large hill. I could see many roots shooting down into the hill, some seemed strong and purposeful while others were rotted or tangled. I asked the Lord what He wanted me to know about what I was seeing, and I wrote in my journal the words I heard in my spirit:

> *My entire body melted into the tear-drenched rug beneath me as I felt the angst release, the shackles unlock, the wounds heal.*

"Those deep roots of bitterness were choking your destiny. They were inhibiting the good roots of this tree of life—this tree that represents your life with Me. I am protecting it, watering, pruning, and caring for it, caring for you. I will continue to help you dig up the roots that are evil and destructive, and help you grow and prosper and create good fruit."

I felt the lavishing love of the Father as He confirmed that He was watching over me, that He would guide me, and that I had nothing to fear. I felt lighter, emotionally untangled, free. I saw the beautiful fruit that He was bringing out of me, for His glory, and all I could do was cry tears of joy as I praised His Holy Name.

Releasing Myself

The day continued with powerful teachings and heartfelt worship. My heart felt lighter and open to more of what God had for me. While one of the speakers shared her story of the loss of her child, I suddenly collapsed onto the floor and began crying uncontrollably. Unsure of what was happening or why I was impacted so significantly by this story, I waited and prayed. *God, what is this all about? What do you want me to know?*

One after another, a slew of distinct scenes from my teenage years appeared in my mind—vivid visuals of various instances surrounding my abortion and my poor choices that resulted in hurting myself or others.

As I recalled each instance, I felt a bristly judgment, anger, and resentment toward my younger self. I heard the all-too-familiar condemning thoughts: *How could you be so stupid? Why did you make those choices or do those things? You should have known better, done better.*

Then I sensed a quick rebuke in my spirit and felt the Lord prompting me, once again, to forgive. This time, to forgive myself.

God showed me His compassion and love for that teenager who was lost, sad, deceived, and confused. He told me to forgive her, to release her, to tell her it would all be okay.

The Lord walked me through memory after memory, and as I paused on the individual moments, I released myself from the bondage that had shackled me for so many years.

With each memory I saw what looked like a dusting of golden light that seemed to wash clean the stains from my past. In the very last visual, as if reaching the climax of a dramatic movie, the Lord took me to my childhood living room where one of my darkest stained memories resided—where I professed my plan to abort my baby.

In my mind's eye, I stood facing my 16-year-old self and, with a compassion that could only have come from the Lord, forgave her for the first time for my abortion.

I looked in her scared and lost eyes and told her that I loved her. I reached through her numb exterior into her distraught and confused soul and cut the contorted cords that tied us together in trauma. I released her of whatever I thought she owed me. Once and for all, I let go of my anger and unforgiveness for myself and severed the ties to that trauma.

Chains binding me to my past sin broke, and my soul lightened. As I praised the Lord for this unexpected healing moment, I suddenly saw an image of a little girl—a sweet child with the cutest round, chubby cheeks and golden-brown curls. She giggled joyfully with a smile that lit up

Once and for all, I let go of my anger and unforgiveness for myself and severed the ties to that trauma.

her whole face as she was lifted playfully into the air with strong, yet gentle hands. My heart flooded with gratitude as I watched this beautiful little girl, my sweet daughter Audrey Marie, thriving in the grasp of her Heavenly Father.

The grim tragedy of my loss, the devastating decision I made to end the life of my first child, and the dark cloud of unforgiveness for myself vanished in an instant as the Lord allowed me to see His goodness, His mercy, and His unconditional love through the heartwarming image of my precious daughter held safely in His arms.

FINDING PURPOSE

*For we are God's handiwork, created in Christ Jesus to do good
works, which God prepared in advance for us to do.
(Ephesians 2:10 NIV)*

19
APPREHENSIVE AMBER

After receiving God's healing and forgiveness from my abortion, I knew that the Lord wanted to use me to help others who had been through a similar experience.

I was consumed with a passion for not only sharing the truth about abortion but also helping men and women who were still living in bondage and shackled by shame and trauma—as I had been.

I continued volunteering at the pregnancy resource center, seeing clients who needed free supplies for their children like clothes, formula, and diapers and providing counseling to men and women who were facing an unexpected pregnancy.

What a joy it was to be in a role actively helping families and serving others in a way that I so wished I would have chosen for myself all those years ago.

I had my first son a little less than a year after I began volunteering at the pregnancy center, promptly leading to a change in my availability to serve. With an infant at home and still working my full-time job at that time, I decided to step away from my weekly evening volunteer shift.

Still devoted to the mission, I pursued other avenues to help at the pregnancy center without taking away from my evenings with my family, such as helping plan the annual fundraising gala, supporting the Walk for Life events, and other initiatives.

Around that time, I was also invited to be a member of the Speaker's Bureau. This group of representatives from the ministry traveled to churches every January, Sanctity of Human Life Month, to share about the offerings of the pregnancy center and touch on the latest abortion statistics and ways to help support families in our communities. These speaking engagements also typically included an abortion testimony, and they asked if I would be willing to share mine.

> *I had found personal healing and forgiveness for my abortion, yes, but did I really want to share my baggage with other people?*

Speaking in public terrified me. I know it's a common fear, but it was a crippling fear of mine. When I was set free from the shame of my abortion and accepted the calling on my life in this area of ministry, I distinctly remember pleading with the Lord, "I will do whatever you want me to do. Just please don't ask me to speak in public!"

Years later and dozens of times sharing my testimony in front of an audience, we can see how well that request worked out. I should have known better than to tell God what I would or would not do for Him!

While merely the thought of sharing my testimony publicly caused twinges of panic to twist my insides into a pretzel, I wanted to follow God, and I truly did want to help others. Still, I had obstacles to overcome.

I had found personal healing and forgiveness for my abortion, yes, but did I really want to share my baggage with other people? A voice in the back of my mind taunted me. *Don't you dare say any of this out loud. You'll be judged. You'll be rejected.*

Fear of man began to rear its ugly head.

But I had faced this fear before, and I wasn't about to let it dictate my decisions anymore. Worrying about what other people thought of me had been one of the driving forces for getting my abortion.

I refused to let that same fear hold me back from doing what God was asking me to do. He *was* asking me to do this. As much as I dreaded it, I trusted and believed that the Lord would use my story for His good. I began to accept this new assignment and resigned to walk it out scared and insecure. After all, His power is made perfect in my weakness, right?[1]

With a resolve in my spirit to step out of my comfort zone and follow God's lead, I joined the Speaker's Bureau and agreed to share my story publicly. I set up a time to accompany a staff member and friend, Julie, to a church to shadow her and see how the process worked. When the day arrived, I eagerly sat in a pew toward the front of the church and observed as my friend and fellow Speaker's Bureau member eloquently shared her abortion testimony and the benefits and offerings of the pregnancy resource center.

My determined demeanor quickly dissolved into apprehension and insecurity as I watched Julie effortlessly stand in front of the crowd and share with passion and articulateness. Berating thoughts bombarded my mind. *I can't do this! I could never do what she's doing as well as she's doing it.* As soon as the church service ended, I escaped to my car and sobbed tears of fear, anxiety, and inadequacy the entire 40-minute drive home.

The moment I arrived at my house, I composed an email to Julie kindly explaining that there was no way I could do what she did, and I was sorry, but I would have to decline being a member of the Speaker's Bureau. Phew! Relief washed over me. Disaster, humiliation, and overwhelming anxiety averted.

Then I received her response. "You'll do great! See you next week!"

What? Did she even read what I wrote?! As much as I wanted to send a response back in protest, I felt a check in my spirit and prayed for God to tell me what He wanted me to know about this, about what I was feeling, and what I should do.

After some contemplation and self-examination, I realized that being on the Speaker's Bureau wasn't about me. God was asking me to do something that made me super uncomfortable, yes. But I had to remember *why* I had agreed to put myself out there in such a public and vulnerable way. I believed with all my heart that the

---

1   2 Corinthians 12:9

Lord wanted to use my story to help others. He couldn't do that if I allowed fear to intimidate me.

I believed with all my heart that the Lord wanted to use my story to help others. He couldn't do that if I allowed fear to intimidate me.

I decided that I would not shrink back. I would move forward with my commitment to speak in churches, even if that meant doing it scared. And that's exactly what I did.

Overcoming Fear

The date arrived. My very first time set to speak at a church for Sanctity of Human Life Sunday. I was as close to being a literal ball of nerves as a human being could possibly be. But I had prepared, I had practiced, and most importantly, I had prayed.

I had completely surrendered everything about this day and my part in it to the Holy Spirit and knew that the only way this could possibly go well was for Him to take over. I released my anxiety, my worry, and my insecurity and laid it all at the feet of Jesus.

In the past, when I had spoken in front of groups for other occasions, my mind had the tendency to go blank. In some instances, I had very little recollection of what I said and had even less control over my shaky voice, hands, and legs.

My nervous reaction to public speaking was interestingly similar to the involuntary tears and shaking I had experienced during my abortion. Had it really been the medication that caused those reactions, or was it my body's natural response to emotional distress and nervousness?

I specifically prayed for God to help me have a clear mind and calm body as I spoke.

Upon arriving at the quaint church, staff members greeted me and directed me to the area where I could set up my ministry table. I methodically organized the display table with brochures and other information about the PRC, thankful for the distraction to keep me occupied, and all the while silently praying for courage.

The time for the service to start neared, and I nestled into a front row seat, full attention and focus forward. As worship began,

I praised God for His goodness outwardly while inwardly praying for peace as I counted down the minutes until I would step up to the podium.

Worship came to an end and the pastor began my introduction. As I accepted his invitation to take my place on the stage and began an ascent up the steps to take my position, I was flooded with an indescribable peace that passed all understanding.[2]

I carefully placed my script on the translucent podium, refusing to be intimidated by this see-through structure that would not hide my shaking body if it happened to betray me. *Thank you, Lord, that you are my strength*, I prayed silently. *I can do all things through Christ who strengthens me.*[3]

I greeted the congregation and confidently began sharing my well-crafted speaking points. Shockingly, the entire time I spoke, my mind was perfectly clear, and I sensed only the tiniest of trembles in my legs, not nearly enough to cause distraction. I made eye contact with the audience and did not lose my place in my script. Even more surprisingly, I felt at ease.

Within fewer than fifteen minutes, my speech concluded, and I made my way down to my seat and sunk into a whirlpool of relief that soothed my tense body. I had done it! Not only did I do it, but I did it well! By God's grace, I made it through my entire fifteen minutes without fumbling over my words, losing track of my thoughts, or shaking uncontrollably!

After the service, I greeted several congregation members who asked questions and thanked me for sharing my story. A couple people even asked how long I had been speaking and remarked how impressed they were with how well I did. *What?!*

I was blown away and completely overwhelmed by God's grace. Not because people thought I was a good speaker but because I was well aware that I wasn't! Only *He* could use a terrified, trembling, blackout-prone ball of insecurity to relay a message for His good *and* allow it to go well.

I felt so loved by God. He was showing me that *He* would do it. That *He* could be trusted, and *He* was bigger than all my fears!

---

2   Philippians 4:7
3   Philippians 4:13

I only had to lean on the Holy Spirit and trust that He was with me, and He would take care of the rest.

I bawled my eyes out the entire drive home—but this time with tears of joy and gratitude. I sang and praised God at the top of my lungs, overwhelmed by what a wonderful Father He is.

20
JADED AMBER

After my first Speaker's Bureau engagement, God continued to bring opportunities for me to run with this mission—to share my story and to work with local pregnancy resource centers. During that time, I also launched a small group called Warriors for Life (the one my pastor Charlie had originally prompted me to start) that gathered locally to pray, serve, and walk out our mission to help families facing unexpected pregnancies and protect the unborn together. God continued to make it clear that He was directing me to the pro-life and abortion recovery realm.

However, similar to my journey of coming back to Christ, my path was not always straight and simple. I often felt hesitant, even resentful at times. I found myself repeatedly resisting this highlighted path[1] in one way or another.

Whether that looked like putting my ministry work on the back burner (there always seemed to be something more pressing to attend to) or avoiding news updates about the topic of abortion (it was just too discouraging to hear about what felt like a losing battle against the propaganda of the abortion industry giant) or disqualifying myself due to lack of experience or skill or influence (surely there was someone more qualified God could use).

---

1 Psalm 119:105

I made plenty of excuses to delay or avoid fully stepping into what the Lord had been prompting me to do.

Unfortunately, I was discovering how immensely unpopular it was to be passionate about protecting the unborn and standing against abortion. Sharing my story in churches full of (presumably) pro-life supporters was one thing, but once I started voicing my pro-life stance in a more diverse setting, like on social media or in conversations with friends and family, I was quickly met with unexpected hostility.

> *I made plenty of excuses to delay or avoid fully stepping into what the Lord had been prompting me to do.*

Unanticipated Opposition

My friends and I cheerfully gathered around a banner and posed for a photo as we rounded the corner for our last lap of the Walk for Life. I dutifully posted the picture on my social media account, hoping to bring some awareness to the important issue of protecting all human lives, especially the most vulnerable (the unborn), as well as to promote the pregnancy resource center.

Within minutes of posting, I received a ridiculing comment from a high school friend claiming that people like me (pro-life advocates, I presume) only care about fetuses and care nothing about children once they are born.

Stunned, I stared at the comment on my phone in disbelief as knots formed in my stomach. Her accusation felt like a slap on the face. How could she think that about me? Let alone about these advocates and organizations that go above and beyond to care for the exact little ones she was claiming they don't care about?

My mind reeled with rebuttals. My first inclination was to defend myself, to protect my image, to make her see she was wrong about me, and everyone like me.

But I had learned the valuable lesson long ago that it was not my job to control what others thought about me.

So, I kept my response short and unemotional. I shared the simple truth that one of the primary goals of pro-life advocates and pregnancy resource centers, like the one I was representing at the Walk for Life, is to care for moms, dads, *and* babies—both before and after a child is born.

I didn't get a response, and that was the last of our interactions on the topic.

That exchange left me baffled. Wasn't the stance of pregnancy resource centers evident in the plethora of free resources, classes, and support they provide?

Do people also not know that Christians and pro-life advocates are responsible for the majority of adoptions and foster care homes and ministries that care for mothers and babies in need?

I felt shocked and disheartened knowing this baseless accusation arises in many pro-choice arguments.

That online run-in was just the beginning of the emotion-inducing incidents that I would face with family, friends, and even strangers as I began to be more open and intentional about my pro-life position.

A Heart Issue

My friend Mary and I filed into the city council building to settle in before the start of the meeting, eager to support our neighboring city. After hearing testimonies from the citizens and council members, the city council would vote on an ordinance to make this a Sanctuary City for the unborn. The ordinance would not only criminalize abortion in the city limits but also publicly profess the city's stance of supporting life and protecting babies in the womb.

The city council meeting room filled up quickly with residents as those of us from surrounding cities took our seats in the overflow room where we could watch the meeting live on a large projection screen.

While we watched the meeting and listened intently to the arguments from both sides, the dissonance and anger in the audience simmered like a pot of water on a hot stove. With each testimony shared, every comment from a city council member, the animosity from the spectators bubbled over and splattered scalding dissention.

Just as I had observed outside the building within mere minutes of arriving, a vast distinction was painstakingly noticeable between the two sides and their respective attitudes, actions, and approaches to defending their cause. I watched as the majority of the pro-life attendees, my friend and me included, remained quiet and dignified. Granted, a couple pro-lifers were baited into a heated argument or two, but for the most part, our side's interactions were peaceful, reserved, and respectful.

On the other hand, the pro-choice campaigners constantly stirred the simmering pot with crude comments and personal attacks targeting the city council members and citizens who testified during the meeting as well as those of us in the audience—like the woman who had barked belligerent remarks inches from my face as I stood silently with my pro-life cohorts outside the building.

I shuddered, recalling the uncomfortable encounter and refocused my attention on the meeting in progress.

Women in the front row turned around frequently to face the crowd and belittle us or spitefully reprimand us for wanting to "take away women's rights" and for "caring more about fetuses than women."

I couldn't believe what I was witnessing. It felt like I had been plopped into a dramatic scene from a movie rather than sitting in an official city council meeting only miles from my hometown.

My thoughts drifted to my many encounters with families seeking help at the pregnancy center—their initial fear and uncertainty about how to handle an unexpected pregnancy and then the relief and deep gratitude expressed once they realized the extent of the resources, care, love, and prayer offered them. The moms and dads who initially faced a flurry of fear about their circumstances, later feeling empowered to raise their children and love them well after receiving counseling and classes that equipped and encouraged them.

I recalled numerous events where passionate pro-lifers gathered to walk, to pray, or to serve others. Each environment, each encounter, each experience full of joy, love, and peace.

I marveled at the stark contrast to what was now portrayed about the nature of the pro-life movement at the city council meeting.

I had heard about these kinds of interactions with pro-abortion crowds but had never experienced it for myself. I realized I didn't want to be there. I wanted to shrink and disappear. I battled tinges of fear of what someone might say or do to me—recalling recent reports of vandalism and threats against pregnancy resource centers and their employees and remembering the pro-life advocates who had been arrested for simply praying outside an abortion facility. I wanted nothing to do with such hostility and hatred and wished for the night to end so I could retreat to the safety and seclusion of my home.

I felt a surge of frustration and defeat swelling up in me. I asked myself, and God, for the thousandth time, *Why this? Why do I have to be called to such a controversial and polarizing issue? How can my voice possibly make a difference?*

While I held back tears of frustration and anger, I sensed in my spirit that I was where I was supposed to be. I recalled the times I had boldly shared my testimony and how every time, without fail, someone followed up to thank me or tell me how much it meant to know they weren't alone.

My mind flooded with the countless conversations, Bible study sessions, and healing prayers where other women, just like me, were set free from the shame and trauma of their abortion.

I glanced at Mary, sitting to my left, to gauge her feelings about all that was happening. I instantly envied her cool, calm, and collected demeanor. She seemed truly unfazed. I reasoned that her decades of exposure to these types of gatherings and her in-depth involvement in pro-life ministry—and legislation in particular—had no doubt prepared her for this night.

I contemplated mentioning to her how I was feeling but worried I would begin crying uncontrollably and draw attention to myself. Instead, I began praying silently.

Lord, this is awful! Please help me through this night. Give me peace that passes all understanding. Help settle my anxious thoughts. Lord, what do You want me to know about what I'm thinking, feeling, and experiencing right now?

After I prayed, I felt a sudden shift in my spirit. Everything in the room seemed to slow down, and the chatter muffled as if I were now watching everything unfold through the narrator's perspective of a paused dramatic scene of a play.

I could see the women in the front row frozen in their furious stances, faces distorted with rage as they shrieked their familiar grievances and fired curses at any adversary within range.

Gradually, as if a curtain lifted and the scene had changed, I began to see these women differently. I saw through their costumes of abrasiveness and spiteful words to their fear and insecurity underneath. I saw women who were misled and lost and who were angry about things that had nothing to do with the current situation.

I was reminded of my 20-something-year-old self who hid behind women's rights and bodily autonomy to make myself feel better about and justify my own choice.

The Lord reminded me that we don't know what we don't know, and that hurt people hurt people.

I had no idea back then how much I was hurting, how wounded I was, or how my selfish actions impacted not only myself but others. I had no idea what I was missing. And neither did these women.

I heard the Lord say in my spirit, "Forgive them for they know not what they do."[2]

I suddenly understood that they *actually believed* what they were saying was true. They genuinely felt threatened. They believed that banning abortion would harm women rather than help them. They bought the lies sold to them about pro-life supporters and Christians caring only about fetuses while disregarding women.

The Lord flooded me with His love for them. I began to see each of these women through His eyes and felt a compassion for them that I didn't know I was capable of feeling. Rather than cringing at the abrasiveness of their comments and insults,

> *The Lord reminded me that we don't know what we don't know, and that hurt people hurt people.*

---

2   Luke 23:34

instead of allowing frustration to pit me against them, I began praying for them.

Lord, please meet each of these women in their woundedness and fear. I pray for the torment and the rage inside of them to subside as they experience Your unconditional love and complete acceptance.

I pray that each of these women, and all the women like them, would have an undeniable encounter with the One True King, and that their hearts and minds would be transformed and healed by Your truth and love. Lord, help me to see my adversaries the way You see them and love them as You would love them. Amen.

I was reminded in that moment that much of what we deal with in this mission for protecting babies in the womb and protecting women from the trauma of abortion is not about making the best argument or proving a point or even passing an ordinance. Abortion is not a religious issue. It's not a reproductive rights or privacy issue. It's not even a women's rights issue.

> *Ultimately, the only way to change minds about abortion is to change hearts.*

At the end of the day, it is a heart issue. Ultimately, the only way to change minds about abortion is to change hearts.

I left that night feeling an unexpected joy and peace. Even though the ordinance ultimately did not pass, I felt hopeful and lighter with a fresh perspective and newfound love for my adversaries.

Learning to Stand

"Amber, you aren't still messaging about that, are you?" Rob asked with concern in his voice. "You have been at this for a long time, and all it's doing is upsetting you."

"I know, but if I can just make this last point, I think I can help her see that we aren't just fighting for the babies' lives, we are fighting to protect women too!" I said in desperation, eyes intently focused on my phone and the response I was carefully crafting to a friend who had challenged my pro-life stance on one of my recent social media posts.

My heart for helping women burned as I battled the propaganda about "my body, my choice" and "reproductive rights." I've watched in dismay for far too long as misled women, like me, make decisions that traumatize their bodies, their minds, and their souls.

Nonetheless, after relentless back-and-forth banter, hours of meticulously responding to messages, enduring hateful and untrue comments spewed at me and at others defending the issue, as well as several restless nights, I fell flat.

Not only were my efforts to defend and explain my position seemingly in vain and my well-thought-out arguments not received, but the comments directed at me and my counterparts had become mean and spiteful. Worst of all, when the discussion finally ended, it left a long-standing friendship feeling wounded and strained. My heart hurt.

All I knew to do was pray and ask God for help.

Lord, search my heart. Show me any way in me that is not in alignment with You. God, reveal my motives and make them pure. Help me to know when to speak and when to listen. I confess feelings of bitterness and resentment toward those who oppose me and release any frustration about not being heard or being misjudged and misunderstood.

I reached out to my friend, Lauren, to confide in her about what I had experienced. I shared openly about my frustrations, my insecurities, and even confessed the discouragement about God asking me to be a part of something so harsh, so difficult.

I pointed out that as my resolve to walk out my mission of speaking truth about abortion and of helping others find healing strengthened, the more drastic and daunting the opposition seemed to become. "When will this internal struggle and this external battle get easier?" I wondered aloud, exasperated.

Lauren lovingly and patiently listened. As our conversation concluded, she prayed for me and shared a scripture that resonated so deeply with my spirit.

> *"You're blessed when your commitment to God provokes persecution. The persecution drives you even deeper into God's kingdom. Not only that—count yourselves blessed every time people put you down or throw you out or speak lies about you to discredit Me. What it means is that the truth is too close for comfort and they are uncomfortable. You can be glad when that happens—give a cheer, even!—for though they don't like it, I do! And all heaven applauds. And know that you are in good company. My prophets and witnesses have always gotten into this kind of trouble."* (Matthew 5:10-12, MSG)

God's word spoke directly to my heart, and I was reminded what it meant to lay down my life, my personal comforts and feelings, to follow Him. To die to my own selfish desires and tendency to self-protect. He reminded me that what I'm doing is not about me and lovingly rebuked me for caring what other people think of me.

I needed that reminder.

I needed to let go of my image management.

I needed to let go of people pleasing.

I needed to hear that what I was doing would not always be easy, but it would most definitely be worth it.

I needed to know that I didn't have to allow the controversy to affect me—that I could choose to be offended, hurt, or frustrated, or I could learn to fully embrace my calling, to stand up for God's truth in love,[3] and rise above the controversy.

> *I could choose to be offended, hurt, or frustrated, or I could learn to fully embrace my calling, to stand up for God's truth in love, and rise above the controversy.*

I resolved to trust the Lord, to lean on Him and not on my own understanding[4] and to

---

3   Ephesians 4:15
4.   Proverbs 3:5-6

charge ahead on this mission in confidence, undaunted and unoffendable, and led by love.

21

ABORTION-GIRL AMBER

I distinctly remember a moment when God made it clear, for about the ten-thousandth time, that I was called to pro-life ministry—more specifically, abortion recovery. I often wonder, *do other people need countless reminders to stay on track or is it just me?*

After a morning of prayer and journaling, I felt the Lord's loving reminder that this is where He was directing me and that my story would help others.

Begrudgingly accepting this truth and simultaneously having a little bit of a pity party for myself for having such a messy ministry calling, I stared at my reflection in my bathroom mirror and said out loud, "Fine. I guess I'm the abortion girl."

The words jolted me, and I felt a swift correction from the Lord in my spirit.

It dawned on me that I had been believing the lie that by agreeing to fully embrace this ministry assignment—to share my story, to stand up for unborn babies, and to help men and women who are wounded from abortion—I was reduced to that one label: Girl who had an abortion.

This was the game the devil was still winning in my mind: that this one part of my life was all I would ever be and now all I had to offer. That was a lie from the pit of hell!

No wonder I was so quick to resist. No wonder I felt a reluctance in my spirit to fully say yes. I was believing a lie about my identity and my worth. Somehow, even after all the progress and healing, my identity was still wrapped up in my previous sin.

> *That is what I did. That is not who I am.*

I went back to prayer and journaling and spending time in God's word, and He reminded me of my value. I had ministered to others in this area and had been teaching this concept for years, but the Lord flipped it back to remind me:

That is what I did. That is not who I am.

Even on the other side—set free and healed—my past does not define me. I am not reduced to this one act, this one sin, or even this one area of redemption. This part of my story is not all I have to offer. The Lord has done so much in my life! My testimony is deep and wide and full of God's redemptive love in so many areas.

I came to that same revelation as I wrote this book. I started off thinking my memoir would be a story all about overcoming the shame and trauma of abortion. Abortion is a part of my story, yes. I am called and equipped to help people heal from past abortion experiences, yes. The Lord has given me a ministry in that specific area, yes.

Yet, while writing this book, with every recounted incident, with every memory I recalled and every breakthrough I shared, it became unmistakably obvious how much the Lord has done in my life beyond healing me from that one trauma.

He has transformed every area of my life and set me free from bondage in a multitude of ways. My story is so much more than overcoming abortion!

God started showing me all the ways I add value and how I can minister to people who have experienced any kind of shame or trauma or loss or brokenness. Through my healing, I can now help others heal.[1]

It just so happens that God has given me the grace, through my experience, to help those who have faced a similar situation. Furthermore, having an area of expertise, something I can speak boldly and confidently about due to my own experience, is a gift, not a burden!

As I pressed in, the Lord began to give me the desires of my heart, and I started to find so much joy and fulfillment in serving women and their families in this way.

Delight yourself in the Lord, and he will give you the desires of your heart. (Psalm 37:4 ESV)

Do You Trust Me?

In 2022, I felt the Lord leading me to make a drastic change. Much to my dismay, God asked me to leave my leadership role at the ministry that Kelly and her husband launched in 2020—one that evolved from the mentorship program she started several years prior. For months, I prayed and fasted fervently. I asked repeatedly for clarity and confirmation.

When I received confirmation, I sobbed—shocked and saddened by the directive that I didn't expect or fully understand. Sure, I had started to become a bit restless in my role in the ministry, but I was convinced those were my own personal issues to overcome.

Surely, God wouldn't want me to leave a group of people who were like family, an environment that flowed with the Holy Spirit's presence and power, and a ministry that was helping individuals find freedom and walk in their authority in Christ. I pleaded with God for compromise. Yet, His instruction remained firm.

Without any real direction for what I would do next, that September I made one of the hardest decisions I have ever made and stepped out of my ministry role and into the unknown. My

---

1   1 Corinthians 1:3-4

friends and co-leaders, while surprised and disappointed by the news, were gracious and sent me off with love and blessings.

But my heart was heavy. While I believed we would still be friends, I instinctively knew it would not be the same. I wondered where I would ever find people so in love with Jesus, people who pushed me to higher levels of knowing Him and following Him. I felt silly for making such a drastic change without any real direction or plan. Most of all, I felt alone.

At the same time that I transitioned out of that ministry, the Lord also prompted our family to change churches. I mourned what felt like a loss of loved ones—leaving connections to ministry leaders and friends, stepping away from a comfortable, familiar place that we had called our church home for sixteen years. While I knew that God was leading us, I wrestled with my emotions. Starting over felt daunting.

For months, I sat with the Lord in solitude, desperate for His presence, His comfort, His direction. I fasted. I prayed. I journaled. I cried. I squirmed in the uneasiness of the unknowns. I doubted my ability to do whatever it was that God would ask me to do. Over and over, I sensed the Lord asking me a simple question: "Do you trust Me?"

God met me in those months of being stripped of my norms, of missing my friends, of feeling aimless and unsure of the future.

He uncovered lies I was believing about myself. He lovingly showed me how to let go of my reliance on other people or circumstances to see and hear from Him. He strengthened my confidence in my connection to Him.

The Lord revealed hidden truths, helped make sense of previously muddled thoughts and emotions, and confirmed this new course. And He helped me release the mindset that the deeds I was doing for Him defined me.

In the searching, in the silence, in the solitude, I gained an intimacy with the Lord that was deeper and more precious than I had ever experienced.

God showed me that, yes, I *could* trust Him. He reminded me that He was my Provider,[2] my Strong Tower,[3] my Refuge,[4] my Comfort,[5] that everything I needed or would ever need was already in me, through His Spirit.

As I grew closer to the Lord, my confidence grew. I knew that I heard His voice clearly and trusted that He would lead the way, even if I didn't know where I was going.

During that season, I continually clung to His word in Hebrews 11:

> *By faith Abraham obeyed when he was called to go out to a place that he was to receive as an inheritance. And he went out, not knowing where he was going.*[6]

An Open Door

I sat across from my dear friend and mentor, Sarah, on her back porch as she shared that she was asked to start an abortion recovery program at a local pregnancy resource center—using the same eleven-week Bible study that I went through years prior. She explained how this opportunity unexpectedly landed in her lap and that she felt a prompting from the Lord to see it through. We chatted excitedly about what God wanted to do through this program, how it would be a blessing to the women in the community, and talked through her next steps.

My heart stirred when she mentioned needing to find a co-facilitator to help lead the Bible study. Carefully tucking the tiny whisper—*What if that's me?*—to the side, we wrapped up our conversation, hugged, and said our goodbyes.

For weeks, I couldn't ignore the sense that I was supposed to help Sarah with this new program. I prayed and God confirmed. Yet, she didn't ask me to help her, so I did not want to impose.

---

2   Genesis 22:14
3   Proverbs 18:10
4   Psalm 9:9
5   2 Corinthians 1:3-4
6   Hebrews 11:8 ESV

I prayed for the Lord to make it clear for both of us and for His timing and for His plan to unfold.

Several weeks after our initial discussion, Sarah and I attended a worship event together. During the lunch break, our conversation casually landed on Sarah's progress with the abortion recovery program. When she mentioned she still needed a co-facilitator, I felt a nudge from the Holy Spirit to speak up. Reluctant, yet hopeful, I blurted out what was on my mind.

"I think the Lord is nudging me to be a part of what you're doing. I don't know what that looks like, but what do you think?"

Sarah's face lit up with a knowing smile, "I have believed all along that you are meant to be the co-facilitator. I was just waiting and praying for God to reveal that to you rather than you hearing it from me."

I felt a flurry of excitement swirling in my spirit. I sensed that God was opening doors and guiding my steps. A surge of encouragement swept over me as I began to see more clearly where God was taking me and what I was meant to do. And I was ready to do it with a joyful, expectant heart.

Where I'm Meant to Be

Within months of that pivotal conversation with Sarah and faithfully stepping into a new role in abortion recovery ministry, I began to see God's hand on my *yes* to His plan.

On my way home from one evening's abortion recovery Bible study, my heart soared, filled with awe and joy. God had shown up, once again, in an incredibly powerful way. I wasn't surprised, but I also didn't take for granted the miracle of how He moved in the hearts and minds of our clients who were seeking Him. The way He brought things only He could know to the surface or how He prompted us to read the perfect Bible verse at just the right time for just the right person.

Over the past year of leading women wounded by abortion through this healing process, we had seen God's undeniable presence penetrate hearts. We witnessed women finding the answers they needed and the healing they had been searching for, breaking through strongholds of anger, resentment, unforgiveness, and shame, and finding a peace that passed all understanding[7] even in the midst of difficult situations.

Tears of joy and gratitude streamed down my face as I felt the Lord confirming that I was exactly where I was supposed to be. After years of grumbling and complaining, after enduring ridicule, heartache, and frustration, after countless times asking "Why me? Why this?" He was revealing the beauty and the impact on the other side.

An image of a pebble thrown into a pond dropped in my spirit. I sensed God revealing that my story is just the beginning of a ripple effect. My healing will lead to another's healing. My sharing will prompt others to share. My yes will lead to others saying yes— yes to faith over fear, yes to letting God heal the shattered places of their hearts, yes to shackles being broken and shame released, yes to forgiveness and redemption for women and their families, yes to freedom and an abundant life in Christ.

My healing will lead to another's healing. My sharing will prompt others to share. My yes will lead to others saying yes.

I became aware, more than ever, that I was chosen for such a time as this[8] and that God wanted to use my trauma and ultimately my healing and transformation for His glory.

The devil intended to harm me, to use my past mistakes, my intentional rebellion, and my trauma to destroy me, but God showed me that He would turn it all around and use it for *His* good.[9] And He will continue to bring healing, transformation, and redemption to one after another, after another.

A word from the Lord resounded and replayed in my spirit as I committed to saying yes to Him and walking boldly wherever He would have me go:

I have called you and equipped you for such a time as this. Set the captives free and glorify My Name!

---

7 Philippians 4:7
8 Esther 4:14
9 Genesis 50:20

REDEEMED

But forget all that—
It is nothing compared to what I am going to do.
For I am about to do something new. See, I have already
begun! Do you not see it?
I will make a pathway through the wilderness. I will create
rivers in the dry wasteland.
(Isaiah 43:18-19 NLT)

22
RESTORED AMBER

When my dad died unexpectedly, it was as if the windshield of my car cracked in an accident. I could still see through it, but not clearly.

I drove on, convinced I could still manage despite my gaping wound and the missing presence of my earthly father. I made many wrong turns as I searched for love, affirmation, and self-worth resulting in more accidents— excessive drinking, sexual immorality, abortion—that ultimately shattered my windshield.

I could not see clearly. I could not drive safely. Yet, I still reasoned that the damage was not extensive enough to stop me from carrying on with my life.

What I failed to recognize in the trenches of my trauma, trauma that left me shattered on the inside, is that my perspective was now skewed. My vision impaired. The way I viewed myself, the world, and others had changed.

God wants us to see clearly. He wants to repair the broken and shattered places in our hearts.[1]

Jesus was crucified so that we could be healed and whole:

---

1   This metaphor is from *Forgiven and Set Free Facilitator's Guide* (Lansdowne, VA: Care Net, 2022).

But he was pierced for our transgressions; he was crushed for our iniquities; upon him was the chastisement that brought us peace, and with his wounds we are healed. (Isaiah 53:5 ESV)

Facing Strongholds

I had to recognize the hard places and go to those hard places to be healed and set free.

Once I began my journey of accepting Jesus Christ as the Lord of my life and seeking His truth, I realized that hastily painting over the dents and scratches of my past and ignoring my injuries was how I coped with the damage.

A flaky, feeble veneer of "everything is fine" no longer sufficed once I desired a beautiful car, an authentic life of fulfillment, joy, and peace.

As I pursued a relationship with Jesus, the fog lifted, enabling me to see clearly that He wanted to heal the broken and shattered pieces of my heart. I would have to face my strongholds and fix what was shattered in order to live the abundant life He had for me.

The thief comes only to steal and kill and destroy. I came that they may have life and have it abundantly. (John 10:10 ESV)

After fifteen years of running from and ignoring my abortion, I collided with the truth of how my choice shattered my life.

I made choices with impaired vision through my shattered heart.

I could no longer discount the pain and grief, deny the shame and regret, or disavow my choice and my sin. Going back to that hard place, the scene of the accident, to face what I had never faced before, was necessary to find healing and move forward.

Nearly thirty years after my dad's death, I had to recognize the dispersed debris of heartache from that tragedy. Not only did I have to acknowledge the father-shaped hole my dad's death had left in my heart, but I also had to see my skewed self-worth, my broken view of myself and others, and realize that I made choices with impaired vision through my shattered heart.

As an adult, I had a fully developed brain that could reason better than my teenage self,[2] so I recognized the need to revisit that place of pain and grief and loss and to address my tragedy from a place of maturity and wholeness and clear vision.

Facing the hard place of my dad's death with Christ as my Counselor and Comforter allowed me to find true healing and to be set free from perpetually poaching from others what only God could provide.

Decades after the damage was done, I had to address the mangled mess that was buried deep in the wreckage of past emotional trauma. I had to sift through and extract bitter fragments and remnants of resentment toward my mom, brother, ex-boyfriends, friends, and others who I felt had hurt or betrayed me. With each prayer of forgiveness, each act of releasing what I felt people owed me, and surrendering my feelings to my Lord and Savior Jesus Christ, my load lightened, my heart restored.

As I deliberately turned off the winding way of emotional trauma and unconfessed sin and veered onto the road to redemption, the destructive patterns of sickness and calamity in my life dispersed. The shards of distress that my shattered soul had sent throughout my body for many years finally dissipated. As I embraced Jesus' invitation to be fully restored—mind, body, and spirit—my vision cleared, and my path straightened.

Along my road to restoration, I encountered potholes, roadblocks, and detours, causing me to pause and reconsider my current route—the lifestyle I was leading and the comforts I clung to. Whether it was my tendency to numb and deflect or the times I allowed sin to go unchecked or when I succumbed to distractions, diversions, insecurity or codependency, each obstruction knocked me off course or delayed my progress.

---

2   The reasoning part of our brains is not fully developed until our mid-20s. See "The Teen Brain: 7 Things to Know," National Institute of Mental Health, accessed February 20, 2025, nimh.nih.gov/health/publications/the-teen-brain-7-things-to-know.

Oftentimes, the Lord revealed repairs that were needed or redirection that was required, lovingly and patiently steering me back into His lane of liberation.

Even recently, I had to face the hard place of shame from my promiscuous past that loomed like a shadowy cloud. I had to recognize the urge to sugarcoat my behavior as I wrote this book, to make myself look better, or to avoid sharing those dark and unfavorable places for fear of what others would think of me.

Like a giant floodlight illuminating the scene of a late-night collision, the Lord exposed a place of internal turmoil and used His jaws of life to extract those residual feelings of shame, image management, and people-pleasing from the wreckage deep within me.

I am willing to face the hard places because I know that a life of freedom filled with peace, power, and purpose is the most enjoyable road trip!

In all my years of grasping for attention, all my desperation for affection, I didn't realize that the only way to fill the emptiness, the only true and healthy way to gain the affirmation I so deeply desired was to open my heart to the love of my Heavenly Father. His love was and still is, the only way for me to find wholeness. His love is pure and unconditional and is everything my wounded soul and shattered heart needed to be restored and to obtain acceptance, peace, and contentedness.

The LORD appeared to us in the past, saying: "I have loved you with an everlasting love; I have drawn you with unfailing kindness." (Jeremiah 31:3 NIV)

I found healing and freedom because I was willing to recognize the hard places and allow my loving Heavenly Father to guide me through each injurious incident. These are a few of the impactful places He has taken me over the years, and I'll likely encounter more potholes as I continue to travel this road to restoration.

I am willing to face the hard places because I know that a life of freedom filled with peace, power, and purpose is the most enjoyable road trip!

What the Lord reveals, He will heal.

23
REDEEMED AMBER

Our pastor taught recently on the passage in John chapter 11 where Jesus raised his good friend, Lazarus, from the dead. One of the most incredible miracles in the Bible, this has always been a favorite story of mine. It's one of those stories, though, that if we're not careful, we can read the words without having a genuine revelation and awe of the Lord or even understand how this pertains to us today.

We're talking about a guy who was dead and in a tomb for *four days* when Jesus showed up and brought him back to life!

Just imagine the scene. Friends and family had been gathered for days, mourning Lazarus' death, grieving the loss of a beloved friend and brother. Then Jesus arrives, too late as far as they're all concerned, and asks them to remove the stone from the entrance of the tomb.

I love how Martha, Lazarus' sister, lovingly warns Jesus. I'm paraphrasing but it went something like, "Um, are you sure that's a good idea? It's going to stink something awful because his dead body has been in there for four days!"

Jesus responds, "Did I not tell you that if you believed, you would see the glory of God?"[1]

---

1   John 11:40 NIV

So, they do what He says and remove the stone. After praying and thanking the Father for hearing His prayers, Jesus calls for Lazarus to come out of the tomb.

Throw Off Your Graveclothes

Like a dramatic war movie where a soldier rises out of the rubble and emerges from what was assumed to be impending death, here comes Lazarus still wrapped in strips of the customary burial linens on his hands, feet, and face.

Then Jesus commands, "Take off the grave clothes and let him go."[2] Another version of the Bible says *unbind him.*[3]

Jesus is giving all of us critical instructions for how to live a new, transformed life of freedom *in Him.*

Because of Jesus, I am unburied.

Because of Jesus, I am unbound.

Because of Jesus, I am rescued, revived, renewed.

When you heard about Christ and were taught in him in accordance with the truth that is in Jesus, you were taught, with regard to your former way of life, to put off your old self, which is being corrupted by its deceitful desires; to be made new in the attitude of your minds; and to put on the new self, created to be like God in true righteousness and holiness. (Ephesians 4:21-24 NIV)

Forever Amber

When I was a young girl, my mom shared with me that she named me after a character in a book she read called *Forever Amber.*[4] It wasn't until my teenage years that I learned that character was a prostitute named Amber St. Clare. We often laughed at the inference, and I jokingly scoffed at being associated with someone with such an undignified profession and past.

---

2   John 11:44b NIV
3   ESV
4   Kathleen Winsor, *Forever Amber* (New York: Macmillan, 1944).

As I began writing my memoir, I became overwhelmingly curious about that book and any connection I might have to my namesake. In fact, the inspiration for my title came from that book but with the revelation the Lord brought to me.

While I obviously have few literal commonalities with a country maid who slept her way into a high-ranking position as a duchess and became a mistress to the king in seventeenth century England, I did discover several noteworthy similarities in our stories.

Amber St. Clare was an orphan, her father absent from birth. She got pregnant shortly after losing her virginity at 16 years of age with a man she loved and presumed she would marry. While she gave birth to her first child, she later had an abortion. She continually put her needs, desires, and goals above everyone and everything else and became an unashamed adulteress.

Amber St. Clare lived a life of selfishness, seeking attention and adoration from others to find significance. She believed her happiness could be found in all that the world deemed important—men, money, popularity, and power—yet despite her lofty achievements and assets, she continually felt empty and unfulfilled. No matter how hard she tried to cling to the one and only man she loved, he inevitably slipped through her grasp, leaving her jaded, insecure, and desperate for acceptance.

With just a little research, I quickly learned that not only was *Forever Amber* a best seller in the 1940s, but it was also highly controversial and had been banned in fourteen states as pornography! Many condemned the story for its indecency and blatant sexual references—for promoting promiscuity and glorifying adultery, illegitimate pregnancies, and abortion.

By today's standards, *Forever Amber* would be perceived as mild when compared to common romance novels. Much, much racier and explicit books and movies are on the market today, highly popular and celebrated for their progressive portrayal of priorities, relationships, sex, and family.

However, in the 1940s, the storylines highlighted and the lifestyle portrayed in *Forever Amber* were far beyond the acceptable early twentieth century moral standards where the majority respected the importance of family, virtue, sexual purity, faithfulness, and integrity.

I was fascinated to learn that the book I was named after is one that is known for normalizing sexual sin and abortion in our American culture. Some critics claim this book deeply impacted our society's view of premarital sex and abortion, leading to declining moral standards and diminishing core value.[5]

I couldn't help but make the connection between our stories and began to grasp why the Lord so clearly directed me to focus so much attention on my sexual sin. As I prayed and asked God to show me the significance of this correlation, my mind flooded with snapshots of the depravity Amber St. Clare and I both endured.

I saw the shifts in cultural norms—self glorified, morals disregarded. I not only saw myself in her character but also in the resemblance of many other women who search for meaning, significance, and acceptance in all the wrong places. The similarities—the depths of dysfunction in our stories and how they relate to our culture—are daunting.

At the end of the book (spoiler alert!) Amber St. Clare excitedly sets off on a journey to America to be reunited with her true love, unaware that he is not only happily married but also that he has always been and will always be utterly uninterested in a future with her.

Everything Amber St. Clare sought after and endured was in vain. She placed her hope in something, in someone, who never would nor could fulfill her. Before I invited Christ to become the Lord of my life, before I knew where to find true hope and fulfillment, my experience was the same.

As I prayed and pressed in, I saw a symbolic vision unfold: I saw the cords that once attached me to my namesake and her persona suddenly and permanently severed. I saw myself released from words that had been spoken over me about who I was or

---

5   Lise Jaillant, "Subversive Middlebrow: The Campaigns to Ban Kathleen Winsor's Forever Amber in the United States and in Canada," International Journal of Canadian Studies (Special issue on Print Culture and the Middlebrow, ed. Michelle Smith & Faye Hammill) 48 (2014): 33-52, November 27, 2024, academia.edu/3765643/Subversive_Middlebrow_The_Campaigns_to_Ban_Kathleen_Winsor_s_Forever_Amber_in_the_United_States_and_in_Canada.

what my life would be like. I saw generational curses broken and attachments to cyclical sin cut off. I saw what the enemy meant to use for evil flipped around for God to use for His good.

As I continued to ponder why the Lord had prompted me to dig so deeply into this connection to a novel written nearly a century ago, I began to see how my story combats all the normalized depravity in that book because, by God's grace, I overcame my past and received freedom in the healing truth of Christ.

Whereas *Forever Amber* is a story of false hope and devastation, I heard in my spirit that *Always Amber* is a story of *transformation* and *redemption*.

Redemption

Just recently, I sat in a folding chair, hunched over, head in my hands, consumed by the lull of worship music that filled the crisp fall night air. "Holy Spirit, you are welcome here. Come flood this place and fill the atmosphere."[6]

Lost in the melody and overcome with contentedness, peace flooded my body from my head to my toes as I soaked in the presence of the Lord. The sound of kids playing and laughing subtly tugged my attention to my physical environment.

I glanced around at the beautiful rustic decor of my friends' worship barn that doubles as an elegant wedding venue. Toward the front of the banquet space, worship leaders stood, strumming instruments and singing elegantly, engrossed in reverence for the Lord. Directly in front of me, Rob sat with his head down and hands open. All around me, friends were lost in worship: eyes closed, hands raised, hearts surrendered.

The revelation came upon me like a gushing wave. This scene was somehow familiar, yet so different.

Here I was late on a Friday night, hanging out with a room full of friends like my parents did with the Camp Crew. My kids were having the time of their lives (like I did with my Camp Crew siblings) wrapped up in an adventure of exploring the property,

---

6   Francesca Battistelli, "Holy Spirit," lyrics by Bryan and Katie Torwalt, produced by Ian Eskelin. *If We're Honest*, Word Entertainment and Fervent Records, 2014.

climbing trees, and playing hide-n-seek with at least a dozen other kids their age.

Tears started to roll down my cheeks as scenes flashed through my mind of all the redemptive changes that had taken place in my life, including this weekend setting—once at a bar partying, now at a barn worshiping. The Lord had transformed me, and in just one generation a routine weekend family outing had been turned for God's glory.

A night of food, fellowship, and worship with a group of laid-down lovers of our Lord Jesus. My heart swelled with gratitude, and I praised God for His faithfulness.

As I sit here now, late on a Saturday night with my family all nestled in their beds fast asleep, I can't help but play that scene over and over. I am overcome with God's goodness in my life. All that He has given me that I didn't deserve but so desperately needed.

Redemption for my childhood.

Redemption for my loss.

Redemption for my trauma.

Redemption for my rebellion.

Redemption for my abortion.

Redemption for my sins.

Redemption for my family.

Redemption for my name.

God doesn't promise us that we will have an easy life, a trouble-free life, or a life without heartache, mistakes, or regrets. He does promise, however, that we can trust Him,[7] that He will never leave us or forsake us,[8] and that He has overcome this broken world.[9]

He is our Redeemer!

But now, this is what the Lord says, He who is your Creator, Jacob, And He who formed you, Israel: "Do not fear, for I have redeemed you; I have called you by name; you are Mine!" (Isaiah 43:1 NASB)

---

7 Isaiah 41:10

8 Hebrews 13:5

9 John 16:33

Even though I ran from God, He never stopped running after me.

Even though I couldn't see the good in myself, God never stopped showing me His goodness.

Even though I didn't grasp the truth, the Truth relentlessly clung to me.

I have always been who God created me to be. I have always been His perfect design, His masterpiece.[10] I am God's beloved daughter—redeemed by Him, named by Him.

I am always His. I am always Amber.

---

10 Ephesians 2:10

THE END

I will change your name; You shall no longer be called
Wounded, outcast, lonely, or afraid.
I will change your name; Your new name shall be
Confidence, joyfulness, overcoming one;
Faithfulness, friend of God, one who seeks My face.

You have changed my name; I will no longer be called
Wounded, outcast, lonely, or afraid.
You have changed my name; My new name shall be
Confidence, joyfulness, overcoming one,
Faithfulness, friend of God, I will seek Your face.
—Mercy Publishing[1]

---

1   Andy Pratt, "I Will Change Your Name," produced by Dan Cutrona and Gerhard
    Barth, *Life,* ABAKUS Music, April 1, 2016.

GOD'S NOT FINISHED YET

At the time of writing this book, specifically writing these words, over five years have passed since my breakthrough at the Her Voice event about my bitter roots with my mom; and I am certain that the Lord prompted me to remember and record that significant memory for a reason.

Revisiting and writing about key moments in my past has stirred so many emotions in me and prompted me to look outside of my personal perspective to seek answers, to dig up things still buried, and to not only gain insight from God but also from the viewpoint of those close to me.

As I have written pages upon pages about my own experiences, feelings, emotions, and trauma, it has become glaringly obvious that my view of my life, my memories, for the most part, are one-sided.

I became increasingly aware that there were several significant conversations that had never taken place, one of which was with my mom. While our family was proficient at stuffing feelings, putting on a happy face, and pressing on with our productive lives, that left little room for dealing with and healing from the root traumas. Emotions and hurts stayed buried, hidden, unchecked.

I had never shared with my mom the feelings of resentment or sense of abandonment that surfaced in my adulthood—those feelings that the Lord so graciously and lovingly revealed and healed in me years ago on the floor of a hotel conference room in Portland, Oregon.

Nor had I ever asked my mom for her side of the story. How did she handle facing the unfathomable circumstance of losing the love of her life and simultaneously being thrust into single parenthood?

What was it like to not only take care of herself but to also care for my brother and me while she was experiencing more sorrow and stress than we could possibly comprehend?

What was going through her mind when her teenage daughter proclaimed her plans to abort her grandchild?

As the realization that my story, my feelings and experiences would eventually be published and available for anyone to read, I felt a sense of urgency about honoring my mom by preemptively clearing the air and addressing some of these much-neglected topics. I began to pray fervently for the Lord to open a door for these conversations to take place. I prayed that my mom and I would have an opportunity to revisit and reconcile the things from our past, to understand each other better, and to reveal and release any hidden grievances or residual guilt, anger, or misunderstandings.

I couldn't quite figure out how this prayer request would come to pass. It presented a challenge because, while my mom and I have a good relationship and see each other frequently, engaging in deep conversations about our feelings is not on a regular rotation in our list of things to do.

Moreover, we are almost always in the company of others, leaving little opportunity to dive deep into a potentially emotionally charged topic. I knew that an intimate, one-on-one setting where we were both willing to be open while also being comfortable, truthful, and unoffendable could only be orchestrated by the Lord.

Closure

In God's perfect timing, that opportunity arose during a recent road trip to the zoo. My mom and I had a rare ninety minutes to ourselves—our husbands at home and my kids preoccupied with the rare treat of headphones and devices during our travels.

"That's where your dad used to work," my mom casually mentioned while pointing out the passenger-side window toward a building tucked off an exit near our city's metropolitan downtown area. "Right over there."

My gaze followed her pointing finger, and I responded to her comment with genuine interest, always grateful for the chance to learn about or discuss my dad.

Immediately my heart stirred, and I prayed for the Holy Spirit to lead me.

Lord, help me. This is the opportunity I have been praying for, but I don't want to force it. Please give me the words, help me to navigate this delicate topic with sensitivity and compassion, yet still speak the truth about my experiences and revelations.

"You know," I added, "writing my book has brought up so many memories and questions about those years." I went on, "I've been thinking a lot about what you must have gone through after Dad died. Now that I'm an adult, married with young children, I see it from a totally different perspective. I can't even imagine how unbearable it all must have been for you."

To my surprise and relief, my mom dove right into the topic with a gentle, humble, and willing spirit. She began sharing some of her innermost feelings and experiences during that time, things that I had never heard before.

She shared depths of her sorrow and loneliness that I didn't even know she experienced. She described the helplessness she battled, not knowing how to manage finances, household responsibilities, or if she even had the resources to do so. She confessed how utterly dependent she had been on her friends and family to carry her through many of her everyday tasks, all the while having to will herself to wake up each day and do it all again.

As a teenager, I saw a mom who seemed broken and sad but who managed to carry on with life somewhat seamlessly and, from what I could tell, did a good job taking care of my brother and me. We never went without. We managed just fine. We were comfortable and content.

Sure, my mom was absent at times and perhaps lackadaisical about rules or supervision, but that was a perk as far as we were concerned. I don't know if I thought it was just her parenting style or if I simply didn't think much of it at all, but I never really considered that there was anything deeper going on than what I could see from my point of view. Leave it to a selfish teenager to think that way. Boy, was I wrong.

Hearing from my mom's perspective of what life was really like for her after my dad's death pulled back the curtain to a hidden expanse of darkness and despondency I had never known existed right in my own home.

A tenderness and compassion for my mom swelled in my heart as I, for the first time, saw a glimpse of those terrible times through her eyes. My admiration and appreciation for her grew as I contemplated all she had endured and yet still persevered.

Carefully choosing my words, I recalled aloud some of the things I experienced at that age, and how it wasn't until many years later that I started to contemplate her lack of supervision or seemingly distant demeanor. I delicately pointed out the lack of guidance or parenting that possibly could have prevented, or at least minimized, some of my most destructive behaviors. I shared that I didn't realize it was there until much later in my life but that I found a resentment and bitterness toward her that I had to deal with as an adult.

"Oh, I was a terrible mom," she stated matter-of-factly. "I was such a mess. I could barely get myself through each day let alone be there for the two of you."

Shocked by her confession, I quickly reassured her that it was an overstatement. "You weren't a terrible mom at all!" I truly never once thought she was a terrible mom, and I did my best to make that clear. I conceded that we had a noticeable lack of guidance and regulation, that we were on our own quite a bit, and that in hindsight I wish she had steered me in the right moral direction on more than one occasion.

Which brought us to the topic that I had been wanting to broach for nearly a decade but hadn't had the opportunity, or the boldness, to address: my abortion.

I continued my silent prayer, trusting the Holy Spirit to give me the words. With genuine curiosity and hunger for the truth, I posed the question, "What were you thinking when I told you I was pregnant and had decided to have an abortion?"

I told her what I remembered of that day, which wasn't much, and that I had never known her true thoughts or feelings around it. I had never even bothered to ask.

Once again, I was shocked by her response. She expressed a sense of guilt and shame she had always felt for not standing in the gap for me and offering to take care of my baby. She admitted how broken and unstable she still was at that time and that the thought of taking care of a child seemed unfathomable.

So, she said, she let me do what I did, resolving that it was I who would have to face God one day regarding my decision. Remorse seeped through her words as she expressed her deep regret for what she perceived as failing me as a mother.

Even as I still process her words and write this now, my heart wrenches thinking about what she has been holding onto all these years. The self-imposed condemnation she has endured and the tormenting thoughts of not measuring up.

At the same time, I'm baffled by how mistaken I have been thinking that her only emotions around my abortion were disappointment and anger toward me. The enemy had succeeded for far too long at allowing that trauma to create a wedge between my mom and me and circulate false beliefs that entrapped us in guilt and shame.

The Lord revealed something so powerful and so precious during our conversation that day. Our discussion was straightforward and unemotional, yet so profound. We were open, honest, and unoffended, just as I had prayed for us to be.

I am amazed at the way the Lord orchestrated each part so that we could speak truth in love, without blame or condemnation.

I hope that my response to my mom that day and my true feelings came across loud and clear. Since that interaction, this message has been on my heart for my mom because I don't want her to ever doubt how loved she is:

Mom, you are not defined by your past (or present or future!) mistakes or inadequacies. Not only have I forgiven you and released you of anything I once thought you owed me, but more importantly, our Heavenly Father has also forgiven you.

I'm so sorry for my selfishness—for compounding your trauma with my own depravity and being oblivious to the depths of your sadness and stress. I pray that you can forgive me. And I pray that our relationship will be strengthened through continued open and honest dialogue. I thank God that He chose you to be my mom, and I am so grateful for your love, sacrifice, and support all my life!

I'm reminded of how powerful Jesus' sacrifice on the cross is, how His blood covers *all*. As soon as we confess to Him what we are feeling, what we have done, and change our hearts to follow Him and His way, we are no longer bound by our sins, our regrets, our shame.

In Him we have redemption [that is, our deliverance and salvation] through His blood, [which paid the penalty for our sin and resulted in] the forgiveness and complete pardon of our sin, in accordance with the riches of His grace. (Ephesians 1:7 AMP)

Since that car ride to the zoo, I have felt chains break, and I pray that my mom has too. I'm no longer bound by the tangles of twisted thoughts or the knots of unknowns and unresolved issues.

Overdue Apology

When I decided to start sharing my abortion story publicly, I asked a mutual friend, Bella, to contact Leo and let him know, just as a courtesy. I told her to assure him that I never intended to share his real name, but since we live in a small town, I knew there was a chance people would make the connection.

Only a slight chance, however, because let's be real—despite how memorable they seem to us, nobody remembers or cares about our high school relationships! Nevertheless, I wanted to make sure that he wasn't blindsided if he heard my story—which is partly his story—floating around.

My phone chimed as I saw a text notification from Bella. "Talked to Leo. Can you chat?"

I quickly picked up my phone and dialed her number, anxious to hear how the conversation went.

"Amber, in all the years I have known Leo, I have never seen him this visibly upset," she shared, still seemingly moved by their discussion.

Bella rehashed her chat with Leo, explaining how angry and hurt he was over my decision to abort our child and how much he has grieved that loss. Shock and guilt punched my gut. My heart shattered.

It suddenly dawned on me that I had never considered Leo's feelings when I was pregnant. I was as selfish as selfish could be and only thought about *my*self and *my* situation.

Quite frankly, I hadn't thought about how Leo felt since my abortion either. If anything, I assumed it was no big deal to him or that he had simply moved on.

As I learned about the unresolved pain and anger he had the past fifteen-plus years, my heart broke for him. I felt such deep remorse over how my actions affected him and grieved the loss I forced him to bear as a father.

I had never even considered that my abortion was a trauma for Leo just as it was for me. Since that realization, not only have I prayed for him many times to find the same healing and closure that I have, but I also now have a brand-new perspective about all the fathers affected by abortion choices.

Fathers who feel helpless or voiceless.

Fathers who don't have a choice to raise their children.

Fathers who are angry and grieving.

I pray for men to stand up for their right to be fathers and to speak up on behalf of their unborn children. I pray that the ones who are hurting, grieving, or holding onto anger or unforgiveness or guilt will seek Jesus for the forgiveness and healing only He can provide.

On behalf of women who have made a choice to end the lives of their unborn children, I want to apologize to the fathers. I'm so sorry for every man who has suffered from the effects of an abortion choice. I'm so deeply sorry for their loss and all they have endured as a result of that choice, whether they had a say in it or not.

My prayer is that any male who has been affected by abortion would explore options for healing and receive the closure he may not even realize he needs.[1]

While I was writing this book—with my memories of Leo and the devastation of our lost baby fresh on my mind—I had an unexpected opportunity for a long-overdue apology.

In true God-incidence fashion, I recently had an unlikely encounter with Leo at a local event. More than thirty years had passed since my life-shattering abortion experience and my relationship with Leo ended. Even though we both live in the same town, I had not seen him or run into him in over fifteen years. Yet, right at the time of writing this story and as I have been intentionally praying for God to make a way for me to apologize to him, a door opened. The timing, the place, the circumstances could only have been orchestrated by God.

After seeing and briefly chatting with Leo in person, I felt released to send him a written apology and to let him know I am praying for him. I don't know how my apology was received, but that wasn't the point. God made it clear to me that I needed to say the words "I'm sorry" to Leo and that He would take care of the rest.

I prayed that the Lord would meet Leo right where He is and that Leo's heart would be open to the love of God. I prayed that Leo receives healing and comfort after the devastating loss of our child—that the shackles of that trauma and any darkness from his past will be broken off him in Jesus' name. I prayed for Leo to experience the inexplicable peace of God, being reassured that his sweet daughter is safe in the loving arms of her Heavenly Father.

---

1   Abortion recovery programs are best done in a group with other post-abortive men with a leader who is also post-abortive. Find a group that fits your needs at H3Helpline h3helpline.org, call or text 866-721-7881 or directly contact the publisher's favorite program, He Found His Grace at shefoundhisgrace.org/mens-healing.

And I praised God for continuing to work out all things for His good, in His perfect timing.[2]

Our Past Does Not Define Us

I can't imagine that anyone would want to be remembered for their worst mistake. I often think about that when I reflect on how much I have changed. I cling to this revelation about the things from my past because it's true and worth repeating:

That is what I did. That is not who I am.

Thank goodness we are not defined by our mistakes! What a beautiful blessing that we can let go of the past—not only our own mistakes, missteps, or faults but those of others as well.

Knowing that I am a completely different person than I was at 16 or 26 or even 36, I try to give others the same grace God gave me. How I remember people or my experiences with someone years ago does not give me an accurate view of who that person is today.

I understand that by sharing bits and pieces of my story, by default, I am inadvertently sharing details about other people as well. Please know—my heart and my motives are pure. I want to ensure that everyone who is mentioned in this book, if they ever happen to read it or hear about it, will feel honored and respected, not blamed or defamed.

I can promise that I will take all responsibility for my actions and the consequences that occurred as a result of my actions. I have long since forgiven any offenses or hurts against me, and I pray that those I have wronged will forgive me as well.

I know there are two sides to every story. I wrote about what *I* experienced and how the events in my life affected *me*. I don't claim to know how these same events were remembered or perceived by others.

I can only imagine how my exes or others in my past would describe me or my behavior back then or how my actions affected them. What a mess I was! So selfish and insecure. So damaged

---

2   Romans 8:28

and lost. I made many mistakes, and I left a wake of destruction in my path.

I would be remiss if I didn't point out that despite the negative experiences I have focused on in my story, there were so many wonderful experiences as well.

My Exes

Each of my relationships had many positive aspects. Leo, Carter, and David were genuinely great guys—loving and kind—and I have fond memories of each of them. I am grateful for the good times, the laughter, the friendship, and the fun. I am blessed to have known each one of them as they are each an important part of my journey. They now have families of their own and even though we no longer see each other, I often pray for them. I pray that they have experienced the same lavishing love of the Father that I experienced. I pray that they, too, have overcome the shadows of the past and have found everything they need in Jesus as their Lord and Savior, living a life of freedom, joy, and peace!

Rebecca

Despite the rough waters Rebecca and I endured during my relationship with Carter, she is still a cherished friend to this day. I thank God that He healed me from the hurt and pulled me out of the pitfall of unforgiveness. Once I realized how self-destructive it was to hold onto my anger, resentment, and woundedness, I was set free from the hold it had on my life.

In a recent God-incidental discussion over dinner with Rebecca, I informed her that I would include the incident with Carter and her in my memoir.

"I hope you understand," I began, "the point is not to focus on the heartache or wrongdoing but to highlight how my life has been transformed by Christ...How He has helped me overcome the hard things and taught me how to truly forgive others."

Tears began welling up in her eyes, and her response was one I had not anticipated. "But have you really forgiven me? I don't understand how you could."

My heart ached as I watched her weep and saw her internal struggle spill out as she confessed her long-held guilt. I had no idea she was still punishing herself, that she still faced feelings of unworthiness even decades after our friendship had been rekindled and the offense forgiven.

"Oh, Rebecca, I really have!" I reassured her. As best I could in a loud, crowded restaurant, I explained to her the power of Christ's love and His sacrifice on the cross that paid for all our sins.

"I could not possibly count the number of times that I have needed to be forgiven, so how could I refuse to fully forgive others?!" I exclaimed. I went on to clarify that it is not in my own willpower but only through Jesus Christ and His mercy and grace that I can grasp forgiveness and give it freely to others.

Be kind to one another, tenderhearted, forgiving one another, as God in Christ forgave you. (Ephesians 4:32 ESV)

Rebecca is one of the most selfless and loving people I know. She cares wholeheartedly and feels deeply and would do anything to help a loved one. She has been like a sister to me since we were inseparable teenagers, and even though the busyness of life and work and family obligations may keep us apart more often than we would like, she still holds a special place in my heart as a dear friend.

My prayer for Rebecca is that she will have a revelation of the unconditional love of God the Father—the kind of love that covers all uncertainty and provides profound peace. I pray that, if she hasn't already, she would invite Him to be the keeper of her heart, to repair any shattered pieces, and fill any holes. May the Lord flood her with the fulfillment and joy that comes from knowing Him so that she can find all she needs in Jesus as her Lord and Savior and allow His truth to set her free.

The Camp Crew

As for the Camp Crew, it's hard to put into words how much this group of people means to me, each one individually and the collective group. They have been family to me since the day I was born.

My Camp Crew family has countless positive attributes that left a lasting impression on my life. I learned friendship and loyalty from my Camp Crew parents. I witnessed these lifelong friends go through innumerable highs and lows, joy and sadness, triumphs and tragedies, and they have been there for each other through it all.

Losing their dear friend, my dad, was devastating for them just as it was for my mom, my brother, and me. Yet, they came alongside our family and poured out love and provided help in small and big ways. I didn't find out until decades later what a significant role they played in helping my mom pick up the broken pieces of her life. My dad had taken care of all the details of managing our home and finances, and my mom felt overwhelmed by the unknowns of her financial stability without him, lost and helpless.

During our car ride to the zoo, my mom told me how her devoted group of Camp Crew friends provided support and peace during that devastating time. They donated money to our family; they created a yearly budget with every single expense written out and when it needed to be paid. Two of her close friends even spent every night for a week at our home to provide tangible comfort for my mom in her sorrow and loneliness.

During hard times and joyful times, our Camp Family has been a constant, providing stability and unconditional love. My bonus parents' dedication to one another is unshakable. Their love for each other is admirable. Their bond strong. To this day, a group of them gets together once, sometimes twice a week for dinner. I am continually encouraged by their example of true friendship modeled throughout my life.

Even though get-togethers with my Camp Crew siblings, parents, and the whole giant gang have become less frequent over the years, I know we will always be there for each other. When I think about my Camp Family, I am overcome with love for them. I know that despite our differences, despite our imperfections, despite geographical distances, and despite various seasons of life that may keep us apart, we have a special bond.

These beloved Camp Crew family members, along with my biological family, are on my heart often, and I pray for each one of them regularly. I continue to pray that the Lord will bless them and keep them, shine His face upon them, and give them peace.[3] I pray, just like I pray for many people in my life, that each one would be flooded with the love and grace of Jesus Christ, that they would discover His truth, surrender their lives to Him as their Lord and Savior, and walk with Him and seek Him with all their hearts!

Sam

When I look back at all my little family went through in those early years, facing the tragedy of my dad's death, I know that each one of us did the very best we could with what we had.

My brother went his own way, as I did, and we each had to face our own demons. I'm so happy to say that he made his way back to the Lord as well and recommitted his life to Christ. Praise God!

Sam is a devoted husband, father, and PeePaw—with almost enough grandchildren to start his own baseball team! On top of being a dedicated family man, he is a savvy entrepreneur running a local game store that he established just out of college. Sam is smart, driven, and passionate; you can always count on him to share vivid stories of his exciting experiences or intricate details of his latest hobby, discovery, or interest.

Sam has a genuine desire to focus on the good, to be a light, and invite others to share in the important facets of his life—including, and most importantly, his love for Jesus.

I still look up to my big brother, but now I see through a clear lens and a whole heart that doesn't require his affirmation to feel good about myself.

While we don't always see eye-to-eye, we have long since moved on from the bullying big brother, tattling little sister duo that we once were. Despite our past grievances or our current differences,

---

3   Numbers 6:24-26

we now have a solid, loving sibling connection. I thank God for all that He has restored in our relationship and in our lives!

I pray that the Lord will continue to move in Sam's heart and in his life as he leads his family and serves those in his sphere of influence. I pray that he will experience an even deeper connection with Christ, a new revelation of healing and freedom, and boldly walk in the profound peace and power of the Holy Spirit.

My Mom

Now that I am a mother of two children and wife of over fifteen years, I am struck by the devastating loss and unimaginable pain that my mom experienced. The complete upheaval and unraveling of the life she had built with my dad for over twenty-two years could have been an excuse to give up, to surrender defeat. She admittedly resisted that temptation regularly.

Even after my dad's death, my mom went through many premature losses and tragedies, including losing her dad to a heart attack, losing her best friend's teenage son to a car accident, losing that same best friend to cancer, as well as the devastating loss of my stepdad, her second husband of over twenty-two years.

My entire life, I have seen my mom persevere. I've watched her overcome, adapt, and move on from each obstacle or tragedy. As a teenager, I couldn't possibly comprehend the depths of her grief, her fears, her loneliness. It was only just recently that I got a glimpse into her severe devastation and struggles. I now have a deeper compassion for her, a greater understanding of her actions, and a growing respect for her as a mom.

I recognize now that when I was consumed with emptiness and loss after my dad's death, I needed more from my mom than she could provide or knew how to, for that matter. She was dealing with her own overwhelming grief, but more importantly, my expectations for her to fill my emotional needs were in vain. That need, that emptiness could only be filled by God. Looking for someone else to fill me up left me disappointed and dejected.

What I see today, through a clear lens, is not only how much I needed the Lord to sustain me but also how incredible my mom was—and still is! While dealing with her own crippling pain and grief, she still worked full time, managed our home, and took care of two reckless and rebellious teenagers.

My mom did the best she could, and her heart was always in the right place. Her imperfections or mistakes serve as encouragement to me, knowing that parenting is a messy and challenging journey. We don't have to get it all right, which is good, because we most certainly won't! Rather, our imperfections as parents are what lead our children to the perfect love of Christ. Only He can fill all the voids and give them (and us) everything they (we) need.

My mom has shown so much resilience. She is a fighter. An overcomer. I admire her perseverance and value her persistent, unconditional love. She has been one of my biggest supporters and encouragers my entire life.

Despite what my mom has gone through, she has always been my dependable and devoted caregiver. I have never doubted her love for me, and I'm so very grateful for her! I pray for her often. I pray that she finds all she has ever needed or wanted in Jesus Christ as her Lord and Savior—that all her past mistakes and heartaches, all of life's regrets or uncertainties, will melt away as she falls into the Lord's loving embrace. I pray for her to experience the sense of security and authentic joy and peace that comes from a life surrendered to Jesus, saturated in His unconditional love, never-ending grace, and life-changing truth.

I'm extremely grateful for the way God held our family together through all the ups and downs of life. I truly believe that each trial makes us stronger. In each difficulty, there is a lesson. With each tribulation, we gain perspective and perseverance. Most importantly, we learn to trust that God will sustain us, no matter what we face.

Consider it all joy, my brothers and sisters, when you encounter various trials, knowing that the testing of your faith produces endurance. (James 1:2-3 NASB)

Revelation for Right Now

As I reflect on the experiences rehashed in this book, I'm struck by how dramatic each test or trial, hurt or heartache, betrayal or breakup, comes across in my stories. I even had someone close to me mention that my recollection of events from my youth seemed overly dramatic at times. As I pondered and prayed about that feedback, and even considered revising to tone things down, I realized I wrote it that way because that is how dramatic it all felt at the time.

My stories are written from the perspective of my younger self, and dramatic though my feelings may seem, they were real to me then:

❖ Believing my life would be over if I had a baby at 16 years old was my perceived reality.
❖ Feeling like my world would fall apart without a certain boyfriend to love me was the truth I trusted.
❖ Thinking heartache and betrayal were too devastating to overcome was the defeat I accepted.
❖ Desperately needing to fit in was the idol my heart bowed to.
❖ Chasing what the world had to offer for fear of missing out was the prescription for fulfillment that I purchased.

As a teenager or young adult with a brain that was still developing[4] and emotions that ran rampant, not to mention lacking an identity rooted in Christ, I was ill-equipped to cope with the traumas I faced. I was in over my head, entrenched in a lifestyle I wasn't meant to lead.

I recognize now, more than ever, how crucial it is for our children and others to have a safe and secure place to express their emotions and to deal with their struggles. While we can look back as mature adults and know that so much of what we went through as teenagers was not significant in the long term or worth stressing about, it doesn't change the fact that it *feels* like a big deal at the time.

---

4   The reasoning part of our brains is not fully developed until our mid-20s. See "The Teen Brain: 7 Things to Know," National Institute of Mental Health, accessed February 20, 2025, nimh.nih.gov/health/publications/the-teen-brain-7-things-to-know.

Without proper guidance and love (and even sometimes with that guidance and love!), we can make devastating choices that will, quite literally, affect the rest of our lives.

Young or old, immature or experienced, whether we have it all together or we are a hot mess, the fact is that human nature creates a hole in our hearts, a hollowness inside that we will continually feel the need to fill.

The only One who can fill that void is God.

We were created to be one with Christ, to have a relationship with Him, and anything short of that connection will leave us longing for more. We can search and search, fill and fill, self-sooth and self-medicate, experiment with alternative sources of spirituality, find fleeting relief in the most recently renowned remedy, and even achieve greatness by the world's standards, but the thirst for something more will always remain. A life without Jesus Christ is dry and deficient and ultimately leads to death, but with Him as our Source, we will be full to overflowing—emotionally, physically, spiritually—and we will have eternal life!

"But whoever drinks of the water that I will give him will never be thirsty again. The water that I will give him will become in him a spring of water welling up to eternal life." (John 4:14 ESV)

Letter to a Friend

Dear friend,

You are not alone. I know the brokenness, the hurt, and the shame that torments you. You may not even be aware of it yet. That was me! I lived many years oblivious of the hurt and destruction that followed in the wake of my choices. Or maybe you have begun to recognize the burden of guilt, shame, and regret and feel a heavy load weighing you down.

Regardless of where you are in your journey, just know that God sees you and He loves you unconditionally. When He looks at you, He doesn't see your mistakes or your flaws. He sees the beloved one He created in His own image, and all you are meant to be.

You are not too damaged, too broken, or too far gone. It doesn't matter what you have done. Your mistakes don't define you. God sent His only son, Jesus Christ, to die for your sins. Past, present, and future. Every. Single. One.

Regardless of how far you have run from God, or if you have never even known Him, He is waiting patiently for you to turn to Him. My prayer is that you will run into the loving arms of your Heavenly Father and receive His freedom and forgiveness.

He saved us, not because of works done by us in righteousness, but according to his own mercy, by the washing of regeneration and renewal of the Holy Spirit, whom he poured out on us richly through Jesus Christ our Savior. (Titus 3:5 ESV)

Freedom, healing, and peace are yours for the taking! You no longer have to be shackled by shame or trauma or unworthiness. You can be a new creation in Christ Jesus!

When you choose to accept Christ as your Savior and Lord and turn from your own way to believe and follow Him, you become a beloved child of the Most High God—redeemed, forgiven, and set free. Receive it and believe it!

Your sister in Christ,
Always Amber

Resources Mentioned in Always Amber

AmberLeraas.com/free-resources

ACKNOWLEDGMENTS

When I felt the Lord nudging me to write my story, I quietly disregarded it, hoping the prompting would pass. When He placed two separate people at two separate times in my path asking me the same question, "Is God telling you to write a book?" and then used the exact same words to encourage me in this endeavor, I knew that I could no longer ignore Him.

From the very beginning of this memoir writing process, I have professed—many times through tears of frustration or inadequacy or sheer overwhelm—that if my book were to ever come together in a coherent, cohesive document, it would be a miracle. I declared that statement many times over the past two years not as hyperbole, but with one-hundred-percent sincerity. Every bit of what I had to do to put my story in writing was beyond my own ability, my own strength, beyond even my own desires, and far beyond my own understanding.

I am here today to testify to that miracle: My book is finished! My story is written. And to the best of my ability, it is written in a compelling way that will share not just the struggles but the victory that is in Christ Jesus. That is my hope and my prayer.

All the glory for this final product goes to God, first and foremost.

To Rob, my amazing and always supportive husband—there are not enough words to express my gratitude for his unwavering dedication. He stands by my side no matter what crazy venture I'm chasing or prompt from the Lord I am pursuing. Thank you, Rob, for loving me unconditionally, for seeing Christ in me and not my past mistakes. Thank you for being such a strong and steady presence in our family and a godly role model for our boys. Thank you for allowing me to walk out this assignment and humoring me as I figured it out on the fly—for all the time spent listening, processing, or just giving me the permission to lock myself away and write. You are my biggest blessing.

To my sweet sons who are warriors in the kingdom—my heart bursts with joy as I watch them grow into the extraordinary young men God has designed them to be. Thank you for graciously giving me the time (countless hours) and space (tucked away in my office/war room either on my computer writing or on my face praying) to focus on this project. Thank you for being two of my biggest fans and for always being eager to celebrate the incredible ways the Holy Spirit moves when we say *yes* to following His lead. It has been a joy to share this experience with you!

Thank you to the spiritual leaders throughout my journey whose experience, wisdom, and courage have not only challenged me to live a life fully devoted and surrendered to the Lord, but who have also inspired me to step boldly into my assignment, confident that He who began a good work in me will carry it on to completion until the day of Christ Jesus.[5]

Thank you to the coaches who came alongside me to hold me up, to reassure me when I felt I was in over my head, and who provided invaluable advice and guidance.

To Cheryl, my writing coach, editor, publisher, co-laborer in pro-life advocacy, and friend—I sincerely could not have gotten through this without you. Without you, this book would still be in heaps of incoherent babblings and pages of stories in disarray! I have your insightful instruction, your diligent editing, and your prayerful encouragement to credit for the final product. I'm so

---

5 Philippians 1:6

grateful for the God-incidence that connected us for this collaboration, and I know that it is just the beginning of great things to come—all for God's glory!

Thank you to Niccie, my business coach and sister in Christ, for your boundless wisdom, Holy Spirit-led strategic planning, and patient teaching as I limped my way through all the nuts and bolts of writing my book and creating a website, marketing plan, and a product that will add value. You have been such a blessing to me!

To my dear friends and mentors, Tiffany and Tara, thank you for selflessly giving of your time and talents to support me in this endeavor, for reading my manuscript and providing constructive feedback, and for sharing valuable insight as I navigated the ups and downs of this book-writing journey. I thank God for placing such amazing, godly women in my life who were willing to pray with me, cry with me, intercede for me, embolden me, and constantly point me back to God's word for strength and truth.

Thank you, Julie, my precious friend and cohort in abortion recovery ministry, for being one of the first to dive into my manuscript and give helpful input. Your devotion to sharing God's word, your powerful prayers, and your loving support have been such a blessing to me from the very beginning.

Thank you to my close friends and those in my prayer groups who patiently listened and lovingly encouraged me as I rode the rollercoaster of emotions during this challenging yet rewarding journey. I'm forever grateful for the countless conversations, the listening ears, the persistent prayers, and the heartfelt encouragement.

Lastly, thank you to my mom for always being my biggest cheerleader. Thank you for so readily agreeing to read my manuscript and provide input even though it meant reliving some of our most painful moments. Thank you for supporting me even when I sometimes choose a path that seems hard or doesn't always make sense. I thank God for you and your unconditional love and support!

ABOUT THE AUTHOR

Amber Leraas is an author, speaker, and restorative healing coach, who is passionate about helping women break free from strongholds and walk in the abundant life of peace, power, and purpose God intends for His followers.

After being rescued and redeemed by Jesus Christ, Amber felt an undeniable burden to share her story of overcoming trauma, shame, and brokenness to help lead women who have been through similar experiences toward healing and lasting freedom.

Since 2010, Amber has been active in pro-life ministry, including serving as a member of the Speaker's Bureau for her local pregnancy center, sharing the center's life-affirming resources and support for women and families facing unexpected pregnancies. She has also led inner healing and abortion recovery ministries for several years, creating safe spaces for women to process their past and their pain and encounter God's restoring love.

With compassion and conviction, she empowers women to face the hard places of their past, receive God's healing, and embrace their true identity, freedom, and wholeness found only in Christ. Her story is a testament to the redemptive love of Jesus—and her mission is to help others experience the same transformation.

Amber lives in Ohio where she cherishes being a wife of over 15 years to her husband, Rob, and mom to their two incredible sons.

Pro-Life Memoir Coaching
workshop or mastermind

Taking Applications Now!

Free 30-Minute Coaching Call

MybodyMyworship.com
/howtowriteamemoir

Raise your Voice Like a Trumpet!
Isaiah 58:1

Cheryl
KRICHBAUM

Invite Amber to Speak
at your next event

Live **F.R.E.E.**

F ace Strongholds
R eceive God's Invitation
E ngage in Restoration
E mbrace Redemption

AmberLeraas.com/speaker

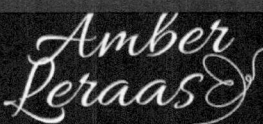

www.ingramcontent.com/pod-product-compliance
Lightning Source LLC
Chambersburg PA
CBHW021613120626
46545CB00001B/208